THE ILLUSTRATED HANDBOOK OF
FLAK

THE ILLUSTRATED HANDBOOK OF

FLAK

GERMAN ANTI-AIRCRAFT
DEFENCES 1935–1945

WEAPONS, EMPLACEMENTS, EQUIPMENTS

JEAN-DENIS LEPAGE

First published 2012
by Spellmount, an imprint of
The History Press
The Mill, Brimscombe Port
Stroud, Gloucestershire, GL5 2QG
www.thehistorypress.co.uk

British Library Cataloguing in Publication Data.
A catalogue record for this book is available from the British Library.

ISBN 978 0 7524 7475 5

Typesetting and origination by The History Press
Printed in Great Britain

CONTENTS

6   AIR RAID PROTECTION SERVICES

ACKNOWLEDGEMENTS

I am very grateful to the competent assistance of my friend Peter de Laet for providing technical data. My deepest thanks go to Jeannette à Stuling, Antoinette Lapaux, Nicole Genessey, Anne Chauvel, Michèle Clermont, Véronique Janty, Jan à Stuling and Siepje Kronenberg. Last but not least thanks to Ben Marcato, Eltjo de Lang and Ben van Luik for their faithful and everlasting support.

INTRODUCTION

No sooner had mankind succeeded in conquering the skies than some soldiers began to contemplate the military applications of aircraft, while others designed weapons to bring such machines down. Anti-aircraft warfare or air defence (any method of engaging military aircraft in combat from the ground) is thus almost as old as military use of aircraft. Just as the Germans were amongst the first to realise and exploit the offensive power of balloons, airships and aeroplanes, so they were amongst the first to provide their armed force with anti-aircraft weapons. The abbreviation FLAK comes from *FlugzeugAbwehrKanone* (anti-aircraft artillery). It entered the vocabulary of the Allies, and in the latter half of the twentieth century became universally used to refer to anti-aircraft fire.

The German Flak arm was built from scratch in the 1930s, and had to work out its own internal arrangements and operating policies. This had to be done within the factional bureaucracy of Nazi Germany, and one of the basic tenets of Hitler's regime was that no single organisation could have sole control over any particular function. However Hermann Göring – chief of the Luftwaffe and second in the Nazi hierarchy – managed to place Flak under his control. So as the Wehrmacht was re-arming, the Luftwaffe Flak was busy doing the same. There was supposed to be a division of responsibilities, with the air force being responsible for defence of the Reich, whilst a newly created Heeres Flak was to defend the ground army in the field. This did not actually happen, and the situation became more complicated when the Navy Flak and Waffen SS Flak were created and operated separately. By the end of the Second World War there were four Flak artilleries resulting in ongoing inter-service squabbles, but they did make a major contribution to the Axis cause. While the Luftwaffe fighting planes dominated the skies early on in the conflict, they met a remarkable reversal as the war proceeded. The result was a phenomenal development of the German Flak artillery whose mission focused on the defence of the Reich from Allied air attacks.

This book is not a specialised full-length academic work, and does not pretend to scholarship, but it makes the claim to cover literally all aspects of German Flak. It should, at least that is the author's purpose, provide an up-to-date and authoritative introduction to the topic of German anti-aircraft gunnery in the period 1935–1945. It is an attempt to cover the full range of Flak providing a visual guide to a key part of Hitler's forces. For ease of reference it is divided into sections dealing not only with weapons and fire-control equipments, but also historical background, organisation and structure, uniforms, both mobile and fixed Flak emplacements including ships, vehicles and fortifications, as well as useful information about civilian and paramilitary air raid services involved in the air war.

The subjects depicted in this book are purely historical and technical; this work must not be taken as an endorsement of the ideology, actions or crimes of Hitler's National Socialist regime. The author firmly distances himself from any organisation or individual who in any manner admires or who would try to excuse, justify or glorify Nazi ideology.

Jean-Denis G.G. Lepage

CHRONOLOGY

1918

11 November : The First World War ends with German defeat

1919

28 April : League of Nations founded
28 June : Signing of the Treaty of Versailles

1921

29 July : Adolf Hitler becomes leader of National Socialist 'Nazi' Party

1923

8/9 November : The Beer Hall Putsch. Hitler arrested, tried and imprisoned for nine months

1925

18 July : Hitler's book *Mein Kampf* is published

1926

8 September : Germany admitted to League of Nations

1929

29 October : Stock Market on Wall Street crashes

1930

14 September : Germans elect Nazis making them the second largest political party in Germany

1932

8 November : Roosevelt elected President of the United States

1933

30 January : Adolf Hitler becomes Chancellor of Germany
27 February : The Reichstag burns

12 March	First concentration camp opened at Oranienburg outside Berlin
23 March	Enabling Act gives Hitler dictatorial power
1 April	Nazi boycott of Jewish-owned shops
10 May	Nazis burn books in Germany
June	Nazis open Dachau concentration camp
14 July	Nazi party declared the only party in Germany
14 October	Germany leaves the League of Nations

1934

30 June	The 'Night of the Long Knives' (elimination of SA leadership)
25 July	Nazis murder Austrian Chancellor Dollfuss
2 August	German President Hindenburg dies
19 August	Adolf Hitler becomes Führer of Germany

1935

16 March	Hitler violates the Treaty of Versailles by introducing military conscription
September	German Jews stripped of rights by the Nuremberg Race Laws

1936

10 February	The German Gestapo is placed above the law
7 March	German troops occupy the Rhineland
9 May	Mussolini's Italian forces take Ethiopia
18 July	Civil war erupts in Spain
1 August	Olympic Games begin in Berlin
1 October	Franco declared head of the Spanish State

1937

11 June	Soviet leader Joseph Stalin begins a purge of Red Army generals
5 November	Hitler reveals war plans during the Hossbach Conference

1938

12/13 March	Germany announces the 'Anschluss' (union) with Austria
12 August	German military mobilises
30 September	British Prime Minister Chamberlain appeases Hitler at Munich
15 October	German troops occupy the Sudetenland; the Czech government resigns
9/10 November	*Kristallnacht* (the Night of Broken Glass)

1939

30 January	Hitler threatens Jews during Reichstag speech
15/16 March	Nazis take Czechoslovakia
28 March	End of the Spanish Civil War
22 May	Nazis sign 'Pact of Steel' with Italy
23 August	Nazis and Soviets sign non-Aggression Pact
25 August	Britain and Poland sign a Mutual Assistance Treaty
31 August	British fleet mobilises; civilian evacuations begin in London
1 September	Nazis invade Poland
3 September	Britain, France, Australia and New Zealand declare war on Germany

4 September	British Royal Air Force attacks the German Navy
5 September	US proclaims neutrality; German troops cross the Vistula river in Poland
10 September	Canada declares war on Germany; Battle of the Atlantic begins
17 September	Soviets invade Poland
27 September	Warsaw surrenders to the Nazis; Reinhard Heydrich becomes the leader of the new Reich Main Security Office (RSHA)
29 September	Nazis and Soviets divide up Poland
October	Nazis begin the euthanasia of sick and disabled in Germany
8 November	Assassination attempt on Hitler fails
30 November	Soviets attack Finland
14 December	Soviet Union expelled from the League of Nations

1940

8 January	Rationing begins in Britain
12 March	Finland signs a peace treaty with the Soviets
16 March	Germans bomb Scapa Flow naval base near Scotland
9 April	Nazis invade Denmark and Norway
10 May	Nazis invade France, Belgium, Luxembourg and the Netherlands; Winston Churchill becomes British Prime Minister
15 May	Holland surrenders to the Nazis
26 May	Evacuation of Allied troops from Dunkirk begins
28 May	Belgium surrenders to the Nazis
3 June	End of Dunkirk evacuation
10 June	Norway surrenders to the Nazis; Italy declares war on Britain and France
14 June	Germans enter Paris
16 June	Marshal Pétain becomes Chef de l'Etat Français (Chief of French State) with capital at Vichy
18 June	Hitler and Mussolini meet in Munich; Soviets begin occupation of the Baltic States
22 June	France signs an armistice with the Nazis
23 June	Hitler tours Paris
28 June	Britain recognises General Charles de Gaulle as the Free French leader
1 July	German U-boats attack merchant ships in the Atlantic
5 July	French Vichy government breaks off relations with Britain
10 July	Battle of Britain begins
23 July	Soviets take Lithuania, Latvia and Estonia
3–19 August	Italians occupy British Somaliland in East Africa
1 August	German bombing offensive against airfields and factories in England
15 August	Air battles and daylight raids over Britain
17 August	Hitler declares a blockade of the British Isles
23/24 August	First German air raids on Central London
25/26 August	First British air raid on Berlin
3 September	Hitler plans Operation *Sealion* (the invasion of Britain)
7 September	German Blitz against England begins
13 September	Italians invade Egypt
15 September	Massive German air raids on London, Southampton, Bristol, Cardiff, Liverpool and Manchester
16 September	US military conscription bill passed
27 September	Tripartite (Axis) Pact signed by Germany, Italy and Japan
7 October	German troops enter Romania
12 October	Germans postpone Operation *Sealion* until the spring of 1941
28 October	Italy invades Greece
5 November	Roosevelt re-elected as President

10/11 November	British torpedo bomber raid cripples the Italian fleet at Taranto, Italy
14/15 November	Germans bomb Coventry, England
20 November	Hungary joins the Axis Powers
22 November	Greeks defeat the Italian 9th Army
23 November	Romania joins the Axis Powers
9/10 December	British begin a western desert offensive in North Africa against the Italians
29/30 December	Massive German air raid on London

1941

22 January	Tobruk in North Africa falls to the British and Australians
11 February	British forces advance into Italian Somaliland in East Africa
12 February	German General Erwin Rommel arrives in Tripoli, North Africa
14 February	First units of German 'Afrika Korps' arrive in North Africa
7 March	British forces arrive in Greece
11 March	President Roosevelt signs the Lend-Lease Act
27 March	Coup in Yugoslavia overthrows the pro-Axis government
3 April	Pro-Axis regime set up in Iraq
6 April	Nazis invade Greece and Yugoslavia
14 April	Rommel attacks Tobruk
17 April	Yugoslavia surrenders to the Nazis
27 April	Greece surrenders to the Nazis
1 May	German attack on Tobruk is repulsed
10 May	Deputy Führer Rudolph Hess flies to Scotland
10/11 May	Heavy German bombing of London; British bomb Hamburg
15 May	Operation *Brevity* begins (the British counterattack in Egypt)
24 May	Sinking of the British ship HMS *Hood* by the *Bismarck*
27 May	Sinking of the *Bismarck* by the Royal Navy
4 June	Pro-Allied government installed in Iraq
8 June	Allies invade Syria and Lebanon
14 June	US freezes German and Italian assets in America
22 June	Germany attacks Soviet Union as Operation *Barbarossa* begins
June	Nazi SS Einsatzgruppen begin mass murder
28 June	Germans capture Minsk
3 July	Stalin calls for a scorched earth policy
10 July	Germans cross the river Dnieper in the Ukraine
12 July	Mutual Assistance agreement between British and Soviets
14 July	British occupy Syria
26 July	Roosevelt freezes Japanese assets in US and suspends relations
31 July	Göring instructs Heydrich to prepare for the Final Solution
1 August	US announces an oil embargo against aggressor states
14 August	Roosevelt and Churchill announce the Atlantic Charter
20 August	Nazi siege of Leningrad begins
1 September	Nazis order Jews to wear yellow stars
3 September	First experimental use of gas chambers at Auschwitz
19 September	Nazis take Kiev
29 September	Nazis murder 33,771 Jews at Kiev
2 October	Operation *Typhoon* begins (German advance on Moscow)
16 October	Germans take Odessa
24 October	Germans take Kharkov
30 October	Germans reach Sevastopol
13 November	British aircraft carrier *Ark Royal* is sunk off Gibraltar by a U-boat
20 November	Germans take Rostov

27 November	Soviet troops retake Rostov
5 December	German attack on Moscow is abandoned
6 December	Soviet Army launches a major counter-offensive around Moscow
7 December	Japanese bomb Pearl Harbor; Hitler issues the Night and Fog decree
8 December	US and Britain declare war on Japan
11 December	Germany declares war on the US
16 December	Rommel begins a retreat to El Agheila in North Africa
19 December	Hitler takes complete command of the German Army

1942

1 January	Declaration of the United Nations signed by 26 Allied nations
13 January	Germans begin a U-boat offensive along east coast of the US
20 January	SS Leader Heydrich holds the Wannsee Conference to coordinate the 'Final Solution of the Jewish Question'
21 January	Rommel's counter-offensive from El Agheila begins
26 January	First US forces arrive in Britain
April	Japanese-Americans sent to relocation centres
23 April	German air raids begin against cathedral cities in Britain
8 May	German summer offensive begins in the Crimea
26 May	Rommel begins an offensive against the Gazala Line
27 May	SS Leader Heydrich attacked in Prague
30 May	First 1000-bomber British air raid (against Cologne)
June	Mass murder of Jews by gassing begins at Auschwitz
4 June	Heydrich dies of wounds
5 June	Germans besiege Sevastopol
10 June	Nazis liquidate Lidice in reprisal for Heydrich's assassination
21 June	Rommel captures Tobruk
25 June	Eisenhower arrives in London
30 June	Rommel reaches El Alamein near Cairo, Egypt
1–30 July	First Battle of El Alamein
3 July	Germans take Sevastopol
5 July	Soviet resistance in the Crimea ends
9 July	Germans begin a drive toward Stalingrad
22 July	First deportations from the Warsaw Ghetto to concentration camps; Treblinka extermination camp opened
7 August	British General Bernard Montgomery takes command of Eighth Army in North Africa
12 August	Stalin and Churchill meet in Moscow
17 August	First all-American air attack in Europe
23 August	Massive German air raid on Stalingrad
2 September	Rommel driven back by Montgomery in the Battle of Alam Halfa
13 September	Battle of Stalingrad begins
18 October	Hitler orders the execution of all captured British commandos
1 November	Operation *Supercharge* (Allies break Axis lines at El Alamein)
8 November	Operation *Torch* begins (US invasion of North Africa)
11 November	Germans and Italians invade unoccupied Vichy France
19 November	Soviet counter-offensive at Stalingrad begins
2 December	Professor Enrico Fermi sets up an atomic reactor in Chicago
13 December	Rommel withdraws from El Agheila
16 December	Soviets defeat Italian troops on the river Don in the USSR
31 December	Battle of the Barents Sea between German and British ships

1943

2/3 January	Germans begin a withdrawal from the Caucasus
10 January	Soviets begin an offensive against the Germans in Stalingrad
14–24 January	Casablanca conference between Churchill and Roosevelt; Roosevelt announces the war can end only with an unconditional German surrender
23 January	Montgomery's Eighth Army takes Tripoli
27 January	First bombing raid by Americans on Germany (at Wilhelmshaven)
2 February	Germans surrender at Stalingrad in the first big defeat of Hitler's armies
8 February	Soviet troops take Kursk
14–25 February	Battle of Kasserine Pass between the US 1st Armoured Division and German Panzers in North Africa
16 February	Soviets re-take Kharkov
18 February	Nazis arrest White Rose resistance leaders in Munich
2 March	Germans begin a withdrawal from Tunisia, Africa
15 March	Germans re-capture Kharkov
16–20 March	Battle of Atlantic climaxes with 27 merchant ships sunk by German U-boats
20–28 March	Montgomery's Eighth Army breaks through the Mareth Line in Tunisia
6/7 April	Axis forces in Tunisia begin a withdrawal toward Enfidaville as American and British forces link
19 April	SS attacks Jewish resistance in the Warsaw Ghetto
7 May	Allies take Tunisia
13 May	German and Italian troops surrender in North Africa
16 May	Jewish resistance in the Warsaw Ghetto ends
16/17 May	British air raid on the Ruhr
22 May	Dönitz suspends U-boat operations in the North Atlantic
10 June	'Pointblank' directive to improve Allied bombing strategy issued
11 June	Himmler orders the liquidation of all Jewish ghettos in Poland
5 July	Germans begin their last offensive against Kursk
9/10 July	Allies land in Sicily
19 July	Allies bomb Rome
22 July	Americans capture Palermo, Sicily
24 July	British bombing raid on Hamburg
25/26 July	Mussolini arrested and the Italian Fascist government falls; Marshal Pietro Badoglio takes over and negotiates with Allies
27/28 July	Allied air raid causes a firestorm in Hamburg
12–17 August	Germans evacuate Sicily
17 August	American daylight air raids on Regensburg and Schweinfurt in Germany; Allies reach Messina, Sicily
23 August	Soviet troops recapture Kharkov
8 September	Italian surrender is announced
9 September	Allied landings at Salerno and Taranto
11 September	Germans occupy Rome
12 September	Germans rescue Mussolini
23 September	Mussolini re-establishes a puppet Fascist government
1 October	Allies enter Naples, Italy
4 October	SS Reichsführer Himmler gives speech at Posen
13 October	Italy declares war on Germany; Second American air raid on Schweinfurt
6 November	Russians recapture Kiev in the Ukraine
18 November	Large British air raid on Berlin
November	Roosevelt, Churchill and Stalin meet at Teheran
24–26 December	Soviets launch offensives on the Ukrainian front

1944

6 January	Soviet troops advance into Poland
17 January	First attack toward Cassino, Italy
22 January	Allies land at Anzio
27 January7	Leningrad relieved after a 900-day siege
15–18 February	Allies bomb the monastery at Monte Cassino
16 February	Germans counter-attack against the Anzio beachhead
4 March	Soviet troops begin an offensive on the Belorussian front; First major daylight bombing raid on Berlin by the Allies
15 March	Second Allied attempt to capture Monte Cassino begins
18 March	British drop 3000 tons of bombs during an air raid on Hamburg, Germany
8 April	Soviet troops begin an offensive to liberate Crimea
9 May	Soviet troops recapture Sevastopol
11 May	Allies attack the Gustav Line south of Rome
12 May	Germans surrender in the Crimea
15 May	Germans withdraw to the Adolf Hitler Line
25 May	Germans retreat from Anzio
5 June	Allies enter Rome
6 June	D-Day landings in Normandy, France
9 June	Soviet offensive against the Finnish front begins
10 June	Nazis liquidate the town of Oradour-sur-Glane in France
13 June	First German V-1 rocket attack on Britain
22 June	Operation *Bagration* begins (the Soviet summer offensive)
27 June	US troops liberate Cherbourg
3 July	'Battle of the Hedgerows' in Normandy; Soviets capture Minsk
9 July	British and Canadian troops capture Caen
18 July	US troops reach St Lô
20 July	German assassination attempt on Hitler fails
24 July	Soviet troops liberate first concentration camp at Majdanek
25–30 July	Operation *Cobra* (US troops break out west of St Lô)
28 July	Soviet troops take Brest-Litovsk; US troops take Coutances
1 August	Polish Home Army uprising against Nazis in Warsaw begins; US troops reach Avranches
4 August	Anne Frank and family arrested by the Gestapo in Amsterdam, Holland
7 August	Germans begin a major counterattack toward Avranches
15 August	Operation *Dragoon* begins (the Allied landing and invasion of Southern France)
19 August	Resistance uprising in Paris
19/20 August	Soviet offensive in the Balkans begins with an attack on Romania
20 August	Allies encircle Germans in the Falaise Pocket
25 August	Liberation of Paris
29 August	Slovak uprising begins
31 August	Soviet troops take Bucharest
1–4 September	Verdun, Dieppe, Artois, Rouen, Abbeville, Antwerp and Brussels liberated by Allies
4 September	Finland and the Soviet Union agree to a cease-fire
13 September	US troops reach the Siegfried Line
17 September	Operation *Market Garden* begins (Allied airborne assault on Holland)
26 September	Soviet troops occupy Estonia
2 October	Warsaw Uprising ends as the Polish Home Army surrenders to the Germans
10–29 October	Soviet troops capture Riga
14 October	Allies liberate Athens; Rommel commits suicide
21 October	Massive German surrender at Aachen
30 October	Last use of gas chambers at Auschwitz

20 November	French troops drive through the 'Belfort Gap' to reach the Rhine
24 November	French capture Strasbourg
4 December	Civil War in Greece; Athens placed under martial law
16–27 December	Battle of the Bulge in the Ardennes
17 December	Waffen SS murder 81 US POWs at Malmedy
26 December	Patton relieves Bastogne
27 December	Soviet troops besiege Budapest

1945

1–17 January	Germans withdraw from the Ardennes
16 January	US 1st and 3rd Armies link up after a month long separation during the Battle of the Bulge
17 January	Soviet troops capture Warsaw
26 January	Soviet troops liberate Auschwitz
4–11 February	Roosevelt, Churchill, Stalin meet at Yalta
13/14 February	Dresden is destroyed by a firestorm after Allied bombing raids
6 March	Last German offensive of the war begins to defend oil fields in Hungary
7 March	Allies take Cologne and establish a bridge across the Rhine at Remagen
30 March	Soviet troops capture Danzig
April	Allies discover stolen Nazi art and wealth hidden in salt mines
1 April	US troops encircle Germans in the Ruhr; Allied offensive in North Italy
12 April	Allies liberate Buchenwald and Belsen concentration camps; President Roosevelt dies; Truman becomes President
16 April	Soviet troops begin their final attack on Berlin; Americans enter Nuremberg
18 April	German forces in the Ruhr surrender
21 April	Soviets reach Berlin
28 April	Mussolini is captured and hanged by Italian partisans; Allies take Venice
29 April	US 7th Army liberates Dachau
30 April	Adolf Hitler commits suicide
2 May	German troops in Italy surrender
7 May	Unconditional surrender of all German forces to Allies
8 May	VE (Victory in Europe) Day
9 May	Hermann Göring is captured by members of the US 7th Army
23 May	SS Reichsführer Himmler commits suicide; German High Command and Provisional Government imprisoned
5 June	Allies divide up Germany and Berlin and take over the government
26 June	United Nations Charter is signed in San Francisco
1 July	US, British and French troops move into Berlin
16 July	First US atomic bomb test; Potsdam Conference begins
26 July	Atlee succeeds Churchill as British Prime Minister
6 August	First atomic bomb dropped on Hiroshima, Japan
8 August	Soviets declares war on Japan and invade Manchuria
9 August	Second atomic bomb dropped on Nagasaki, Japan
14 August	Japanese agree to unconditional surrender
2 September	Japanese sign the surrender agreement; V-J (Victory over Japan) Day
24 October	United Nations is officially born
20 November	Nuremberg war crimes trials begin

HISTORICAL BACKGROUND

EARLY GERMAN FLAK ARTILLERY

Modern anti-aircraft artillery can trace its origins back to the Franco-Prussian War of 1870 during the siege of Paris when some daring and ingenious Frenchmen used hot air balloons to operate a mail service to other parts of France. The most famous of these balloon flights was that of the prominent statesman and Minister of the Interior, Léon Gambetta (1838–1882). On 7 October 1870, Gambetta left Paris in a balloon (named *Armand-Barbès*) and landed at Tours, where he organised further resistance in the provinces. After a few balloons had safely got out of Paris, General Moltke ordered the production of a suitable weapon to shoot them down. The Krupp Company quickly manufactured a heavy one-inch rifle mounted on a pedestal set on a horse-drawn wagon. Primitive as it may sound this was the first recorded anti-aircraft weapon.

Krupp went on to design several anti-balloon pieces, which originally were little more than existing field guns placed on high-angle carriages, but soon the company was instrumental in developing specific weapons with high elevation for use against airships and aeroplanes. At the Frankfurt International Exhibition in 1909, Krupp presented three different anti-aircraft guns (65mm, 75mm and 105mm), while the Erhart Company exhibited a 50mm quick-firing cannon mounted inside an armoured turret placed on a gas-engine vehicle.

Later years saw the use of military planes for aerial reconnaissance and observation, stimulating the market for anti-aircraft weapons. A few years before the First World War, the German Army had the embryo of an anti-aircraft artillery organisation, known as *Ballonabwehrkanonen* (Bak, anti-balloon artillery) consisting of eight batteries of 7.7cm guns plus a dozen light horse-drawn batteries.

◆ The Krupp anti-balloon piece (1909). Exhibited during the Frankfurt International Fair of 1909, this 7.5cm 12-pounder flak gun was designed for a static role, and placed on a concrete platform.

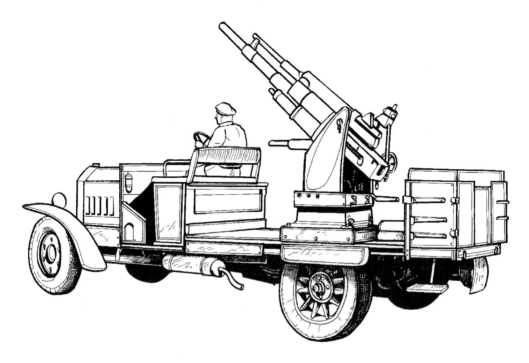

✦ The Krupp-Daimler Balloon destroyer (1909). Soon weapon designers reasoned that high mobility was necessary for pursuing and engaging moving flying targets, which dictated the fitting of the gun on a vehicle. This 7.5cm gun was similar to the 7.5cm field gun with modified trunnions moved back near to the breach to give the necessary elevation. The gun had a telescopic sight, and could fire a 14.33lb shell with a velocity of 2130 feet per second to a range of 13,000 yards at 45 degrees elevation. To show up the shell trajectory to the gunners, Krupp engineers designed a round which emitted smoke in flight, assisting the gun layer to correct his aim between shots. The gun was placed on a modified standard commercial Daimler 50hp truck, which had a top speed of 30mph. The rear of the truck included a platform with a rotating gun, ammunition lockers and seats for the crew.

✦ Krupp Kraftwagenflak with 7.1cm L/30 gun (1910).
A refinement was to protect driver, gunners and
ammunition by adding armoured plates to the truck.
Such a mobile anti-aircraft system, armed with a
7.7cm L/27 or L/30 gun was the Krupp-Daimler
armoured Flak truck. The Germans used this
sort of vehicle in the First World War,
though later refinements included
the provision of jacks to
stabilise the truck when
the gun was firing.

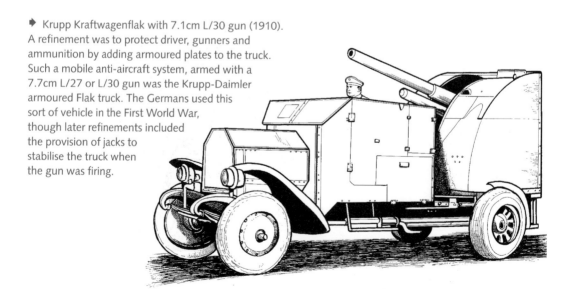

THE FIRST WORLD WAR

The introduction of balloons, airships and aeroplanes in the First World War inevitably led to the development of anti-aircraft guns. However, at the outbreak of the conflict in September 1914, the major powers had very few aeroplanes and thus very few anti-aircraft weapons available, and as a result, anything that could fire upwards was used. The first anti-aircraft weapons were the infantrymen's rifles, machine guns and a few artillery pieces hastily adapted to an anti-aircraft role used against strafing fighters and reconnaissance aeroplanes. They were served by artillery ground forces and were thus part of the army.

These primitive weapons were generally ineffective. With little experience in the role and no ability to spot the fall of their rounds with accuracy, early Flak gunners proved unable to get the correct altitude and most rounds fell well below their targets. Useless in practice, these ad hoc solutions merely helped to sustain the morale of troops subjected to the new experience of being attacked by aircraft.

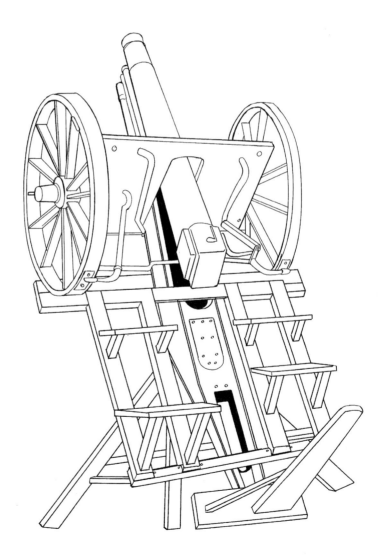

◆ The 7.7cm Flak gun was the standard German field gun at the start of the First World War, and it therefore made sense to adapt it for an anti-aircraft role. The 7.7cm is shown here on an improvised steel framework enabling the standard field gun to fire at a high angle against aircraft. It had an elevation of 70 degrees, a vertical range of 14,000 feet and a rate of fire of eight rounds per minute.

◀ A First World War Flak alarm. At the same time as new weapons were developed, primitive detection and rudimentary alarm devices were introduced.

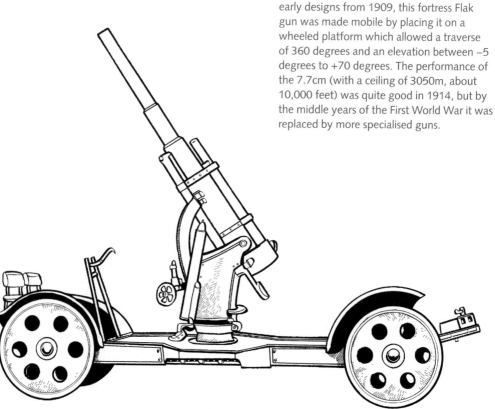

◀ German 7.7cm Flak (1914). Based on early designs from 1909, this fortress Flak gun was made mobile by placing it on a wheeled platform which allowed a traverse of 360 degrees and an elevation between –5 degrees to +70 degrees. The performance of the 7.7cm (with a ceiling of 3050m, about 10,000 feet) was quite good in 1914, but by the middle years of the First World War it was replaced by more specialised guns.

◆ MG 08/15 heavy machine gun. The
Maschinengewehr MG 08 was the German Army's
standard machine gun in the First World War. An
almost direct copy of Hiram S. Maxim's original 1884
Maxim gun, it was designed in 1908, manufactured
by the Deutsche Waffen und Munitionsfabriken,
produced in a number of variants during the
war, and remained in service until 1942. The
MG 08 weighed 62kg (137.7lbs) and was thus
unsuitable for offensive action, but it proved an
excellent weapon in a static defensive role. It
could reach a firing rate of up to 400 rounds
per minute using 250-round fabric belts of
7.92mm ammunition; it was water-cooled
using a jacket around the barrel that held
approximately one gallon. Its practical
range was estimated at 2200 yards. The
MG 08 was mounted on a heavy tripod,
and some were put to some use as
anti-aircraft weapons on improvised
mounts.

In October 1916, because of the increasing importance of the air war, a
special corps was founded, known as *Kommandierender General der Luftstreitkrafte*
(Commanding General of the Air Combat Force), which united in one service all
army defensive and offensive weapons in the field and homeland. This marked the
birth of both the German air force and the *Flugzeugabwehrkanone* (Flak in short, anti-
aircraft artillery).

Soon the first specialised anti-aircraft guns appeared, characterised by a long
barrel (and thus a higher muzzle velocity), a pedestal mount enabling a full 360-
degree traverse, and mobile platform. Using rudimentary sighting devices enabling
the user to aim at attacking enemy planes; early Flak guns were, however, far from
efficient. Nonetheless, when the First World War came to an end in November 1918,
the German Flak had destroyed or damaged 1590 Allied aircraft, and it had also
made its first successful anti-tank hits.

The war made it clear that the increasing capabilities of aircraft would require
bespoke methods of shooting them down. Lessons had been learnt and a pattern had
been set: anti-aircraft weapons would be based around heavy weapons engaging
high-altitude targets, and heavy machine guns and lighter quick-firing guns would
be used when they came to lower altitudes.

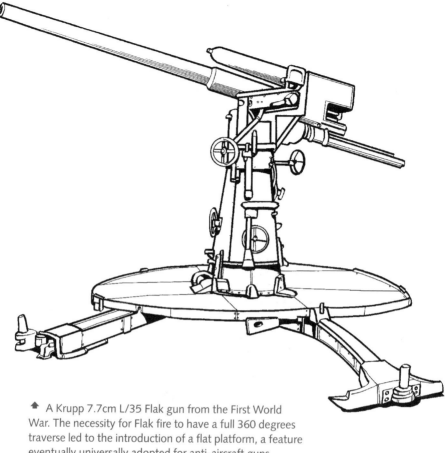

⬆ A Krupp 7.7cm L/35 Flak gun from the First World War. The necessity for Flak fire to have a full 360 degrees traverse led to the introduction of a flat platform, a feature eventually universally adopted for anti-aircraft guns.

HITLER'S REARMAMENT

The DLV and the Creation of the Luftwaffe

The First World War had shown the direction in which anti-aircraft artillery had to go in order to be successful, although there was a period when some opinion prevailed that Flak gunnery was only a panicky attempt at defence, and that it could be abandoned and replaced by small, heavily armed fast and manoeuvrable interceptor/fighters. Other voices opined in favour of Flak artillery, however, and anti-aircraft gunnery started a period of experimentation and trial in the 1920s and 1930s. The Treaty of Versailles (1919) restricted Germany to an army of 100,000 men with no air force, no heavy artillery and no anti-aircraft artillery except that in the navy, and heavy 8.8 and 10.5cm guns in the fortress of Königsberg. But General Hans von Seekt (1866–1936), the Chief of the new Reichswehr, set to work to turn the tiny army into an embryonic body capable of rapid expansion, an elite corps into which a large conscript army could rapidly be drafted when the time came. Von Seekt's secret planning and clandestine preparation formed the basis of Hitler's later Wehrmacht.

In 1918 the German artillery was disbanded, and the existing Flak guns and personnel were converted to field artillery and used to equip seven motorised batteries (each including four 7.7cm guns) attached to the permitted Reichswehr's artillery regiments. In 1928, the mobile batteries were armed with improved 7.5cm Flak guns, ostensibly built commercially for export but surreptitiously acquired by means of dummy German companies. Equipped with fire control instruments, these guns were positioned in remote regions where they would not be noticed, and used in clandestine training in an anti-aircraft role.

The Treaty of Versailles naturally disrupted the German armament companies. The two major firms, Friedrich Krupp AG and Rheinische Metallwaaren und Maschinenfabrik (later renamed Rheinmetall-Borsig AG), were strictly limited in the designs and number of weapons they could produce. On the other hand, the Treaty ensured the German military authorities were not burdened with obsolete First

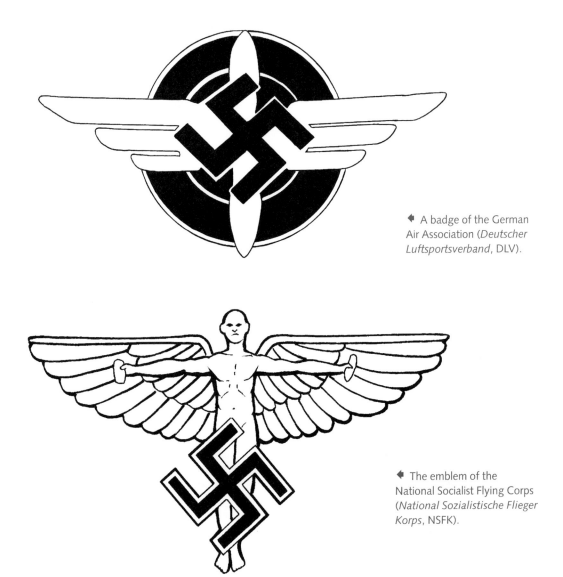

◀ A badge of the German Air Association (*Deutscher Luftsportsverband*, DLV).

◀ The emblem of the National Socialist Flying Corps (*National Sozialistische Flieger Korps*, NSFK).

World War stocks of weapons and ammunition as was the case with the victors. This meant that the Germans were not committed by economic considerations to a policy of using up the obsolete weapons. In order to evade restricting regulations Krupp made a fruitful arrangement with Svenska Aktiebolagst Bofors of Sweden. As for Rheinische Metallwaaren und Maschinenfabrik, they set up a company in Switzerland named Waffenfabrik Solothurn AG.

In 1932 secret Flak training with guns and machine guns was expanded and continued under the cover designation of *Transport Abteilungen* (transport units) operating under the sponsorship of the *Deutscher Luftsportsverband* (DLV, German Air Association). The DLV, tightly controlled by the Nazis, was an important scientific institution during the years of forbidden military aviation, as it promoted interest and stimulated the development of air sport. The DLV offered its members, most of whom had previously been in the armed forces, the active disciplined life for which they yearned, to such an extent that in November 1933 Hitler granted the DLV its own uniform with rank and trade insignia. Under the direction of this organisation the members learned aeronautical skills: model building, educational classes related to aeronautics followed by building and flying gliders and balloons, and parachuting. In 1933 Hitler and Göring placed reliance on the DLV to train new personnel for the clandestine Luftwaffe. From the start there were therefore close links between the Luftwaffe and the Nazi Party. Its leader, Hermann Göring was second in the Nazi hierarchy and appointed Hitler's successor. Until the middle of the war, he was one of the most influential men in the Third Reich.

In 1934 the Ministry of Air Transport (RLM) took control of the clandestine Flak units. As the Nazi Party assumed an iron grip on Germany, Hitler became more confident on the international stage, and on 26 February 1935 he announced the official formation of the Luftwaffe. All the secrecy that had surrounded it was blown away. By that time, the Luftwaffe – who now were unofficially responsible for Flak defence – had a fully organised department, ready for a fresh start, and all that was then needed was a paper transaction to bring the secret organisations back under Göring's control, followed by an injection of funds, personnel and weapons to bring them up to strength. By late 1935, Flak Regiments 1 through 13, and 22, 23 and 25 came to existence. Most had only one battalion, but they gradually grew; a second battalion was soon added, and a third in 1938.

The DLV was disbanded and all its former members transferred or were encouraged to join the newly created *National Sozialistische Flieger Korps* (NSFK, National Socialist Flying Corps), which was introduced in its place. In this manner the Nazi Party brought together under its control all of the country's flying clubs into one, essentially paramilitary, organisation. The NSFK could thus operate side-by-side with the fledgling Luftwaffe, and both were able to grow and gather strength together. The Luftwaffe indeed owed its existence to the Nazis, for it was they who helped develop the force first in secrecy, and it was they who gave it priority in expansion after 1935.

Air Power Theories

Between 1918 and 1939, air power was the subject of conflicting theories, and the use of modern bomber planes in a future war was much discussed. One of these theories received the most attention: the Italian General Giulio Douhet (1869–1930) in his book *Il Dominio dell'Aria* ('The Command of the Air') published in 1921, recommended a massive use of strategic bombing, based on his own experience during the Turco-Italian War in Libya in 1911. Douhet recognised aircraft as the ultimate offensive weapons because of their independence of surface limitations and superior speed. Convinced that no defence against bombers could be possible, he

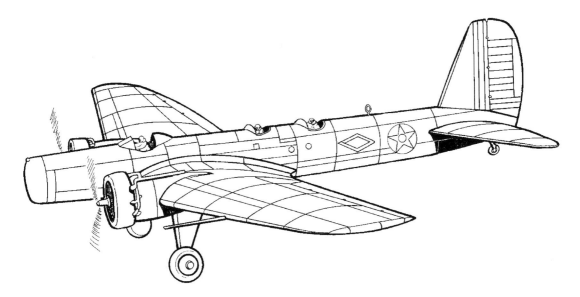

♣ The American Boeing Y1-B-9A aircraft made its first flight in May 1931. It was the first US Army twin-engine bomber to have a low-wing cantilever design. It carried a crew of three, all seated in separate open cockpits along the length of the fuselage. It had a length of 51ft 6in (15.7m), a wingspan of 76ft 10in (23.4m), a height of 12ft 8in (3.86m), a wing area of 954 square feet (88.6m²) and an empty weight of 8941lbs (4056kg). It was powered by two Pratt & Whitney R-1860-11 Hornet radial engines, 600hp (450 kW) each, with a maximum speed of 188mph (163 knots, 302kmph) and a range of 540 miles (870km). Armament included two .30in (7.62mm) machine guns and a bomb load of 2200lbs (1000kg). Production was carried out from 1931 to 1933; only seven were built.

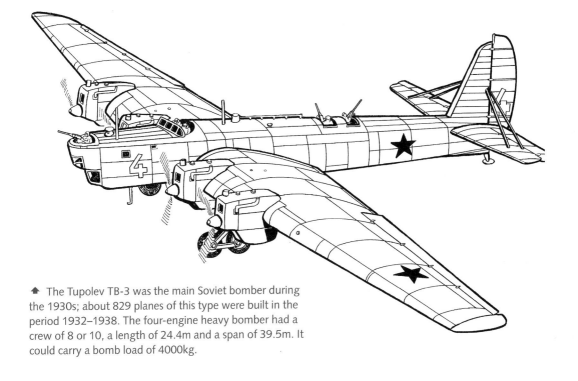

♣ The Tupolev TB-3 was the main Soviet bomber during the 1930s; about 829 planes of this type were built in the period 1932–1938. The four-engine heavy bomber had a crew of 8 or 10, a length of 24.4m and a span of 39.5m. It could carry a bomb load of 4000kg.

therefore advocated violent and surprise air attacks to break an opponent's will by terrorising his vulnerable civilian population. Large air fleets of long range bombers would attack cities, ports, dams, oil stores, railway junctions, industrial and power plants, commercial and distribution centres, and any other targets that helped, directly or indirectly, the war machine of the enemy, with a rain of high explosives, gas and incendiary bombs until civilian morale cracked. This would unravel the social basis of resistance, and pressure citizens into demanding their governments surrender. By blanketing the enemy's civilian centres with bombs, Douhet argued the war would become so terrible that the common people would rise against their government, overthrow it with revolution, and then sue for peace. In the Douhet model, the damage inflicted would be thus as much psychological as physical with enormous social and political consequences. Control of the air could win a war regardless of land or sea power, and conventional ground troops would simply have the task of mopping up.

Douhet was appointed Commissioner of Aviation when Mussolini's Fascist Party assumed power in Italy but he soon gave up this bureaucrat's job to continue writing, which he did up to his death from a heart attack in 1930. Douhet's theory had a mixed reception, but it was endorsed by Hugh Montague Trenchard (1873–1956), chief of the British Air Staff and by William Mitchell (1879–1936) of the US Army Air Service, who took Douhet's theories seriously. These theorists were preoccupied with consideration of the bomber and failed to credit the fighter as an effective method of defence, and underestimated the potential of anti-aircraft artillery. In the end, Douhet and Mitchell's gloomy predictions as to the extent of civilian demoralisation through air raids failed to come true, and theories emphasising the role of the bomber were found wanting, notably during the Battle of Britain in 1940.

Just as the Germans were the first to realise and exploit the offensive power of

◆ The French bomber Potez 540, designed in 1933, could carry four 225kg (496lbs) bombs on external racks or ten 55kg (110lb) bombs in a bomb bay. With a maximum speed of 193mph (310kmph) and a range of 777 miles (1250km) it was also used as a reconnaissance aircraft. The post-First World War Potez 540, the Boeing Y1B-9A, as well as the British Vickers Virginia and Handley-Page Heyford, the American Keystone B-4, the Russian Tupolev TB-3 and the German Dornier Do 23 and Junkers Ju 52 were designed to meet policies of strategic bombing as advocated by the Italian air warfare theorist Giulio Douhet.

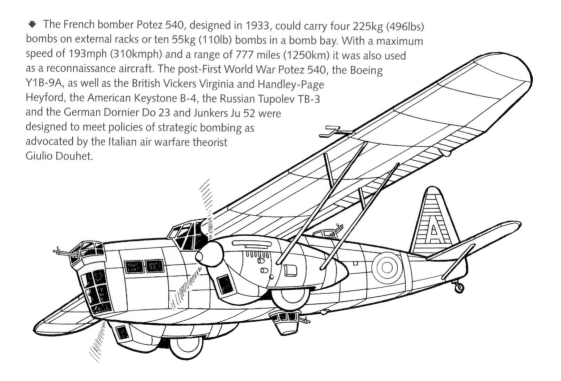

◆ *Top*: Hitler's Third Reich adopted the eagle as Hoheitszeichen (national symbol), in common with previous German governments and several other European countries. Originally, the design was to show the eagle's head facing to its right when used as a national symbol, and to its left when used as a Nazi Party symbol, but this convention was discontinued. The eagle's claws were to grasp a wreath of oak leaves surrounding a swastika. The Luftwaffe had a special and distinctive version of the Hoheitsabzeichen. It represented a diving eagle (flying to the right) holding a swastika in one of its claws. The emblem (in transfer, metal or embroidered cloth form) varied in quality according to rank. It was worn at the front of soft headgear, on the left side of the steel helmet (in that case the eagle was flying to the left), and on the right breast of tunics, jackets and coats. *Bottom*: An early issue of the Luftwaffe emblem had the eagle with heavier and shorter wingspread and drop-dragging tail. The eagle – flying to the left – indicates a transfer stencilled on the left side of the combat helmet.

aircraft, so they were amongst the first to provide their armed force with Flak guns. After the Nazi takeover, General von Blomberg (Minister of Defence) made plans regarding which arm of service the Flak should belong. The ground army was to be responsible for protection against aircraft in the field; the navy was responsible for protection at sea and along the coast; and the (then still clandestine) Luftwaffe was entrusted with the aerial defence of Germany. However, due to lobbying by Hermann Göring, the existing DLV Transport Abteilungen was transferred in 1934 to the *Reichsministerium der Luftfahrt* (RLM, Minister of National Aviation) as stated above. The RLM, formed in April 1933, was the department in charge of development and production of aircraft until 1945. As was characteristic of government departments in the Nazi era, the Ministry was personality-driven and formal procedure was often ignored in favour of the whims of the Minister, Reichsmarschall Hermann Göring. As a result, development progressed only slowly and erratically during the war, until the RLM was taken over by Minister of Armaments and War Production Albert Speer (1905–1981) who successfully managed to increase Germany's war production despite massive and devastating Allied bombing.

As previously stated, in 1935 the existence of the Luftwaffe was officially made public and, in spite of protest from the navy and ground army, the whole German Flak

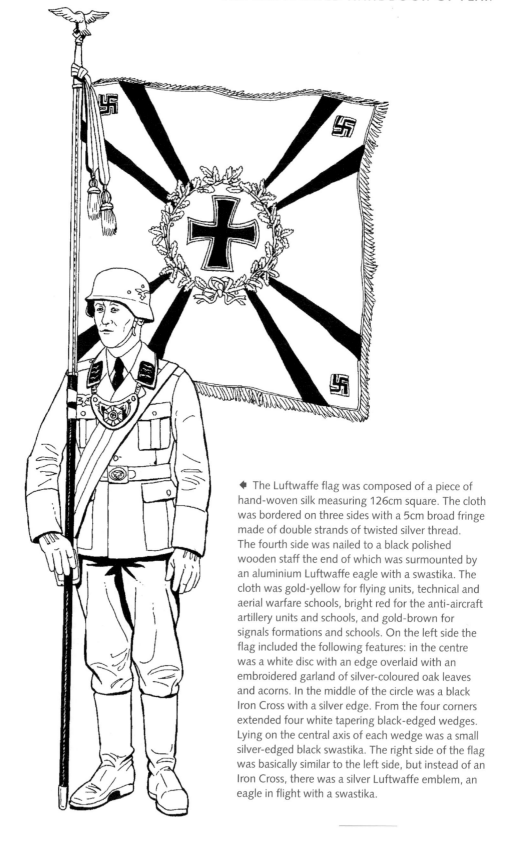

◀ The Luftwaffe flag was composed of a piece of hand-woven silk measuring 126cm square. The cloth was bordered on three sides with a 5cm broad fringe made of double strands of twisted silver thread. The fourth side was nailed to a black polished wooden staff the end of which was surmounted by an aluminium Luftwaffe eagle with a swastika. The cloth was gold-yellow for flying units, technical and aerial warfare schools, bright red for the anti-aircraft artillery units and schools, and gold-brown for signals formations and schools. On the left side the flag included the following features: in the centre was a white disc with an edge overlaid with an embroidered garland of silver-coloured oak leaves and acorns. In the middle of the circle was a black Iron Cross with a silver edge. From the four corners extended four white tapering black-edged wedges. Lying on the central axis of each wedge was a small silver-edged black swastika. The right side of the flag was basically similar to the left side, but instead of an Iron Cross, there was a silver Luftwaffe emblem, an eagle in flight with a swastika.

◆ Legion Condor Flak gunner. Germany was not officially at war against Republican Spain so German soldiers' service uniforms were rather neutral in appearance. This artilleryman wears the German standard shirt, trousers and jackboots, and a Spanish summer light hat called a *chambergo*. He also wears a thick leather protective glove on his right hand for loading the 8.8cm Flak 18 gun. He is armed with a P08 pistol.

was placed under Göring's Luftwaffe. From then on, its growth was steady. From the original seven Abteilungen in 1933, the strength of the Flak rose to 18 battalions in 1935 and to 115 in 1939, armed with 8.8cm, 2cm and 3.7cm Flak guns.

THE SPANISH CIVIL WAR

During the Spanish Civil War (1936–1939), Nazi Germany supported the rebellious Nationalists headed by Generalissimo Francisco Franco Bahamontes (1892–1975), justifying their involvement as part of a 'fight against international Judeo-Bolshevism'. A special force, named Condor Legion, was created, with volunteers placed under the command of General-Major Hugo Speerle. The Condor Legion included a *Panzergruppe* (armoured unit equipped with small PzKfw I tanks), aircraft (fighters, dive and medium bombers and reconnaissance), and a Flak detachment, coded F/88 with an establishment of 1400 men. This was divided into a searchlight platoon, 20 light Flak guns headed by Wachtmeister Hakenholt, and four heavy batteries of 8.8cm guns commanded by Oberleutnant Aldinger. Originally exclusively intended to defend the German airfields in Spain, the Flak detachment (soon increased to regimental size and known as Flakregiment 9) was also employed with success in battle, notably at Malaga, Santander, Gijon, Toledo, Cartagena, Madrid and Valencia.

The Spanish Civil War was the Lutfwaffe's most intensive period of combat experience before the Second World War, providing them with the opportunity to test new weapons and tactics. Some of the most significant lessons learnt from the intervention in Spain were the importance of logistics; the need for adequate radio communications; the use of air transport to move entire units; the tactic of low-level attacks; mass-bombing (as advocated by Douhet); dive-bombing (utilising the Junkers Ju-87 Stuka); the development of navigational aids essential for bad weather and night operations; and the use of Flak guns in the mobile ground artillery role, notably the use of the new and formidable 8.8cm Flak gun as a Pak (anti-tank) weapon. The results achieved by Flak Abteilung F/88 and Flakregiment 9 revealed the huge potential of German anti-aircraft guns, which was fruitfully exploited during the Second World War. The years 1937 to 1939 were also a period during which the German Luftwaffe High Command developed, organised and improved weapons, recruitment, training and the administrative structure of the Flak arm.

ORGANISATION OF LUFTWAFFE FLAK

The Luftwaffe Flak was administratively attached to the four *Luftflotten* (air-force fleets). It was organised into various units as follows. *Flakkorps* (corps) operated entirely in the field, and included two to four divisions with subordinate regiments. *Flakdivisionen* (divisions) were of two main types: static and motorised, the latter composed of two to four regiments in field operation. *Flakbrigaden* (brigades) commanding two to four regiments, mainly confined to fixed defence. *Flakregimenten* (1500–9000 men) numbered from 1 to 70, were composed of a headquarters and two to six *Flakabteilungen* (battalions).

The *Abteilungen* could be detached and allotted to other combat units or defence areas. A battalion was usually mixed, containing generally three medium or heavy batteries (24 guns), two light batteries (24 guns) and one or several searchlight batteries. In addition there were *Ersatzabteilungen*, responsible for repairs and replacement of weapons, equipment and personnel. The battalion was divided into *Flakzüge* (platoons of 80–100 men) and *Truppen* (squads of 10–20 men), which formed *Flakbatterien* (batteries) and other units with varying functions (signals, transport etc). In theory a heavy battery of four or six 8.8cm guns consisted of two *Züge*.

There was also a *Lehrregiment* (training regiment), and special detached Flak units allotted to the protection of Nazi VIPs. It should be noted, however, that the formations described above were not fixed, and while the composition of batteries were usually standardised, the formation of these into higher units was subject to variation. Often the sizes of these units depended on the importance of the defended area.

The Luftwaffe divided Germany into *Luftgaue* (operational command for static defence in air regions) in similar fashion to the army's *Wehrkreise* (military regions). During the Second World War, the areas covered by the Luftgaue could be approximated to the army Wehrkreis regions as follows:

Luftgau I/II	Wehrkreis 1 (East Prussia), 2 (Mecklenburg and Pomenaria), 20 (Danzig), 21 (West Poland) and the General Government of Poland
Luftgau III/IV	Wehrkreis 3 (Berlin and Brandenburg) and 4 (Saxony and Thuringia) together with portions of Wehrkreis 2 and 7 (southern Bavaria), 9 (Thuringia and Hessen) and 11 (Brunswick)
Luftgau VI	Wehrkreis 6 (Westphalia and Rhineland) and part of 9 (Thuringia and Hessen)
Luftgau VII	Wehrkreis 5 (Wurttemberg and Baden) and 7 (southern Bavaria), as well as parts of 18 (Austria) and eastern France
Luftgau VIII	Wehrkreis 8 (Silesia) and a large part of Poland
Luftgau XI	Wehrkreis 10 (Schleswig-Holstein) and parts of Wehrkreise 2, 6 and 11
Luftgau XII/XIII	Wehrkreis 12 (Eifel, Sarre, Lorraine, Luxemburg), 13 (northern Bavaria and Bohemia) and parts of Wehrkreis 9
Luftgau XVII	Wehrkreis 17 (Austria and Moravia), and parts of Wehrkreise 18 (Austrian Tyrol and Slovenia) and Czechoslovakia

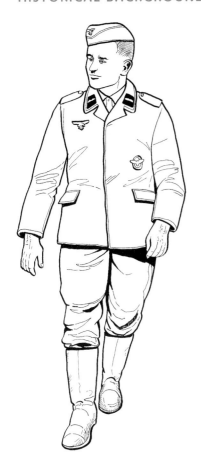

◀ Basic Luftwaffe service uniform. This man wears the *Fliegermütze* (peakless field cap) and the *Fliegerbluse*. This short tunic, originally intended for wear by aircrews only, was designed so that no buttons, patch pockets or cuffs would catch on projecting parts of aircraft. It was short-waisted, cuffless, fly-fronted (fastened by four buttons) sometimes with two side slash pockets. The collar could be worn open or closed. Collar patches indicated rank, in this case a Hauptgefreiter (Sergeant). The *Fliegerbluse* was sufficiently convenient and smart that it became universal for all air force personnel, including ground personnel and Flak artillerymen. This man also wears a pair of *Tuchhose* (trousers), which were cut full and yet tapered slightly towards the bottom so as to fit easily into boots; they had two side pockets and were generally worn with braces. Grey shirts of mottled grey-blue thread were worn with a black tie (not always worn in the field). The shirt might be fitted with shoulder straps to indicate rank. Footwear consisted of the three-quarter length *Marschstiefel* (marching boot) made of black leather. The purchase, quality control, distribution and sale of items was handled by the *Luftwaffe Bekleidung Amt* (Air Force Clothing Office). Like the other Wehrmacht forces that operated in extreme climates and which carried out a wide range of functions, the Luftwaffe (and of course its Flak artillery) eventually adopted many other different forms of combat uniforms.

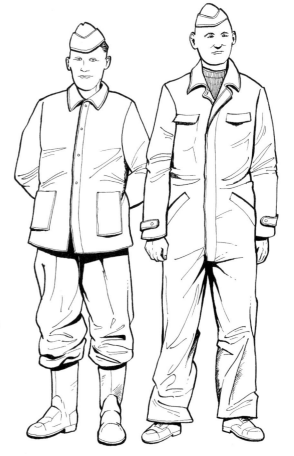

◆ Men engaged in dirty jobs, manoeuvres, weapon cleaning, equipment maintenance, instruction or training wore hardwearing overalls or the *Drillichanzug* (fatigue or work suit) including a simple shapeless single-breasted tunic with a turn-down collar, and matching trousers made of easily washable, strong materials like cotton-linen-rayon or herringbone twill. These items were black, dark blue or light grey, and generally without insignia and badge. The man in overalls (right) wears a Luftwaffe woollen sweater; this had a blue band around the neck to distinguish it from the army version.

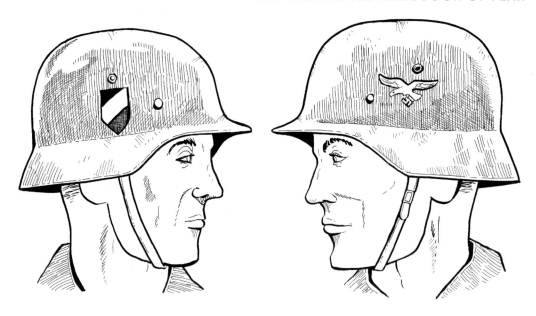

◆ Stahlhelm M35. Derived from the First World War model 1918 helmet, the compact steel helmet model 1935 was universally worn by the German armed forces during the Second World War. The lining and adjustable chinstrap were of leather, the strap generally being dyed black on the outer surface. The Luftwaffe version had the national emblem transfer on the left side, while the right side bore the shield in national colours: black, white and red. The Luftwaffe helmet transfer eagle was reversed from its direction in all other insignia, so that it was seen 'flying forwards' (from right to left, and not 'retreating backwards', which would have had an embarrassing symbolic connotation) on the left side of the helmet. After 1942, steel helmets were often manufactured without any insignia.

The German Flak was a well organised, large and effective force. In 1939, it had 6500 light guns and 2450 medium and heavy guns. In June 1944, the time of maximum strength, the Flak totalled 30,463 light guns and 15,087 medium and heavy guns. The Flak was also charged to deploy *Luftballonen* (balloons). It was equipped with both heavy artillery to deal with bombers flying at high altitude, and light artillery intended for combat against low flying aircraft and dive-bombers. Based on the experience gained during the Spanish Civil War, a large number of German Flak guns were dual-purpose: they could be used against both aircraft and ground targets.

Luftwaffe Flak units – like paratroopers, the elite Hermann Göring armoured division and Luftwaffe infantry field divisions – were part of what may be termed Göring's private ground army. They were allocated to the other two arms of the Wehrmacht according to battle requirements but the Heer, Kriegsmarine and the newly-created Waffen SS also possessed their own Flak artillery, as will be described below.

EARLY CAMPAIGNS 1939–1941

At the outbreak of the Second World War in September 1939, the German Flak artillery was standardised on a few calibres, and the weapons were in general of sound and well-tested design. The Flak artillery was built around the 2cm and 3.7cm

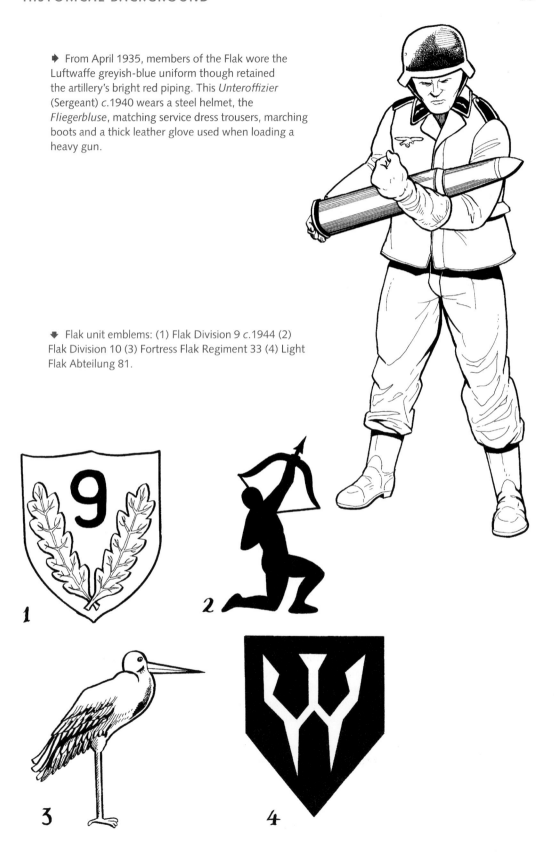

◆ From April 1935, members of the Flak wore the Luftwaffe greyish-blue uniform though retained the artillery's bright red piping. This *Unteroffizier* (Sergeant) *c*.1940 wears a steel helmet, the *Fliegerbluse*, matching service dress trousers, marching boots and a thick leather glove used when loading a heavy gun.

◆ Flak unit emblems: (1) Flak Division 9 *c*.1944 (2) Flak Division 10 (3) Fortress Flak Regiment 33 (4) Light Flak Abteilung 81.

1

2

3

4

light guns, and the 8.8cm and 10.5cm heavy guns. Several improved designs were undergoing routine development with the intention of bringing them into service as and when the need arose. By 1939, the Luftwaffe *Flakartillerie* totalled some 107,000 men, NCOs and officers serving 2600 heavy guns (mostly 8.8cm), 6700 light guns (2cm and 3.7cm) and about 3000 searchlights (60cm and 150cm). The German forces engaged these modern weapons during the attack on Poland. During this first *Blitzkrieg* ('lightning war' based on the use of swift-moving armoured vehicles supported by attack aircraft) that lasted only 18 days, the Germans enjoyed total air supremacy and Flak units had little to do in the anti-aircraft role. They were thus engaged against ground targets such as fortifications and bunkers, and achieved good results notably at Graudenz, Mlawa near Warsaw, and Bezura. These first successful combats made infantrymen and Flak gunners closer to each other, a nearness that only increased as the war went on.

Flak units took part in the invasion of Denmark and Norway in April 1940 without having to fire a round, but the units sent to the region of Petsamo in Finland distinguished themselves by protecting nickel ore mines against British air attacks.

During the 'Phoney War' on the Western Front (September 1939 to May 1940) the German Flak was deployed to protect strategically important points in German cities such as bridges, stations, marshalling yards and factories from British and French air attacks that never came. They were also placed in the so-called *Luftwaffeverteidigungszone West* (LVZ-W Western Air Defensive Zone). The LVZ-W – formed in 1938 – was part of the Westwall (also known as 'Siegfried Line', a belt of obstacles and fortifications facing the French Maginot Line, built in the late 1930s to secure the German western flank). The LVZ-W was intended to be approximately 10–30km deep. Parallel to the Westwall, it stretched from the Black Forest to the Saar and later extended, first to Aachen, then to the Heligoland Bight and finally to Schleswig-Holstein. The zone was intended to include observatories, a massive deployment of light and heavy anti-aircraft guns, and air strips from which fighter planes could intercept all intruders. According to German propaganda the LVZ-W was a formidable barrier. In reality its strength was grossly exaggerated and, until 1940 at least, the LVZ-W was not developed beyond an elementary stage.

Events became serious for the Flak in May and June 1940 when Hitler launched the invasion of the Netherlands, Belgium and France. For this campaign, more Flak troops were engaged than had previously been the case: Flakkorps I (headed by *Generaloberst* Hubert Weise), and Flakkorps II (commanded by *Generalmajor* Otto Dessloch) each included four regiments, signal troops and liaison units with the air force, infantry and Panzer forces. A specially trained unit, the Flakgruppe Aldinger (named after its commanding officer Hauptmann Aldinger) operated as support to the paratroopers and combat engineers who captured the heavily defended Belgian fort of Eben-Emael on 11 May 1940. In coordination with the Heer's Panzer Group von Kleist, Flakkorps I supported the offensive across the Sarre region, against the French Maginot Line bunkers facing southern Luxemburg, and after the breakthrough at Sedan, continued its 'lightning' advance with Guderian's Panzergruppe to Boulogne, Calais and Dunkirk. By the end of the victorious campaign, Flakkorps I – still attached to Guderian's force – had advanced as far as Dijon in Burgundy.

Meanwhile Flakkorps II, attached to 6th and later to 4th Army, moved into Holland and later into France as far as the Loire river. Flak soldiers were at the spearhead of the offensives attacking centres of resistance and fortified positions with their '88s', and covering the sky with their light guns. Examples of Flak achievements include Oberleutnant Karl Götz, who destroyed French batteries and nine tanks at Cambrai, and Oberleutnant Harras, commander of a battery of Flakregiment 18, who made a breach with his 8.8cm in the walls of the citadel of Boulogne forcing 6000 French soldiers to capitulate. Unteroffizier Nelcke, a veteran of the Condor legion, took prisoner 97 French and British soldiers, an exploit rewarded with the Knight's Iron Cross.

At the end of the campaign by the end of June 1940, the German Flak artillery had proved its worth as much against enemy aircraft as against ground targets. Flakkorps I had downed 372 Allied aircraft (and destroyed 252 planes on the ground), knocked out 47 tanks, smashed 30 bunkers and sunk one warship. The achievements of Flakkorps II were equally impressive: 214 aeroplanes, 284 tanks, 17 fortified positions and bunkers and 7 troop transport ships. It had lost 24 guns and suffered 312 wounded, and 106 killed and missing in action. On 28 June 1940, Generaloberst von Kluge declared:

> The name of Flakkorps II and that of his chief are for ever linked to our successes in the West. I thank them for their faithful comradeship. The IVth Army will never forget Flakkorps Dessloch and I express my warmest and best wishes to all of you for the future.

The months immediately following the astonishing victory of June 1940 were used to adapt to the new situation, notably to support the air war against Britain. Most of the motorised units of the Flak were maintained in France, the Netherlands and Belgium, and regrouped under the designation of VIIIth Flakkorps headed by General von Richthoffen (the nephew of the celebrated First World War ace, the 'Red Baron'). The purpose was now to form a line of defence from the North Sea to the Gulf of Biskay, aiming at protecting all airfields from which the Luftwaffe operated during the Battle of Britain, and supporting the preparation of Operation *Seelöwe* ('Sealion' the never carried-out invasion of the British Isles). For the purpose of *Sealion*, the OKW (*Oberkommando der Wehrmacht*, Armed Forces High Command) had decided to create *Flakkampftruppen*, special assault and anti-aircraft detachments which received special training as they were to closely cooperate with storm infantrymen and combat engineers in the invasion. However, by October 1940 it was clear that the Germans had failed to shake the British will; the Royal Air Force had won the Battle of Britain and Operation *Sealion* was cancelled. The special *Flakkampftruppen* were disbanded and returned to their units of origin.

In November 1940, a small part of the Luftwaffe Flak stayed in the west and was placed in static batteries whose mission was to combat British aeroplanes; the bulk was repatriated to Germany and put in operational reserve, while some units were deployed to Romania to defend the important oilfields of Plesti and Oefelder. Then the British launched their air raids on Hitler's Reich. Berlin was attacked for the first time on 8 October 1940, a raid that was followed by many others until 1945. From then on, it was clear that the capital of the Nazi empire, but also industrial centres, ports and major cities were potential targets. As a result, the OKL (*Oberkommando der Luftwaffe*: Air Force High Command) was confronted with a new challenge: to lay the foundations and develop in earnest the structures of a defensive organisation aimed at the protection of the Third Reich.

NORTH AFRICA AND THE MEDITERRANEAN

Benito Mussolini, dictator of Fascist Italy, had allied with Hitler's Nazi Germany (forming the 'Axis' Berlin-Rome). The Italians attacked Greece but were given a defiant reply. Hitler, concerned by his ally's failure, decided to intervene. At the beginning of April 1941, German troops invaded Yugoslavia and Greece. Some

⬇ A gunner in North Africa, 1942. A special tropical uniform was designed for use by forces serving in hot and arid climates. Worn in North Africa (but also in summer in the Crimea, Italy and Greece), this included a light khaki cotton twill tunic with an open collar, four front buttons and four patch pockets, a light khaki shirt with two patch breast pockets, matching baggy trousers or khaki shorts. This man wears a shirt, shorts and a *Tropische Kopfbedeckung* (tropical pith sun helmet). This item proved uncomfortable, unwieldy and of little protective value. It was soon discarded and replaced by the popular *Einheitsmütze* (light peaked cap) and the standard M35 steel helmet in action.

⬆ Paratrooper, Crete 1941. German *Fallschirmjäger* (paratroops), a specialist force of highly trained men, came under the command of the Luftwaffe. As such they were issued with both regular air force uniforms as well as a number of items of specialist dress required for their airborne role. Their basic uniform included the Luftwaffe blue-grey *Fliegerbluse*, field grey trousers and black leather, side lacing, rubber soled jump boots. Their weapons and equipment were basically the same as those used by the infantry but they had a special jump smock either olive green or camouflaged; this was a step-in type with fixed legs and a plain zip front. Paratroopers also wore a special compact heavily padded steel helmet with visor and ear guards cut down to eliminate the protrusive parts for air manoeuvring; the helmet was secured to the head by a special harness which prevented it from slipping during the jump and landing. It could be worn with several different patterns of cover depending on the theatre of operations. After the costly invasion of Crete in May 1941, virtually all paratroopers were taken off jump status and employed as elite assault infantry until the end of the war.

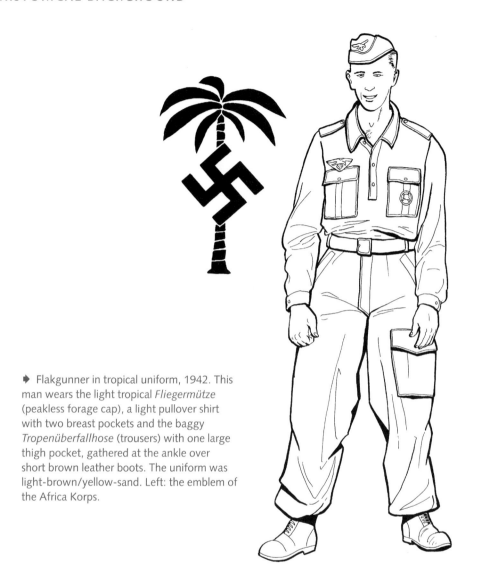

◆ Flakgunner in tropical uniform, 1942. This man wears the light tropical *Fliegermütze* (peakless forage cap), a light pullover shirt with two breast pockets and the baggy *Tropenüberfallhose* (trousers) with one large thigh pocket, gathered at the ankle over short brown leather boots. The uniform was light-brown/yellow-sand. Left: the emblem of the Africa Korps.

motorised units of Flakkorps II, attached to von Kleist's Panzergruppe, participated in this campaign. They fought notably at Rupel and along the fortified Metaxas Line held by the Greeks. When the campaign ended in early May, these units went to Romania and Bulgaria, some elements participating to the conquest of the Greek island of Crete (Operation *Mercury*). They eventually formed Flakregiment 58 under the leadership of Colonel Massing.

Since February 1941, the first batteries of Flakregiment 33, headed by Captain Fromm, were deployed in Libya with General Erwin Rommel's famous Afrika Korps. This unit was reinforced by Flakbataillon 606, and soon by other Flak troops placed under command of Generalleutnant Müller. The whole Flak force deployed in Libya became in August 1942 the 19th Afrika Flakdivision, successively commanded by Generalleutnant Burchardt and Generalleutnant Frantz. The fighting in Libya lasted for two years, the war became a seesaw struggle, and Tripoli, Benghazi and Tobruk were major prizes in any advance.

Campaigning in the desert was done under extremely testing conditions and demonstrated the importance of fast-moving troops carried in vehicles. Tactically armoured fighting vehicles were the key to success in a terrain with few 'tank proof' places for infantry to shelter, and in which major natural obstacles were few and far between. Mobility was all important to bypass and encircle strongholds which fell as soon as the defenders' supplies ran out. Tanks and wheeled armoured cars with their speed and long range were therefore very useful during the different desert moves, withdrawals, pursuits, retreats and counter-offensives. For this purpose some light motorised Flak assault units were formed (known as *Sturmflak*) which accompanied tanks and infantry, in both anti-aircraft and anti-tank roles. Here again, the famous 8.8cm Flak gun 18, used in an anti-tank role, was one of the trump cards of the Afrika Korps. However, notwithstanding the power of German Flak, the North African campaign ended in May 1943 when the Axis forces were defeated.

THE RUSSIAN FRONT

Ideologically Nazi Germany and Soviet Russia were arch enemies, each fearing the growth of the other's strength. In August 1939 they surprised the world by signing an agreement not to attack each other, and instead to join forces to crush, dismantle and divide Poland between them. This cynical pact was only temporary though, and after his victory in the West, Hitler turned his attention to the East. On 22 June 1941, a huge concentration of German forces launched Operation *Barbarossa*, the invasion of the Soviet Union. At first things went well; the Germans made tremendous advances, wiping out all resistance, defeating large but ill-prepared armies, conquering vast territories and towns, and taking hundreds of thousands of prisoners. Both Flakkorps were involved and incorporated into von Kleist's Panzergruppe I, Guderian's Panzergruppe II, Hoth's Panzergruppe III as well as into Army Group Centre and Army Group North.

Fierce battles took place, and by mid-September Flakkorps I (headed by General von Axthelm) had already destroyed 300 Russian planes and about 3000 vehicles including an important number of tanks. Flak units attached to Guderian's forces advanced almost to Moscow where the German offensive was brought to a halt due to strong Soviet resistance, problems of supply and the early bitter winter cold. The battle at the gate of Moscow marked the end of the successful Blitzkrieg. The Soviet Union, although having suffered enormous casualties and prisoners and lost a lot of war material and supplies, was not defeated. From then on, the conflict became a world war, a chaotic and gigantic war of attrition, particularly when the US entered the conflict at the end of 1941. With Britain intact, the Red Army battered but unbowed, and the US rapidly arming, time was no longer on the side of the Nazis.

Between June and November 1941, the German Flak destroyed about 2000 Soviet aeroplanes. As the war went on, the Flak artillery, as with the rest of the German Army on the Russian Front, was progressively forced into a defensive attitude, marked by numerous retreats, disastrous encirclements (like Stalingrad in the winter of 1942/1943), and a few strong offensives (such as Kursk in the summer of 1943) which increased casualty numbers. During the Battle of Stalingrad the 9th Flakdivision destroyed 600 Russian planes and 826 tanks, but local successes could not conceal the fact that the war was already lost.

◀ This Flak gunner wears a blue-grey version of the army *Mantel* (overcoat), which was worn by Luftwaffe personnel and Flak artillerymen in cold weather. The greatcoat was calf-length, double-breasted, slightly waisted, fastened by two rows of buttons, with two side slash pockets and flaps, deep turned-back cuffs and a deep single vent at the rear. Rank patches were usually placed on the large collar which could be worn closed or open. The *Mantel* was a garment which proved adequate in the climate of western Europe, but failed to offer sufficient protection in the Russian winter.

◆ Flak gunner on the Eastern Front (*c.* end of 1942). The Luftwaffe used the various army winter uniforms, and improvised in the same way as the elder service. The depicted gunloader wears a woollen toque under the Stahlhelm M35, and the reversible winter uniform (standard for Heer and Luftwaffe) including a jacket with attached hood and trousers made extra thick for warmth. A very heavy sheepskin surcoat was often worn by Flak sentries in very exposed positions. This coat might be worn by the entire gun crew, if necessary. It was, however, too heavy for infantry combat use.

DEFENCE OF THE REICH

The Allied Air Offensive

At the outbreak of the war in 1939, caution and restraint were the watchwords, and the British restricted themselves to attacking military targets in daylight raids. But when the Germans attacked London during the Battle of Britain, Prime Minister Winston Churchill ordered a retaliation on Berlin, and the escalading air war began. The British were rapidly forced to switch to night bombing because of crippling losses, and evolved a bombing strategy that was hoped would win the war: mounting large scale attacks that would destroy Germany's ability to fight and her will to do so. This was advocated by Chief of RAF Bomber Command, Air Marshall Sir Arthur Harris who believed it could achieve victory independently of ground armies and navies. He said: 'The Nazis entered this war under the rather childish illusion that they were going to bomb everyone else and nobody was going to bomb them ... They sowed the wind, and now they are going to reap the whirlwind.'

From 1942 on, the RAF and later the USAAF adopted a controversial strategy based on large scale area bombing. The Allies had developed long range bombers, such as the British Avro Lancaster and Handley-Page Halifax, and the American B17 Flying Fortress and later B24 Liberator. Progressively deadly air raids were launched over the Reich. Soon attacks by forces of over 1000 bombers became frequent. As Harris said, the German people, who were used to always dealing blows and never receiving them, began to feel the might of the combined Allied air forces. The tide was turning.

In three months of 1943, the RAF dropped over 20,000 tons of bombs on Berlin alone. The RAF (at night) and the USAAF (during the day) massively bombarded German towns and industrial centres. The aim was to crush enemy war production, thus diminishing fighting capability and creating a collapse of German morale. In short, the air war, as advocated by Douhet, was to bring an end to hostilities. Massive bombardments often paralysed transportation means, and reduced many German towns into smoking ruins, but they did not win the war. The air war over Germany was one of the most controversial campaigns of the entire Second World War and cost many thousands of Allied and German lives.

Main Allied Air Attacks on Germany

15 May 1940	Ruhr
17 December 1940	Mannheim
28 March 1942	Lübeck
17 April 1942	Augsburg
30 May 1942	Cologne
6 March 1943	Essen
16 May 1943	Möhne and Eder dams in the Ruhr
25 July 1943	Hamburg
14 October 1943	Schweinfurt
18 November 1943	Berlin
8 March 1944	Berlin
30 March 1944	Nuremberg
13 February 1945	Dresden

The air offensive – which was intended to win the war quickly and without the need for an invasion of mainland Europe – did not live up to expectations. However, for years it was the only way the war could be carried home to the German people, and this was of great importance to Allied morale. After the war, Albert Speer (Hitler's architect and eventually Minister of Weapons and Ammunition Production) declared:

the real importance of the air war consisted in the fact that it opened a second front before the invasion of Europe. The front was the skies over Germany. Every square metre of the territory we controlled was a kind of front line. Defence against air attacks required the production of thousands of anti-aircraft guns, the stockpiling of tremendous quantities of ammunition over the country, and holding in readiness hundreds of thousands of soldiers, who in addition had to stay in position by their guns, often totally inactive and idle for months at a time.

By the end of 1943/early 1944, the Allies had undisputed air superiority, sufficient to enable them to inflict an unprecedented degree of destruction on the enemy homeland. Most of Germany's big cities were laid waste, and the air war caused many casualties amongst German civilians (estimated at 600,000) and Allied airmen but it did not stop German war production. Owing to Minister of Armament Albert Speer's skills – through a policy of rationalisation and dispersal – German industrial production remained astonishingly high till the end of 1944. Factories and industrial sites were scattered, concealed and camouflaged, protected in concrete shelters and bunkers. The main impact was probably the destruction of the Reich's synthetic oil production, which further lamed both the German Army and the Luftwaffe.

It was the destruction of the transportation system, rather than of the factories themselves, which led to the defeat of Germany. In preparation for D-Day (the Allied landing in Normandy in June 1944), roads, railroads, railways stations, canals, bridges and docks were massively bombarded in order to isolate Normandy, and to weaken German supply lines. At the same time a deception air offensive was launched in the Pas-de-Calais in northern France to make the Germans believe that the landing would come further north. If the air strikes largely contributed to the success of D-Day, they were not always accurate and the European occupied civilian population suffered a great deal.

Over time the tactics of the Second World War evolved. Modern technology and strategic advancements changed the rules of combat allowing for widespread attacks from the ground, the sea and the sky. The air war above Germany stimulated a tremendous boost in air defence, an increase in numbers, technical development and automation, with mechanical computers, predictors and radar for ranging and tracking, as well as the first ventures into developing and using ground-to-air rocket-powered missiles for shooting down Allied bombers. The Germans also developed massive reinforced concrete Flak towers bristling with Flak weapons, and cities became fortresses. In a secret decree of 4 November 1944, Hitler ordered the immediate increase of anti-aircraft weapons and ammunition, radar and predictor devices, and the mobilisation of the (slave and forced) labour forces employed to carry out the various Flak programmes. It was easy to command, but difficult to achieve, and in spite of developments and high priority, the German military situation was critical at the end of 1944 and desperate in the spring of 1945.

If the Allied bombardments spread fear amongst the German population, they never caused the expected total collapse of morale. The German people went stoically on with their business and – on the whole – obeyed the Nazi regime until the very end.

German Defence

The German response to the air war launched by the Allies rested on two pillars: interception aircraft (both day and night fighters) and anti-aircraft artillery. By 1944 the Luftwaffe aeroplanes became increasingly unable to carry the fight to the

◀ This Flak *Unterfeldwebel* (an intermediate rank between Corporal and Sergeant) from 1943 wears the standard Luftwaffe uniform with model 1935 steel helmet, *Fliegerbluse* (short jacket), *Tuchhose* (trousers) and *Marschstiefel* (marching boots). On the left lower sleeve he wears a proficiency badge (machine-embroidered in light grey thread on grey-blue cloth) indicating a Flak gun crew.

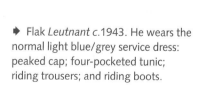

◆ Flak *Leutnant c.*1943. He wears the normal light blue/grey service dress: peaked cap; four-pocketed tunic; riding trousers; and riding boots.

enemy or even to defend the homeland against Allied air attacks. Like so much in the Third Reich, the Luftwaffe was not ready for the type of war that developed after 1941, and serious preparations were only put onto an efficient footing when the war had effectively been lost. Luftwaffe Chief Hermann Göring fell gradually from grace, and withdrew from direct command of operations.

German technology made revolutionary breakthroughs in military aviation in the latter years of the war but these technical advances (the Messerschmitt Me 262 jet aircraft, V1 flying bomb, V2 supersonic missile) were too little too late and ill-employed. This left the defence of Germany mainly a task for the Flak arm. Flak was, in the end, the only remaining, steadfast defender of the German skies as German fighter aircraft succumbed to dwindling numbers, a lack of experienced pilots and sporadic fuel shortages. By June 1944, the air defence of the homeland against British and US bombers absorbed thousands of guns and huge numbers of personnel. So as the Allies' air raids on Germany escalated in frequency and destructiveness, and the Luftwaffe aircraft efficiency decreased, so the ranks of Luftwaffe 'regular' Flak units had to be increased by recruiting thousands of *Flakhelfer* (auxiliaries), boys and girls of the Hitler Youth, young men and women of the *Reichsarbeitsdienst* (RAD, National Labour Service), *Flakhelferrinen* (volunteer women), drafted civilian workers and even volunteer foreigners.

◆ British Mosquito shot down by Flak. The two-seat De Havilland DH-98 Mosquito Mark VI was powered by two Rolls-Royce Merlin XXI engines. It had a span of 16.47m, a length of 12.3m and a height of 4.6m. It was armed with eight machine guns, had a maximum speed of 600kmph and a maximum range of 1980km.

According to the French historian Patrick de Gméline, in the autumn of 1944, the Flak personnel totalled 662,000 officers, NCOs and soldiers, as well as 478,000 auxiliaries. The latter included 350,000 German civilian men, 128,700 women, and 98,200 foreign volunteers. The number of heavy batteries in 1942 was 984, and 2123 in 1943; in the same period the total of light batteries went from 568 to 1460. In early September 1944, the Flak had 2170 heavy batteries and 1311 light batteries. According to Wolfgang Dierich, by the end of the war the German Flak totalled 31,559 guns including: 14,708 light guns (2cm); 4682 medium guns (3.7 and 5cm); 12,169 heavy guns (8.8cm, 10.5cm and 12.88cm); and 16,010 searchlights of various diameter. According to Ian V. Hogg, in June 1944, at the time of maximum strength, the German Flak totalled 45,550 guns, 30,463 of which were light weapons.

The defence of the Reich against British and US strategic long-range bombers had top priority, mobilising 33,345 guns of all kinds, and representing 73 per cent of the total strength. The result of the effectiveness of the German Flak is illustrated by the following table showing the damages done to 8th US Air Force bombers.

Period	Planes Damaged	Planes Destroyed
May–August 1943	1594	88
September–December 1943	2670	135
January–February 1944	2878	98
March–April 1944	5969	281
May–June 1944	7920	286

GROUND FORCES' FLAK

The bulk of the German anti-aircraft artillery, inclusive of anti-aircraft searchlight units, was an organic part of the Luftwaffe, which was responsible for the air defence of territorial Germany as well as important installations in occupied countries. At the start of the Second World War, it was also the Luftwaffe that provided protection for ground forces against enemy air attack in the field, but it soon appeared that this task could not be fulfilled with total efficiency. Luftwaffe Flak units were attached to army formations but this arrangement never satisfied the Heer (ground army) and it never stopped agitating for its own anti-aircraft gunnery. In the autumn of 1941 the Heer were at last allowed to form their own Flak units for the use and protection of German Army units against air attack.

Two sorts of formations were developed: first the *Heeresflakbataillonen* troops belonging to the infantry arm and whose men wore its distinctive white piping. There were two different types of *Heeresflakbataillonen*: the battalion of six companies in which the company was the tactical unit, and the battalion of three companies in which the battalion itself was the tactical unit, although its companies could on occasion be found operating independently. The battalions were equipped with standard machine guns and either 2cm (both single- and four-barrelled) or 3.7cm Flak guns, all on self-propelled mounts. These guns were available for additional use in Pak (anti-tank) or other roles against ground targets.

The second formation type was the *Heeresflakabteilungen,* troops belonging to the artillery arm and whose men wore red piping. Heeresflak battalions were usually mechanised, and in most cases consisted of three heavy batteries each of four 8.8cm guns, and two light batteries each of either twelve 2cm guns or nine 3.7cm guns. All equipment could be used in Flak, Pak and other ground roles. The operational control of these special types of Flak units was extremely flexible. They were normally allotted from a headquarters pool to an army, corps or division for permanent anti-aircraft protection.

The supply of weapons, ammunition and equipment to the Heer's troops was still the Luftwaffe's responsibility, while inspection, training and replacement of personnel was dealt with by the Heer. Neither the air force nor the ground army were satisfied with this arrangement which created administrative difficulties, caused delays and rivalry, and duplicated efforts – especially when the Heer set up its own Flak schools and training grounds. Problems increased as Waffen SS units entered the Flak equation (see below). Units bound for the field would often find their equipment and ammunition hijacked by other units, and Heer Flak formations would generally find themselves at the bottom of the pile.

The engagement against enemy aerial reconnaissance, artillery observation, air attacks on personnel and important installations was regarded as primary, but as long as the Germans enjoyed air supremacy the Army Flak batteries (both light and heavy) were a precious addition to the divisional field and Pak (anti-tank) artillery engaging ground targets in battle. In the period 1939–1941 German Army Flak guns were often employed as a highly mobile striking force in conjunction with armoured, motorised and infantry formations, such as in forcing river crossings, attacking fortified positions and supporting tank attacks. But when the Allies increasingly dominated the sky by 1943 onwards, Heer Flak units were obliged to revert to their original anti-aircraft role. New Heer Flak units were created and from then on they were exclusively used for anti-aircraft defence. These light motorised brigades and battalions, escorting troop columns and supply convoys, included detachments armed with machine guns and light quick-firing guns mounted on soft-skin vehicles and halftracks.

Moved by tractor or truck, the average marching speed of motorised Flak guns was 5–20mph depending on the vehicle used and the terrain encountered. Horse-drawn Flak guns were used by units contending with fuel shortages or travelling on damaged roads. The war also saw the appearance of the *Flakpanzer* (a Flak gun mounted on the chassis of a tank) escorting armoured divisions in combat.

By 1944 the Heeres Flak counted 60 Flak-MG Bataillone (machine-gun battalions), 33 battalions of motorised 2cm and 3.7cm guns, 12 fortress machine-gun battalions (of which three were motorised), 55 'classical' Flak detachments (each including mixed batteries of 8.8cm, 2cm and 3.7cm), and 11 detachments of Panzerflak. Tactically the Heer also had control of the Eisenbahn Flak (anti-aircraft artillery mounted on trains), which will be further described in Chapter 4.

◀ Heer Flak loader with overcoat. This man wears the standard double-breasted greatcoat (*Mantel*).

WAFFEN SS FLAK

The *Schutz-Staffeln* (Protection Squads, SS in short), created in 1925, were originally the elite personal bodyguards of Adolf Hitler. When Heinrich Himmler (1900–1945) was appointed Reichsführer SS in January 1929, the SS was expanded, growing in size and specialisation. In the 1930s it included a ruthless intelligence service (*Sicherheitsdienst*, SD headed by Reinhardt Heydrich); the *Rasse und Siedlungshauptamt* (RuSHa, Race and Resettlement Central Office created in 1931, intended to check the 'racial purity' of the SS members and to establish the racial standards required of good German stock); a ceremonial regiment, Leibstandarte Adolf Hitler, (LSSAH formed in 1933 under command of Josef 'Sepp' Dietrich); a secret state police (the Gestapo); and an embryonic army *Verfügungstruppe*, SS-VT, an armed, uniformed and barracked police task force at the disposition of the Nazi Party). When the first concentration camps were created in 1933, special warden units were formed as well, known as *Totenkopfverbände* (Death's Head Detachments).

When Himmler combined the office of Reichsführer SS and the function of chief of all German polices in June 1936, his power was boosted enormously. From then on and until 1945, the SS became a formidable machine for the repression of real and supposed 'enemies' of the Reich, and eventually for the extermination of the European Jewish community, putting absurd racial theories into terrifying practice. The SS also became a conglomerate of fruitful businesses employing slave labour from the concentration camps, virtually a state within the state, and as Hitler described them 'the pillar upon which my house stands'.

The SS also became an elite army within the Wehrmacht. Himmler was determined to form a special SS military branch that could be totally relied upon, and that should become the nucleus of a post-war German national police and army service. From the ceremonial LSSAH, armed SS-VT, concentration camp wardens,

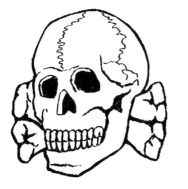

◆ Waffen SS insignia. Eagle/swastika worn on headgear and upper left sleeve; SS rune insignia worn on right collar patch; Totenkopf (Death's Head) worn on headgear.

◆ Waffen SS Flak gunner *Untersturmführer* (Second Lieutenant). The Waffen SS uniform, as well as all equipment and weapons, were the same as those used by the Heer, but a trademark of the armed SS was the wearing of a *Tarnjacke* (camouflage smock) above the standard jacket. The smock, whose design was slightly modified during the course of the war, was a short, baggy pullover manufactured from water-repellent linen duck. It was reversible; one side was predominantly green for use during the spring and summer whilst the reverse was printed with browns and tans for use in the autumn.

and drafted policemen, four SS military divisions were formed in 1939, respectively the 1st Leibstandarte Adolf Hitler, 2nd Das Reich, 3rd Totenkopf, and 4th Polizei. In 1940, they became known as the Waffen SS (Armed SS). From the start it was decided that the Waffen SS would be totally independent, and thus would have its own Flak. The first anti-aircraft artillery group was formed in May 1939 equipped with machine guns and three batteries of 2cm guns. This unit took part in the invasion of Poland and achieved modest results.

The Waffen SS also developed their own Flak units for the use and protection of their formations on the field against enemy air attack, and this added to the rivalry and problems which already existed between the other arms of the Wehrmacht. Equipped with 8.8 and 3.7cm guns, the Waffen SS Flak participated in the attack on Belgium, the Netherlands and France in May and June 1940, and destroyed twelve enemy aeroplanes. During 1941, the Waffen SS Flak increased its personnel and equipment. In July, it counted 205 officers, 870 NCOs and 4500 men who served 32 heavy guns, 60 medium and 170 light guns. The personnel were formed at Bad Tölz, Brunswick and Arolsen training centres. Although the regular Heer watched the SS with dislike and distrust and although the generals tried to obstruct him, Reichsführer Heinrich Himmler managed to constitute a formidable force, which had grown to 38 divisions by the end of the war.

After 1940, the Waffen SS was opened to *Volksdeutsche*. These 'racial' Germans from central and northern European Germanic lands (Skandinavia, Holland and Flanders) were considered people of 'similar blood'. They were encouraged to volunteer in newly created units: the 5th Division Wiking and the 6th Mountain Division Nord. Where power was at stake, even a meddlesome and finical perfectionist like Himmler could abandon racial quality for quantity. After 1942, as the war progressed and casualties rose, the ranks of the Waffen SS were opened to 'racially unpure' volunteers from western and eastern Europe (from more than 40 different nationalities). Even Russian mercenaries and Muslims from the Balkans

➧ M35 steel helmet. The standard German Army helmet is shown here with camouflaged cloth cover fitted with loops to hold fresh cut foliage.

➧ Waffen SS rifleman. There were several camouflage patterns used, notably 'splinter' (shown here), 'fading watercolour', 'tiger' or 'motley'. There was also a cloth helmet cover in matching pattern.

were encouraged to enlist. The Waffen SS became an international mercenary force dedicated to the triumph of National Socialism, and engaged in a 'crusade against Judeo-Bolchevism'. However only a few Waffen SS were elite units, and on the whole the achievements of many of these foreign legions proved a ludicrous failure. The Waffen SS was virtually a private Nazi army with its own staff (*SS-Führungs Hauptamt*), and it was organised separately from the regular Heer and had its own badges of ranks, regalia and emblems.

The Flak artillery of these SS units was engaged in Russia, and had many successes even as the front collapsed. By October 1943, for example, the Flak gunners of Division Das Reich destroyed their 142nd enemy aeroplane. In January 1944 the SS-Flak Abteilung 1 of Division Leibstandarte SS Adolf Hitler destroyed 20 Soviet tanks in a few hours at Jitomir. In June 1944 the SS-Flak Abteilung of the 12th Division Hitlerjugend (headed by Hauptscharführer Ritzel) destroyed 20 Allied planes and 4 tanks during the Battle of Caen. In December 1944 the SS-Flak Abteilung 18 of the 18th Division Horst Wessel, commanded by Obersturmführer Lipinski, destroyed 24 Russian tanks at Szezeny.

For the year 1944, the Waffen SS Flak artillery counted some 20,000 men serving 270 heavy guns, 330 medium and 770 light guns, scoring 1037 enemy aircrafts destroyed. In spite of their successes, the glamorous and much-admired Waffen SS was, however, a highly controversial army. It built up a reputation of hard fighting soldiers, but they were not ordinary combatants, they were not an ordinary corps or – as has been often suggested – merely a fourth service of the Wehrmacht. Waffen SS men were often fanatical Nazis, trained to be unquestioningly obedient, ruthless and without emotion, indoctrinated to have contempt for all 'racial inferiors' and for those who did not belong to the SS order. As a result, the Waffen SS committed numerous unsoldierly acts, atrocities and war crimes, both on and off the battlefield. The Waffen SS was therefore declared a criminal organisation by the tribunal of Nuremberg in 1946.

HERMANN GÖRING DIVISION

The Hermann Göring Division, an elite Luftwaffe ground force unit, originated from the Prussian motorised *Polizeigruppe Wecke* (paramilitary police militia) established in February 1933 by Hermann Göring (then Secretary of the Interior). The unit continually expanded before and during the war. In 1935 the detachment grew to regimental size (named Regiment General Göring), and consisted primarily of Flak and searchlight batteries with a motorcycle company and a ceremonial guard battalion. From a regiment it grew to a powerful infantry combat elite unit (soon a brigade and later an armoured division), built on a core of former paratroopers with a draft of 5000 Luftwaffe selected conscripts to bulk it out. Remaining a Luftwaffe unit, its ethos was however close to that of the Waffen SS. Well-equipped, powerfully armed and competently led, the Hermann Göring Division won a reputation as an excellent fighting formation in North Africa in 1942, Sicily in 1943, and – enlarged into a two-division corps   on the Eastern Front for the rest of the war.

From 1933–1935 the men of the police group wore 'police green' uniforms. In the transitional period 1936–1940 the soldiers of the Regiment General Göring wore various Luftwaffe and German Army uniforms. In the period 1943–1945, Waffen SS camouflaged smocks and camouflage tunics were issued. The tropical uniform was worn in Northern Africa in 1942–1943 and various winter dresses on the Russian Front in 1944–1945. When the Hermann Göring Division was expanded to an armoured formation, crews of armoured vehicles wore the black Panzer uniform (see Chapter 4). Equipment, headgear, weapons, artillery, vehicles and tanks were

◀ Flak gunner of the Hermann Göring Division. This man wears the soft peaked cap, the special three-quarter length fly-fronted Luftwaffe camouflage jacket for ground troops in standard Wehrmacht splinter pattern material, standard grey-blue trousers, canvas anklets and ankle boots.

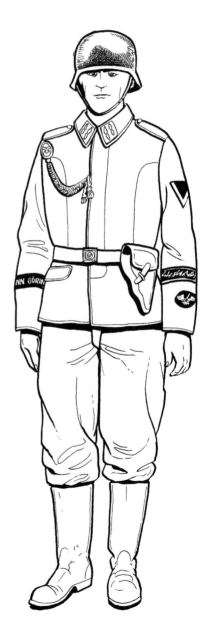

▶ *Gefreiter* (Private 1st Class) Führer-Flak-Abteilung, Hermann Göring Division. This Flak artilleryman of the Hitler Flak Regiment based in Berlin wears the basic Luftwaffe blue/grey uniform with marksmanship lanyards, a divisional black cuff band with the inscription 'Hermann Göring' on the right sleeve as well as, on the left sleeve, an inverted chevron indicating rank, a cuff band bearing the word '*Führerhauptquartier*' in Sütterlin script and a Flak gunner speciality badge.

the same as those used by the Heer and Waffen SS. But all through the war the original Luftwaffe 'diving' eagle emblem was retained, as well as typical Luftwaffe rank badges displayed on white collar-patches (with appropriate *Waffenfarbe*). In addition the elite character of the Hermann Göring Division was emphasised by a black cuff-title worn on the lower right sleeve carrying the name 'Hermann Göring' in silver letters.

MARINE FLAK

The German Navy traced its roots back to the *Reichsflotte* (Imperial Fleet) of the revolutionary era of 1848–1852 and more directly to the Prussian Navy, which later evolved into the *Norddeutsche Bundesmarine* (Northern German Federal Navy) in 1866–1871, and became the *Kaiserliche Marine* (Imperial Navy) in 1872–1918. From 1919 to 1921 it was known as the *Vorläufige Reichsmarine* (Temporary Imperial Navy) and then became the *Reichsmarine*. It was known as the *Kriegsmarine* (War Navy) from 1935 to 1945. The Kriegsmarine was one of three official branches of the Wehrmacht, but was by far the weakest of the German armed forces in the Second World War. It was – on the whole – a neglected arm as Hitler did not conceive of a European war that would hang in the balance because of a few ships. Germany had thus only a few excellent large surface vessels but they were no match in the face of overwhelming British and subsequent American strength. It was the German submarine arm that claimed the greatest degree of success, particularly in the Atlantic Ocean.

The German Navy had a tradition of independence, and the specificity of its task and the conditions in which it operated required its own anti-aircraft artillery. Experiments with aircraft successfully attacking warships had been carried out in the 1930s, and it was proved that dive-bombers or aeroplanes carrying torpedoes could hit, damage or even sink major battleships. Flak guns manned by navy crews would have to be part of the armament of modern warships: the armoured cruiser *Admiral Graf Spee* (launched in June 1934 and scuttled off Montevideo in December 1939) was equipped with eight 3.7cm and ten 2cm Flak guns; the heavy cruiser *Prinz Eugen* (launched

◆ German sailor/Flak gunner. This gunner of the *Marineflakabteilung* (MaFla) wears the traditional navy dark blue service uniform, including a peakless hat, a warm woollen short pullover blouse with navy collar and matching trousers.

◀ Navy Flak gunner in a *Drillichanzug*. Men engaged in dirty jobs (training, cleaning and maintenance) were issued with the *Drillichanzug* (fatigue suit) made of strong black or dark blue material. The blouse was fly-fronted, with or without two large pockets, and the collar could be worn open or closed. In general no insignia were worn. The trousers of matching material were full cut with two side pockets.

in August 1938, damaged in 1944) had 17 4cm Flak 3.7cm L/83, and 28 2cm Flak guns; the battleship *Tirpitz* (completed in 1941, damaged in 1944) had 16 4.1-inch anti-aircraft guns, 58 2cm, and 16 3.7cm guns; the battleship *Bismarck* (completed in late 1940 and sunk in May 1941) was defended by 16 4.1-inch, 16 3.7cm, and 36 2cm Flak guns; the heavy cruiser *Admiral Hipper* (launched in February 1937) had 17 4cm/56 Flak 28, 8 3.7cm L/83, and 28 2cm L/64 Flak MG; and the pocket battleship *Deutschland* (launched in May 1931, later renamed *Lützow*) had eight 3.7cm and ten 2cm Flak guns.

Most submarines were armed with anti-aircraft guns too – either a 3.7 or a 2cm mounted in the conning tower. But the Kriegsmarine also wanted its ports and naval installations to be protected. Created in 1940 and called *Marineflakabteilung* (in short MFLA or MaFla), the German Navy anti-aircraft artillery was deployed

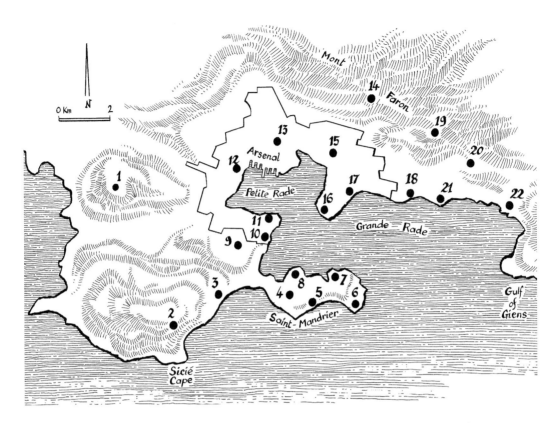

♠ Flak defence around Toulon in 1944. After November 1942, France's chief naval port in the Mediterranean was occupied and fortified by the Germans as part of the Südwall ('Southern Wall'). Units of Luftwaffe-Flak-Abteilung 355 and Marine-Flak-Abteilung 819 installed anti-aircraft defences in former French positions and created new batteries. Right before the Allied landing in Provence in August 1944, the German Flak defences included the following: (1) Heavy battery of Six-Fours (2) Battery of Peyras (3) Heavy battery La Verne (4) Heavy battery Le Lazaret (5) Heavy battery La Renardière (6) Heavy battery Cap Cepet (7) Light battery Craux Saint Georges (8) Light battery La Piastre (9) Light battery Fort-Napoléon (10) Light battery Balaguier (11) Light battery Eguillette (12) Heavy battery Brégaillon (13) Heavy battery Malbousquet (14) Heavy battery Fort de Croix-Faron (15) Heavy battery La Rade (16) Light battery Fort Lamalgue (17) Light battery Fort Saint Louis (18) Heavy battery Cap Brun (19) Heavy battery Sainte Musse (20) Light battery Pont de la Clue (21) Heavy battery Fort Sainte Marguerite (22) Heavy battery Pin de Galle.

near all important harbours, shipyards, U-Boat bases, supply dumps, main coastal batteries and any other maritime-related facilities. Just like the Luftwaffe Flak, the Navy Flak personnel included specialists (range-finders, calculators, gunners, code-users) who were trained in three main *Marineflugabwehrschule* (formation centres) at Swinemünde, Kiel and Wilhemhaven as well as in regional instruction centres. They used the same weapons as the Luftwaffe Flak, although some equipment was slightly modified to suit the navy's specificities. The MaFla batteries (light and heavy) could be either mobile units (mounted on barges and Flak ships) or permanent static ground positions (often in concrete bunkers) for the protection of approaches to vital naval installations, as will be seen further in Chapters 4 and 5.

HEIMAT FLAK

Flak Defence Men

Intended to complement the naval blockade in striking at the base of Germany's economic strength, the massive Allied air raids on Germany, as discussed above, aimed to destroy the Nazi military, industrial and economic system, dislocate its communication systems and undermine the morale of the German people. The power of the German Flak had thus to be constantly increased when Allied bombing on Germany – at first little more than a nuisance – began to have a punishing effect. By May 1944, about 3.3 million German men were dead, missing, taken prisoner or wounded, and sullen foreign forced labour could not replace them, whatever means of coercion were used. At the same time, to ease the strain of manpower imposed by Germany's war effort, large numbers of trained anti-aircraft personnel were transferred to ground combat units to serve as infantrymen or field artillerymen. So, were men to be withdrawn from the armed forces to produce weapons or withdrawn from industry to fight?

The answer to this question – a clear indication of the desperation that heralded Germany's defeat – was the introduction of the *Heimat Flak* (Home Air Defence Units). Organised at Luftgau level within the framework of Germany's air defence system, the Heimat Flak involved the partial replacement of regular anti-aircraft artillery personnel by factory and office workers, known as *Flakwehrmänner* (Flak Defence Men). The average age of the men serving in these Flak militias was between 50 and 60. Their weapons were positioned near their workplaces so as to be operated without delay when there was an attack, the men going straight from their workbenches to combat emplacements. As these units were very *ad hoc* in nature, they did not receive a great deal of training, if any. In the best cases, civilians were trained to use Flak artillery for a period of 2–3 months by NCOs from regular Flak units. Training was done after working hours and during their spare time. Some had no previous experience, others were ex-servicemen (some ex-Flak gunners) discharged from the armed forces, the latter relinquishing their former service rank and also helping in training.

The *Flakwehrmänner* were equipped with only light anti-aircraft guns of 2cm or 3.7cm calibre. They also lacked fire control equipment, so they functioned more than anything in the barrage role, sending as much fire into the air as possible in the path of oncoming Allied aircraft. They served much better against lower flying aircraft because of this. It is not known exactly how many of these units were formed during the Second World War, or how well they performed in general, but it can only be assumed that their services lacked the punch and training to have been as effective as was hoped.

When the war continued to go disastrously for Hitler's armies, another desperate measure was taken in October 1944: the creation of the *Volkssturm* (Home Defence Militia), which ordered the drafting of all men aged from 16 to 60 to defend their villages and districts with any weapons that could be found.

Hitler Youth and Women Auxiliaries

Other civilians involved in the Heimat Flak were boys and girls of the *Hitler Jugend* (HJ). This was a paramilitary organisation of the Nazi Party founded in 1922 with the aims of indoctrination and military preparation of youth for war. Membership in the Hitler Youth Movement for children from the age of ten to eighteen was compulsory from 1939. The *Hitler Jugend* was drafted from 1943 into the Heimat Flak to serve as *Luftwaffe-Helfern* (air force auxiliaries) for anti-aircraft duties,

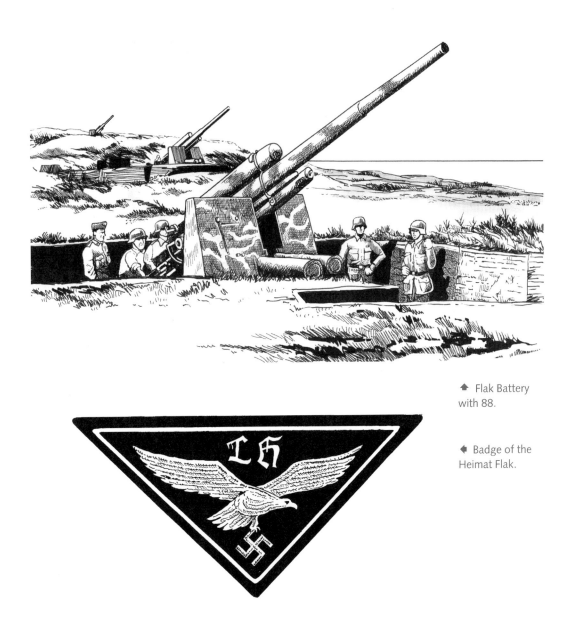

↑ Flak Battery
with 88.

◀ Badge of the
Heimat Flak.

to man searchlight batteries, to bring ammunition and supplies and to carry
dispatches.

German women and female members of various government-controlled
organisations, notably the *Nationalsozialistische-Frauenschaft* (NSF, Nazi Women's
Association, created in 1931) were also encouraged to serve in the German Air
Force. The Second World War brought a change in role for many women in the
Third Reich; where before they had been expected to occupy themselves exclusively
with their duties as wives and mothers, as war depleted the male workforce, women
were called upon to replace them. Since its official creation in 1935, the Luftwaffe
was the only German arm employing females en masse in uniform (*Helferinnen*

◀ Flakhelfer. When uniforms were available, Heimat Flak personnel wore a steel helmet or a cap, and the greyish-blue Luftwaffe dress or various tunics and overalls with the red collar patch of the Luftwaffe anti-aircraft artillery. Note the standard leather report/map case carried on the waist belt.

▶ Hitler Youth Flak auxiliary. This young man of the Hitler Jugend wears a Luftwaffe M35 service steel helmet (a woollen dark blue ski peaked cap when not in service) and the uniform of the HJ including a short dark blue pull-over jacket, matching trousers and gaiters. On the left arm he wears the HJ triangular district badge, the HJ armband (black swastika on red-white-red background) and an armband bearing the words 'Im Dienst der Deutschen Wehrmacht' ('in service of the German armed forces'). On the breast he wears the HJ Shooting Award and the HJ Proficiency Award. He has a HJ knife attached to his service waist belt.

♠ This RAD *Haupttruppführer* (Sergeant) wears the brown M1935 RAD uniform with spade-shaped badge indicating battalion and company numbers and red armband with black swastika in a white disc. Top left: RAD insignia; bottom left: Insignia of the RADwJ (Female Labour Service). Introduced by law in June 1935 the *Reichsarbeitsdienst* (RAD, National Labour Service) enforced six months' labour service for all young men between the ages of 19 and 25. The RAD was intended to toughen young men physically, instil Nazi values such as discipline, while performing useful public works. Men called for labour service generally worked in agriculture or public works including swamp draining, forest maintenance, ground clearing and building canals, roads and irrigation systems. Women, who were later included, were used in domestic and medical services, and agricultural tasks. Both male and female branches of the RAD were part of the *Deutsche Arbeitsfront* (DAF, German Labour Front), a huge organisation set up in 1933 originally to replace the dismantled trade unions. The DAF and its many sub-organisations were placed under the leadership of Robert Ley. With the outbreak of the Second World War hundreds of RAD units were employed as Wehrmacht support troops. Later in the war RAD units were increasingly trained and used into post-raid rescue and clearance duty. They were also pressed into military roles including anti-aircraft gun crews under the control of the Luftwaffe. Many saw service along the Western Front in the form of RAD Flak batteries, while others saw service in the East as ground combat units against the advancing Soviet Army. In October of 1944, at least 60,000 RAD troops are known to have served in Luftwaffe Flak batteries. When serving in Flak service, the troops were known as *Luftwaffe-Flakhelfer* (air force auxiliary artillerymen).

about 100,000 in 1944) serving as auxiliaries in air warning, plotting operators, intelligence service assistants, searchlight crews, filing clerks, medical assistants, Flak artillery, radio operators, telephone and teletype departments auxiliaries. Helferinnen was a generic term applied to female auxiliaries in service to all branches of the Wehrmacht (Heer, Kriegsmarine and Luftwaffe).

◀ RAD *Flakhelfer* in overalls. Supplementing the Luftwaffe Flak, this RAD man wears a steel helmet and dark blue overalls with a yellow arm band bearing the words '*Deutsche Wehrmacht*' in black Gothic letters indicating that while on duty he was classed as a member of the German armed forces.

◆ Female Flak signal auxiliary, 1943. Women were recruited and employed as auxiliaries in the Luftwaffe in more capacities than in any other branch of German military. The women's uniform stayed consistent with those of the Luftwaffe's blue-grey colour. This *Luftnachrichtenhelferin* (signal auxiliary woman) wears the standard Luftwaffe female blue-grey uniform composed of a *Fliegermütze* (forage cap) with the ubiquitous eagle/swastika insignia, a single breasted, three-button jacket (with eagle/swastika on the right breast) and matching skirt. On the upper right sleeve she displays the qualified radio operator badge and just under it the two chevrons indicating her rank of *Oberhelferin* (Corporal).

Luftwaffen-Helferinnen were the most numerous of all women in service to the Reich and were the most publicised. *Flugmelde-Helferinnen*, who were engaged in detection, tracking and control of aircraft, enemy and friendly, were especially utilised. They were often nicknamed *Blitz Mädel* ('lightning girls') because of their insignia, a 'blitz' (lightning bolt symbol) indicating the function of *Luftnachrichten* (radio operator).

Although the image of the uniformed female soldier was not compatible with the National Socialist conception of womanhood, the reality of the period 1943–1945 contradicted official doctrine. Recruitment of women into auxiliary units continued and increased. Uniforms for women auxiliaries were issued but it was specified that obvious and apparent makeup, and the wearing of any type of conspicuous jewellery, brightly coloured gloves, bright purses, umbrellas and the like were forbidden when in service. Alcohol, tobacco and cosmetics were strongly discouraged in Nazi

◀ Flak *Helferin c.*1944.

➡ Originally most of the female Luftwaffe recruits wore skirts and jackets, but they switched to trousers when practical dress was needed. This woman wears a functional blue-grey Luftwaffe uniform for outdoor activity including a field peaked cap (a helmet in combat conditions), a three-quarter length jacket, baggy ski-style trousers and heavy ankle boots. Insignia displayed are the Luftwaffe emblem on the right breast, the trade qualification badge and a 5mm braid chevron indicates rank of *Helferin* (Auxiliary 1st Class) on the left arm.

🔺 The Luftwaffe dagger was awarded to officers and certain high-ranking NCOs. The fittings were generally produced in a grey finish, although nickel or silver plating was available. The dagger had an aluminium top pommel featuring a swastika on both sides, and a matching cross guard that depicted an eagle in flight clutching a swastika in his talons. The grip was white or coloured celluloid. The steel scabbard was usually in a matching finish with pebble panels and oak leaf lower section. These daggers were often worn with a *portepee* (a decorative tassel wrapped about the grip).

➡ Introduced in 1944, the M44 uniform marked a break with traditional German dress. Rather similar to the British Army battledress uniform, it consisted of a short, two breast pocket jacket with matching trousers. Due to economic pressures it was of inferior quality, and issued to both male and female Heer and Luftwaffe auxiliaries.

◆ This German Armed Forces armband – worn by those who served as auxiliaries in the Deutsche Wehrmacht – was yellow with black gothic lettering.

◀ Luftwaffe trade badges. Top: direction-finder operator; bottom: signal personnel.

◆ Anti-aircraft crew badge worn by RADwJ personnel (female branch of the Reich Labour Service).

female organisations from the outset of their establishment. Good behaviour was mandatory as auxiliaries were 'female representatives of German nationhood'. Curfew was 11:00pm for German female auxiliaries, and there was to be no visiting of bars and cafés and 'no linking arms on the street'.

Some female Luftwaffe auxiliaries were the targets of acrimonious name-calling. They were called 'war prolongers', 'nymphomaniacs', 'Blitz whores', 'Wehrmacht mattresses', 'slit soldiers', 'gun-women' and 'unfeminine Amazons', pejoratives that belied the *Volksgemeinschaft* ('unified national community') the Nazis were so fond of extolling. However, when the war started to go against Germany and women were drafted en masse to work in the armament industry and the military auxiliary forces, Fritz Sauckel (the Plenipotentiary-General for the Utilisation of Labour) decreed that only a certificate of pregnancy could exempt women from service; the products of this directive were popularly known as 'Sauckel children'. During the last year of the Second World War, the Wehrmacht could claim over 500,000 female civilian auxiliaries, along with an additional 80,000–100,000 members of various Nazi organisations helping in various service capacities, plus another 50,000 RADwJ (female members of the RAD, Reich Labour Service) serving in the Home Flak. Despite their uniforms, ranks and badges, and their often dangerous assignments, female auxiliary personnel never received military status in any branch of the Wehrmacht.

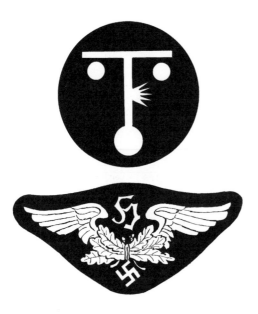

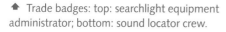

♠ Trade badges: top: searchlight equipment administrator; bottom: sound locator crew.

♠ Trade badges: top: Flak personnel; bottom: range-finder crew.

➡ Trade badges: left: graduate from signal school; right: telephone operator.

HITLER'S HEADQUARTERS FLAK

Hitler had a *Führersonderzug* (special command train) used in the period 1939–1941, codenamed 'Amerika'. The train was composed of two locomotives, a *Flakwagen* (flat car with anti-aircraft guns), a baggage and supply car, a sleeping car for Hitler himself, a *Befehlswagen* (a command car furnished with maps and communication means), a *Begleitkommandowagen* (a car for Hitler's SS bodyguard escort), a restaurant car, two cars for guests, a *Badewagen* (with showers, bath, and washing facilities), two other sleeping cars for personnel, and a second *Flakwagen*.

Throughout the war, Hitler had about 20 permanent *Führerhauptquartiere* (Command Headquarters abbreviated to FHQu). There was no planned construction programme, the headquarters being built according to the fluctuation of the war, and they greatly varied in size and degree of protection. Some were never completed and some were never used, while others (Wolfschanze at Rastenburg, East Prussia, or the Führer's Bunker under the Chancellery at Berlin) became dwelling places where Hitler spent much of his time. Hitler also directed operations intermittently from Castle Klessheim near Salzburg, and from FHQu Berghof, his pre-war holiday home at Berchtesgaden (Obersalzberg).

Hitler's residences were protected by fortifications, electrified fences and barbed wire, and controlled by *SS-Füher-Begleit-Truppen* (SS escort security troops). As Allied air raids against FHQus became a threat, the security troops also included anti-aircraft batteries. At the outbreak of the war the air defences was entrusted to Reserve-Festung Flakabteilung 321 which consisted of 600 men serving five batteries, three equipped with 10.5cm guns and one with 3.7cm and 2cm guns. In July 1943, for example, the Flak defences at FHQu Obersalzberg included 60 guns (12 10.5cm, 24 3.7cm, 6 2cm, and 2 2cm Vierling) sited on various favourable heights. In addition there were smoke-spreading installations and a *Führerflugmeldezentrale* (air raid warning centre) placed underground, and linked to the national system showing enemy air movement over the Reich in real time. If aircraft approached to within 100km of the FHQu the alarm went off.

MEDALS

Hitler considered that a lot could be done with medals and human vanity. Medals were (and still are) the tokens of a nation's esteem. In time of war, medals fell into three categories and the following examples are only a small selection of German Second World War medals.

Medals for Bravery

The first category comprised the world's most famous and coveted medals: the French Légion d'Honneur and the Croix de Guerre, the British Victoria Cross, the US Medal of Honor, and the German Pour le Mérite. These were awarded for outstanding bravery, gallantry and valour to men who had performed exceptionally on the field. After the defeat of 1918, all existing military orders and decorations for bravery were forbidden in Germany.

In September 1939 Hitler reinstated the order of the *Eiserne Kreuz* (Iron Cross, originally a Prussian decoration) with four grades: Grand Cross (only awarded to Hermann Göring); Knight's Cross (*Ritterkreuz*, about 6973 awarded); Ritterkreuz First Class; and Ritterkreuz Second Class. As the war progressed higher grades of the Ritterkreuz were added to bridge the gap between the Grand Cross and Knight's Cross: Knight's Cross with Oak Leaves was introduced in June 1940; Knight's Cross

◆ The Iron Cross Second Class was instituted in 1939. On the first day of award it was worn in the second button hole and after that the ribbon only was worn. The inner was black; the outer was white and red. In full dress the cross was worn above the breast pocket suspended from its ribbon.

◆ *Kriegsverdienstkreuz* (War Merit Cross) First Class. Awarded with or without sword, it was worn on the left breast.

◆ The Flak *Kampfabzeichen* was a medal awarded to gunners. It represented an 8.8cm gun turned to the sky, hemmed with oak leaves and crowned with the swastika held in the claws of a 'diving' Luftwaffe eagle. The medal, issued in January 1941, was awarded to gun crews having shot down a minimum of five enemy aircrafts and later on a point basis: two points for each aircraft, and a total of sixteen points to obtain the medal. There was also a *Heeres-Flakabzeichen* counterpart intended for ground troop anti-aircraft gunners instituted in July 1941 with a similar service requirement.

◆ Instituted in November 1942, the *Nahkampfsprange* (close-combat clasp) was awarded for distinguished frontline combat. It was gold for 50 hand-to-hand actions, silver for 30 and bronze for 15. The clasp was worn above the left breast tunic pocket.

◆ The *Panzerkampfwagen Abzeichen* (Tank Assault Badge) for 25 engagements. Introduced in December 1939, it was awarded for three tank engagements on three different days. It was silver for Panzer units and bronze for other motorised formations, including Flak units. After July 1943 further grades were issued for 25, 50, 75 and 100 engagements against enemy armour.

◀ The *Infanterie Sturm Abzeichen* (Infantry Assault Badge). Introduced in December 1939, it was awarded for three successful assault operations on three different days; it was silver for rifle and mountain infantry units and bronze for motorised formations. It was worn on the left tunic pocket.

◆ The *Sturm Abzeichen* (Army General Assault Badge). Introduced in June 1940, it was awarded to troops supporting tanks having taken part of assaults made on three different days. After July 1943 further grades were issued for 25, 50, 75 and 100 engagements.

◀ The *Verwundeten Abzeichen* (Wound Badge). Reinstituted by Hitler in May 1939 for German volunteers wounded in the Spanish Civil War of 1936–1939, it was awarded during the Second World War in three classes: gilt for five or more wounds, for total disablement or permanent blindness; silver for three or four wounds, or for the loss of a hand, foot or eye or for deafness; black for one or two wounds. The wound badge, worn on the left breast without ribbon, was similar to that of the First World War but with a swastika added to the steel helmet.

◀ The *Cholmshild* (Cholm Campaign Badge). Introduced in July 1942 by Hitler, it was awarded to the defenders of Cholm situated in Russia in the neighbourhood of Novgorod near the river Lavat. The garrison composed of 5500 miscellaneous troops under Generalmajor Scherer's command held the place from 21 January 1942 to 5 May 1942 against numerically superior enemy forces.

with Oak Leaves and Swords was introduced in June 1941 (only 150 awarded); Knight's Cross with Oak Leaves, Swords and Diamonds in December 1944. The Iron Cross was fitted to a ribbon round the collar, hung on the left breast pocket or worn on the second button of the tunic (only the ribbon, the cross itself not being shown). Other new decorations included the German Cross (DK) in two classes and the War Merit Cross (KVK) in five grades.

There were also badges for wounds in three classes according to disablement. Others tokens were awarded for military actions, and given the fact that Flak artillerymen often fought along infantrymen and tank units, they were eligible

▲ This *Krimschild* badge was awarded to soldiers who participated in the Crimean campaign of 1941–1942.

▲ This Flak medal was awarded for the air defence of Danzig.

for distinctions related to ground war operations. These medals were awarded for destruction of one or more tanks (*Panzerkampfabzeichen*); shooting down one or more low flying aeroplanes; participation in infantry assaults; anti-partisan operations; and to qualified snipers and marksmen.

Campaign Medals

The second category of medal was campaign medals. Whereas gallantry decorations were usually in the form of a cross, the campaign medals were mostly circular, oval or shield-shaped; they were awarded without reference to a soldier's performance but merely in recognition of the fact that he had been involved in a specific campaign. These campaign rewards also took the form of cuff-titles, consisting of a cloth band worn on the right sleeve. They illustrated combats such as Spain (1936), Africa (1941), Crete (1942), Metz (1944) and Kurland (1945).

Service Medals

The third category included medals for services rendered to the war effort or for the welfare of the nation. While the first two categories were awarded to military, the service medals were mostly awarded to civilians such as mothers who gave birth to numerous children, skilled workers, sportsmen, zealous administrators and members of the Nazi Party.

WEAPONS

AIR WARFARE

The battleground of the air is vast, being unhindered in three dimensions. On land, a hill, a defile, a marsh, a thick forest or a sheet of water may hinder movement, but the whole sky is available for combat, and free for the passage and attack of aircraft. Routes do not have to be defined, there are no set lanes along which hostile aircraft can approach, and their movements in one direction need not necessarily mean that their target is where their noses point. For purposes of air defence, artificial restrictions have to be created in the air space. During the Second World War these limits in the sky were set by interceptor planes (fighters), as well as by anti-aircraft weapons and balloons. Both Flak guns (and eventually ground-to-air missiles) and balloons were barrages, the former active, the latter passive. Balloons set the limit below which an enemy aircraft would not attempt to attack, while the fire of Flak artillery put up a fence around definite areas.

German Flak artillery utilised a smaller variety of weapons than the other classes of artillery, but what it lacked in diversity it made up for in numbers. Flak artillery was basically divided into two main categories, each with its own zone of employment and main effectiveness.

First, the light and medium Flak artillery was especially useful in combating close-range surprise attack by low-flying enemy aircraft. With machine guns and calibres from 2cm to 5.9cm automatic guns, they could be put into action very rapidly. Second, the heavy Flak artillery (from 6cm to 15.9cm calibres) was intended to fire at high-flying level bomber planes. It featured heavy calibre guns such as the 8.8cm or 10.5cm guns.

The Germans also utilised many machine guns, light and heavy anti-aircraft guns captured from defeated nations. As the Second World War proceeded, the main preoccupation of the German Flak was to get more firepower out of their light guns, and more performance out of their heavy ones.

BASIC TECHNICAL DATA

Before discussing the specific Second World War German Flak weapons, it might be useful for the reader to be familiar with a few technical concepts connected to artillery in general.

A gun is a tube closed at one end (breech) in which a charge of powder is burned and brought to explode in order to blow a projectile (bullet) out of the other end (muzzle). Ballistics is the science of projectiles. The technique of aiming does not mean simply pointing the barrel straight at the target. This works if the target is very close and if the forces of gravity, wind and air resistance, temperature and pressure have not time to take effect. If the target is farther away the projectile drops short, and the gun has therefore to be elevated above the 'line of sight' (the straight line drawn from the gun to the target) to an angle sufficient for the projectile to reach the target.

The elevation is the distance a gun can be moved vertically. The traverse is the distance a barrel can be moved horizontally. The 'effective range' is the farthest distance a weapon can be accurately aimed.

When gunners engage a target they can see with a clear line of sight, this is called 'direct fire'. Cannons fire in what is termed the 'lower register', or 'grazing fire', below 10 degrees. Mortars fire in the 'upper register', that is over 45 degrees. Halfway between conventional gun and mortar, the howitzer fires with a high angle of elevation in the 'middle register' (between 10 and 45 degrees).

When the target cannot be seen – 'indirect fire' – the gunners receive instructions from an observation post, which is placed in a position enabling the observer to have a good view of the target. Indirect fire (often carried out by mortars and howitzers) thus relies upon good communications between the gunner and the observer.

Until the middle of the nineteenth century, guns were 'muzzle-loading': that meant that the powder was poured into the muzzle of the barrel and pushed down with a ramrod, a wad was placed over the powder and the (solid metal round) shot rammed down upon it. Between rounds the barrel had to be swabbed out with a wet sponge to remove fouling and burning bits of wad. Since the 1860s most guns were breech-loading: the fixed round – a single unit composed of a cartridge case (propellant charge) and shell (projectile) – is loaded and fired at the breech by means of various mechanisms (e.g. block or screw system).

The 'recoil' is the violent force that drives a gun several feet backwards when fired. This means that the gun has to be manhandled back into position and re-aimed before firing the next shot. To counteract this force (and thus increase rate of fire), since the end of the nineteenth century guns have been fitted with various forms of recoil buffer systems. Guns were placed on a wheeled carriage or fixed mount (*'Lafette'* in German) often fitted with a shield to protect the gunners. The trail of the carriage was fitted with a traversing handspike, a recoil spade and a towing eye for transport. Some German guns were fitted with a 'muzzle brake'; this was a four-port brake placed at the end of the gun, which deflected and exited the gas behind the projectile to reduce the recoil force.

Guns – particularly those used in casemates, tanks and self-propelled guns – were often fitted with a 'fume extractor', a device creating a vacuum exhausting gas and fumes through the muzzle. A 'flash suppressor' is a device that minimises the visible flash from the gun when fired.

The speed at which a gun propels its projectile is called the 'velocity'. The 'calibre' is a complicated and a somewhat confusing notion. It is the gun's barrel size, the diameter of the bore measured across the lands (the higher portions of the bore left between the rifling grooves). Since the 1860s, cannon bores are 'rifled', with spiral ridges and grooves imparting a spinning motion to the projectile for greater accuracy. A barrel that does not have rifled grooves is called a 'smoothbore'.

The German practice was to designate gun types in terms of calibre expressed in centimetres rather than millimetres. Figures indicated the length of the barrel or the diameter of the projectile: e.g. 8.8cm, 5cm or 30.5cm SK L/50 or 40.6cm SK C/34 (L/52). The formula was as follows: length x calibre = total length (e.g. 50 x 30.5 = 1525cm or 15.25m). Additional letters showed the kind of gun:

K	*Kanone*	gun
FK	*Feldkanone*	field gun
LAG	*Landeabwehrgeschütz*	field gun
Mrs or M	*Mörser*	mortar
GrW	*Granatwerfer*	grenade launcher (mortar)
PaK	*Panzerabwehrkanone*	anti-tank gun
SK	*Schiffskanone*	navy gun
TbtsK	*Torpedobootkanone*	torpedo boat gun
U or UbtsK	*Unterseebootkanone*	gun mounted on a submarine
FlaK	*Flugabwehrkanone*	anti-aircraft gun
leFH	*leichte Feldhaubitz*	light field howitzer
sFH	*schwere Feldhaubitz*	heavy field howitzer
KwK	*Kampfwagenkanone*	gun mounted on tank
MG	*Maschine Gewehr*	machine gun

Figures gave the year the gun was designed (e.g. /34 = 1934; /42 = 1942). Additional figures indicated possible improvement (/34/38 = designed 1934, improved 1938). During the Second World War, captured foreign guns pressed into German service were given a number and indicated by a letter placed between brackets as follows: (e) englisch (English); (r) russisch (Russian); (t) tcheschisch (Czech); (i) italienisch (Italian); (a) amerikanisch (American); (h) hollandisch (Dutch); (f) französish (French).

MACHINE GUNS

The most basic form of protection against low-flying enemy aeroplanes was the machine gun, and it was utilised by the German light Flak artillery. During the Second World War, the Germans did not produce separate heavy or light machine guns but used the dual-purpose air-cooled *Maschinengewehr* MG 34 and *Maschinengewehr* MG 42. The MG 34 and MG 42 machine guns were the standard armament for infantry, bunkers and most German fighting vehicles. However, the German demand for machine guns was so great that large numbers of captured automatic weapons were pressed into service (notably from Austria, Czechoslovakia, Denmark, the Netherlands, France and Russia).

Instead of firing with the aid of tracking devices, machine guns were fitted with sights in order to keep up with the flying target. They were fired by eye for short engagements. Ammunition for the anti-aircraft role was usually fed in the ratio of one tracer, two armour piercing, and two incendiary bullets. The machine guns had a high rate of fire, enabling them to put up a devastating curtain of fire, particularly when used as an infantry weapon, but in the anti-aircraft role their efficiency was rather limited. They lacked punch and range so could only be engaged against small, slow and low-flying targets.

MG 08/15

The *Maschinengewehr* 08/15, designed in 1915, was a revised version of the famous MG 08, the German Army's standard machine gun during the First World War. It featured a bipod rather than the tripod mount, plus a pistol grip and a shoulder stock. At 18kg (39lbs), it was lighter and less cumbersome than the 08 and was intended to provide assault troops with mobile firepower on the battlefield. It nevertheless remained a bulky weapon that was chiefly used for defensive purposes. It was, however, still in service during the Second World War and put to some use as an

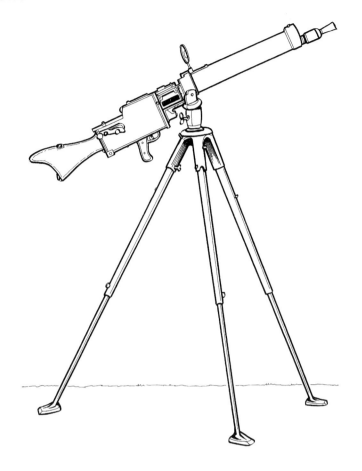

anti-aircraft weapon mounted on a tripod. The MG 08/15 was water-cooled (using a jacket around the barrel that held approximately one gallon), and was fed by a 50, 100 or 250-round fabric belt. It used the 7.92 x 57mm (0.312in) Mauser cartridge, had a rate of fire of 400 rounds per minute, and an effective range of 2200 yards.

MG 15

The MG 15, designed in the late 1930s by Rheinmetall and Solothurn, was widely used as a manned aeroplane machine gun in such medium bombers as the Heinkel He 111, the Junkers Ju 88 and the Dornier Do 17. It had a calibre of 7.92mm (0.31in), a length of 1.33m (52.5in), a weight of 12.7kg (28lbs) and a rate of fire of 850 rounds per minute. It was air-cooled and fed by a 75-round saddle drum. There were conversions to ground and anti-aircraft roles, which included a bipod and a short stock, as well as a quadruple mount version. The MG 15 was also licence-built by the Japanese, known as the Type 98 and used in aircraft.

MG 34 and MG 42

The *Maschinengewehr* MG 34 originated from a Swiss machine gun designed by the Solothurn Company, a sister firm of the German Rheinmetall. The MG 34 weighed 12.1kg (26lbs 11oz), its length was 1.21m (48in) and it shot about 800 rounds per

◆ MG 15
machine gun.

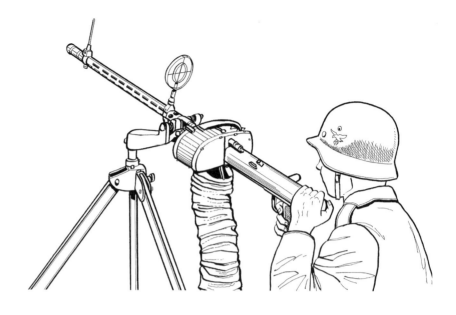

◆ MG 15 on
an improvised
mount.

minute. The MG 34 was an excellent weapon but it was complicated to manufacture, and was sensitive to mud, dust, rain and snow. The production of the MG 34 continued until 1945, concurrent with the later MG 42.

The MG 42 was probably the most famous machine gun of the Second World War. Born out of the need to simplify the manufacture of the MG 34, the MG 42 was designed by Dr Grunow of the Grossfuss-Werke armament company. It was much cheaper to manufacture, using stamped metal and spot-welding to speed production. It weighed 11.5kg (25lbs 8oz), had a similar muzzle velocity and range but a much

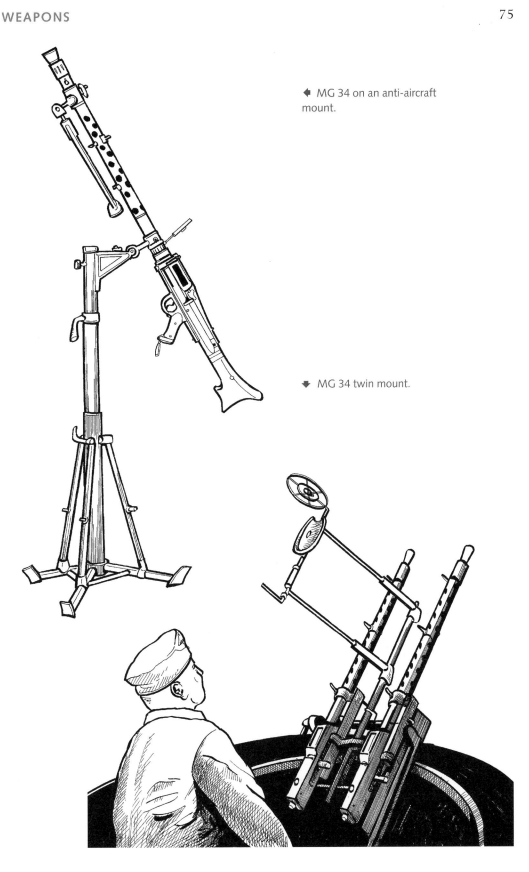

◀ MG 34 on an anti-aircraft mount.

◀ MG 34 twin mount.

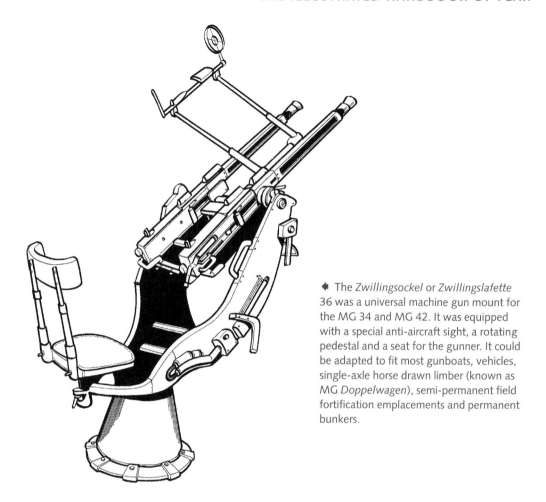

◀ The *Zwillingsockel* or *Zwillingslafette*
36 was a universal machine gun mount for
the MG 34 and MG 42. It was equipped
with a special anti-aircraft sight, a rotating
pedestal and a seat for the gunner. It could
be adapted to fit most gunboats, vehicles,
single-axle horse drawn limber (known as
MG *Doppelwagen*), semi-permanent field
fortification emplacements and permanent
bunkers.

higher cyclic rate of about 1300 rounds per minute, and this high rate of fire was
important, particularly in anti-aircraft role when engaging a fast moving aerial
target. However in an infantry support role, the prodigious rate of fire encouraged
an equally prodigious use of ammo. As a result, most members of infantry squads
would carry extra belts of rounds for the MG 42.

About 200,000 MG 34s were produced in the period 1934–1945 and more
than 750,000 MG 42s for the period 1942–1945. Both the MG 34 and MG 42
were general-purpose weapons combining the characteristics of a light machine
gun (limited weight, easy use and portability) and the formidable fire rate of
a heavy machine gun. Both used the standard German 7.92mm cartridge fed
either by a *Gurttrommel* (cylindrical magazine) containing 50 projectiles or by a
250-cartridge belt. Both machine guns could be adapted on various mountings: as
a light infantry weapon they had a folding bipod and shoulder butt; in a defensive
role they were fixed on a complicated tripod with a long-range sight. In an anti-
aircraft role they were installed on various mounts including a *Zwillingslafette*
(twin mounting) fitted with a circular sight. A horse or vehicle-drawn limber large
enough to accommodate one gunner with twin MG 34s was part of the German
Army inventory.

MG 151/15

Designed by Mauser and manufactured by Rheinmetall, the MG 151/15 was originally an aircraft weapon mounted on such fighters as the Messerschmitt Bf 109 and Focke-Wulf Fw 190. In spite of its good construction and excellent performance, the MG 151/15 proved too weak to arm aircraft, and more powerful weapons were fitted to fighters. Output was diverted to bolster Flak defences late in the war. The MG 151/15 was particularly employed as triple or twin mount on the SdKfz 251/21 half-track (see Chapter 4). The weapon had a calibre of 15mm (0.59in), and was fed by linked 50-round belts. It had an overall length of 1.91m (75.4in), a weight of 42kg (92.6lbs), a muzzle velocity of 790m/s (2600ft/s) and a rate of fire of about 700 rounds per minute.

Heavy MG 151

The Heavy MG 151 was originally an aircraft heavy machine gun that was later used in a ground role. The weapon, produced by Mauser since 1940 in the version MG151/15, had a calibre of 15mm, a length of 191.7cm, a barrel length of 125cm and weighed 41.5kg, which required the use of a small two-wheeled mount. The rate of fire was originally 700 rounds per minute. It was fed by a disintegrating metal-link belt, and used *Panzergranaten-Patrone* 15mm ammunition. Most of the MG 151s

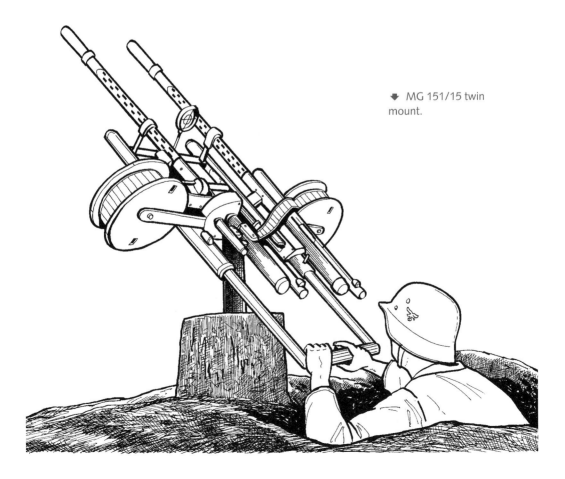

◆ MG 151/15 twin mount.

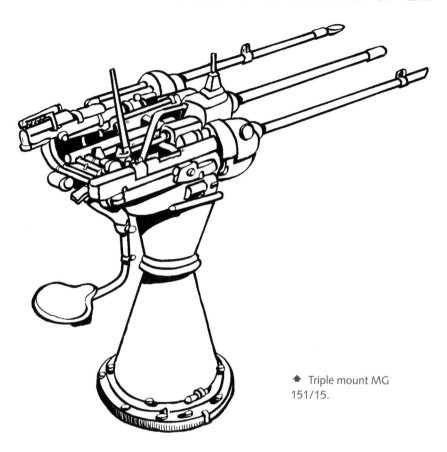

▲ Triple mount MG
151/15.

employed in a ground role were used as air defence mounts. Again, numbers of
army conversions are unclear; even total production of the MG 151 15mm is hard to
estimate since the production number of 249,609 includes many MG151/20s, the
20mm version of the same type (both weapons are identical apart from the calibre),
which was only rarely used in the ground role (in fixed anti-aircraft emplacements).
An efficient variant included a triple mount carried on an armoured halftrack type
SdKfz 251/21.

MG 271 (f)

The MG 271 was in fact the captured French 13.2mm Mitrailleuse Model 1930.
Designed and produced by the Hotchkiss Company in 1930, the weapon was used
by the French Army but also exported to Poland, Russia, Romania, Yugoslavia and
Greece. It was intended for several roles including anti-tank, infantry use, cavalry
support and anti-aircraft. Each version was provided with an appropriate mounting
(two-spoked wheel or tripod). The Japanese produced a copy known as the Type 93.
The Hotchkiss model 1930 had a calibre of 13.2mm (0.51in), a length of 2.41mm
(95in), a weight of 37.5kg (87lbs) – without mount – and a rate of fire of 450 rounds
per minute. It was air-cooled, and fed by 30-round box magazines, or 15 or 20 round
strips. The anti-aircraft version was mounted on a heavy *affût-trépied* (tripod mount)
with a complex sighting device. It existed in both single and twin-mount. After the
defeat of France in June 1940, a number of Hotchkiss model 1930S were captured
and put into German service.

Czech 7.92mm ZB vz/26

Introduced in the Czech armed forces in 1926, the ZB vz/26 light machine gun was designed by the Czech firm Ceskoslovenska Zbrojovka, based in Brno. This gas-operated magazine-fed model was so reliable and well-designed that it became extremely popular and was exported to numerous countries, notably China, Lithuania, Yugoslavia, Romania, Russia, Spain, Sweden, Turkey and Japan. Many other states manufactured it under licence, and the model eventually led to the famous British Bren gun. The ZB vz/26 had a calibre of 7.92mm (0.31in), a total length of 1.161m (45.75in), a rate of fire of 500 rounds per minute, and it was fed using a 20 or 30-round box magazine. With a weight of only 9.6kg (21.3lbs), it could

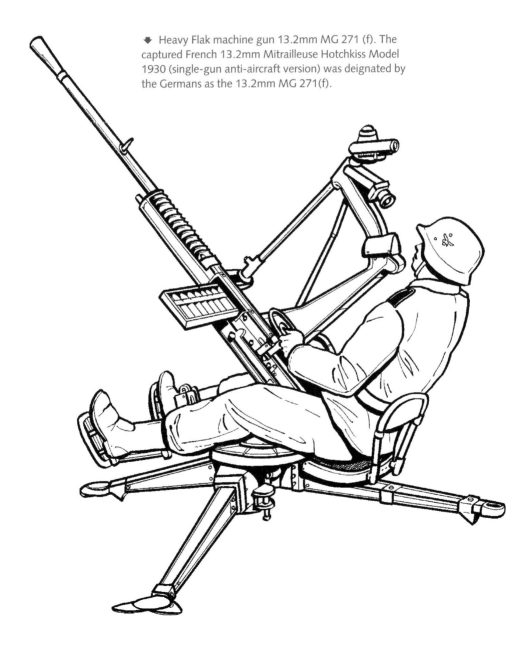

Heavy Flak machine gun 13.2mm MG 271 (f). The captured French 13.2mm Mitrailleuse Hotchkiss Model 1930 (single-gun anti-aircraft version) was deignated by the Germans as the 13.2mm MG 271(f).

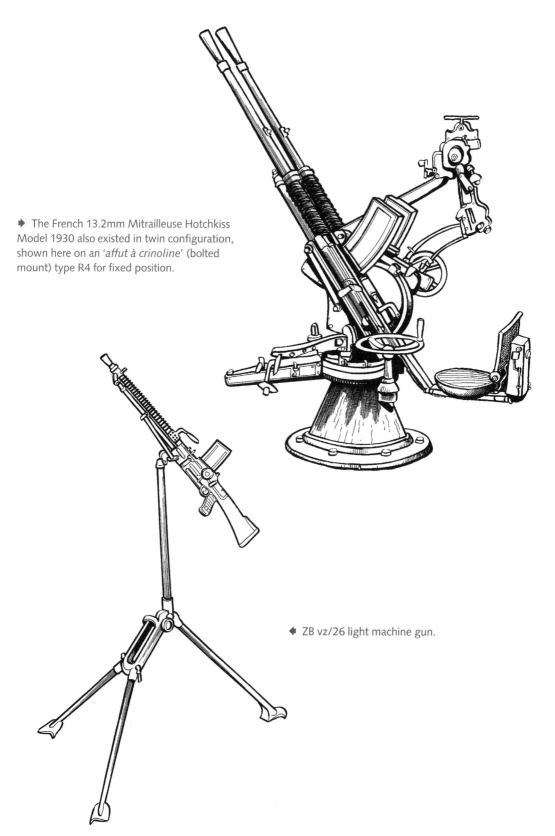

▶ The French 13.2mm Mitrailleuse Hotchkiss
Model 1930 also existed in twin configuration,
shown here on an 'affut à crinoline' (bolted
mount) type R4 for fixed position.

◀ ZB vz/26 light machine gun.

be carried by a single infantryman in battle, and there was a version on a tripod for an anti-aircraft role. After the annexation of Czechoslovakia in 1938, many were commandeered and used by the Germans throughout the Second World War.

LIGHT FLAK GUNS

Schnellfeuerkanone (automatic quick-fire light guns) were weapons with a calibre of 2cm or more, which were more effective than machine guns in the Flak role. Still small enough to have a high rate of fire, the projectiles they fired were large enough to carry a significant explosive charge, enough to inflict severe punishment on low-level fighter-bombers, ground attackers, dive-bombers and light bombers. Hedge-hopping aircraft appeared and disappeared very quickly, so light Flak crews had to react rapidly and be able to deliver sustained fire, putting the maximum amount of metal and explosive into the air in the shortest possible time.

The accepted way of dealing with low-flying, fast-moving aircraft was sustained fire and dispersing shells to increase the possibility of a hit. The speed of aircraft meant that it was very difficult for light Flak gun crews to traverse their weapons quickly enough, even assuming they had warning of an aircraft's approach. Although many thousands of rounds were wasted for every hit, light Flak guns had much more punch than machine guns, and they posed a formidable threat to low-flying aeroplanes.

Light Flak guns engaged targets flying up to 640kmph (400mph), at ranges of 900m (1000 yards) or less, and therefore had a high rate of traverse and wide elevation because at relatively close ranges the angular rate of change of the target was very fast. They were aimed by hand with several types of sight, notably the open 'cartwheel' type, but also with magnifying optical sights (*Linearvisier* 21, *Flakvisier* 38 or the *Schwebekreisvisier* 30/38).

All German light Flak guns were recoil operated and could fire single shots or bursts fed by 20-round box magazines. Some guns were fitted with nets to retrieve empty cases, so that they could be collected later for recycling. As stated above, light Flak guns could be used both against flying and ground targets – in the role of super heavy machine guns – with devastating effect. They therefore used different types of ammunition according to their role.

The most common shell type was high explosive, commonly referred as HE. It had a strong steel case, a bursting charge and a fuze. The fuze detonated the bursting charge, which shattered the case and scattered the pieces (fragments, splinters) at high velocity. Most of the damage done to the aeroplane was caused by the blast, but also by the shrapnel.

To guard against the danger of the shells coming back down to earth after missing a target, light Flak guns fired self destroying projectiles fitted with an adjustable time fuze, which exploded the rounds in the air.

⬇ Cross-section of a fixed round with explosive shell: (1) primer (2) cartridge case (3) propellant (4) steel shell (5) driving band (6) high explosive filling (7) fuze.

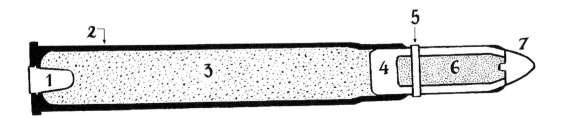

➡ Tracer (here
shown fired by
2cm Flak Vierling
38).

HE-tracer shells were interspersed with ordinary rounds and burned in flight, making it possible to see the projectile's trajectory and therefore allowing the gun crew to improve their aim at the anticipated position of an aeroplane. HE-incendiary was a type of ammunition filled with flammable liquid specially designed to pierce armour, injure crewmen and ignite readily combustible materials (ammunition or fuel), causing a fire inside the target aircraft. The incendiary also quickly depleted the oxygen in small contained areas such as within a plane, tank or shipboard compartment, which could mean the crew suffocated. Armour piercing (AP) ammunition was used against tanks and ground targets. Shells designed for this purpose sometimes had a greatly strengthened case with a small bursting charge, and were sometimes solid metal, i.e. shot. In either case, they almost always had a specially hardened and shaped nose to facilitate penetration into armour.

Light Flak guns were often fitted with armoured shields to protect the gunners, but this was usually discarded on weapons used in fixed positions. Light Flak guns had a prodigious rate of fire, but consequently they were extremely voracious in ammunition and this could lead to supply problems. All light Flak guns and their mountings (a triangular base which was lowered and stabilised by levelling jacks) were relatively lightweight allowing their installation on a two-wheel carriage, or as mobile weapons mounted on trucks, halftracks, tanks and warships. German light Flak artillery included a relatively limited number of homemade guns and a few foreign models pressed into Wehrmacht service.

2cm Flak 30

The 2cm Flak 30 was designed by Rheinmetall-Borsig in the early 1930s. It went into production in 1934 for use by the German Navy, and a year later it was taken into use by the Luftwaffe as a field Flak gun. The 2cm Flak 30 – little more than an over-scaled machine gun – was good and reliable but it had a rather low practical

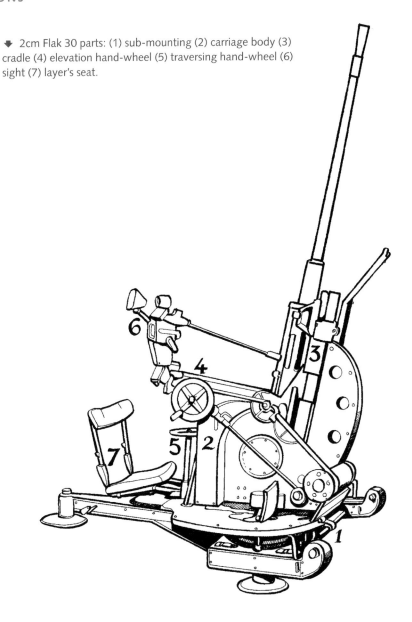

➧ 2cm Flak 30 parts: (1) sub-mounting (2) carriage body (3) cradle (4) elevation hand-wheel (5) traversing hand-wheel (6) sight (7) layer's seat.

rate of fire – about 120 rounds per minute – that was not particularly fast for a weapon of this calibre. It weighed only 483 kg in firing position and was transported on a two-wheeled trailer (the *Sonderhänger* 51 that could be towed by almost any vehicle), upon which fitted the basic mount proper. This triangular platform could be removed quickly and simply by withdrawing a shackle pin, tipping the trailer to disengage two anchoring lugs, and pulling it clear to leave the mounting on the ground. It could then be levelled by the three adjustable feet and was ready to fire. In an emergency the 2cm Flak could also be fired from the trailer.

The gun was recoil operated, and could fire either automatic bursts or single shots. Ammunition was fed from 20-round box magazines. It fired a 120g (4.23oz) 20mm HE projectile with a contact detonating fuze. A pyrotechnic relay detonated the projectile after a set time as a safety measure, limiting the effective ceiling to 2200m (6630ft). The 2cm Flak 30 was also issued drill rounds with wooden bullets for training, and combat incendiary rounds, as well as PzGr40 *Panzergranate* (Armour-Piercing Shell 40) ammunition for anti-tank use until supplies of tungsten dwindled later in the war. The gun had a calibre of 2cm (0.79in), a maximum ceiling (vertical range) of 2200m (6630ft), an overall length of 4.08m (160in), an elevation of −12 to +90 degrees, a traverse of 360 degrees, a muzzle velocity of 900m/s (2953ft/s) and a practical rate of fire of 120 rounds per minute.

Sighting was via a *Flakvisier* 35 (Flak Sight 35), which required a constant supply of range information from a crewmember operating a portable range finder. This was replaced in 1941 by the *Linealvisier* 21 (Linear Sight 21), which was similar but had gunner's reference markings for specific speeds instead of relying on manual input. As the war progressed, these cumbersome arrangements were simplified with a basic optical cartwheel sight and corrections based on tracer observation.

The 2cm Flak 30 was usually served by a crew of six or seven, although fewer men often crewed motorised self-propelled installations. The *Geschützführer* (Gun Leader) chose where to place the gun and how to camouflage it, and was responsible for maintaining contact with other units. In action, he selected targets and estimated their speed, calling it out to the rest of the crew. *Kanonier 1* (Gunner 1) aimed the

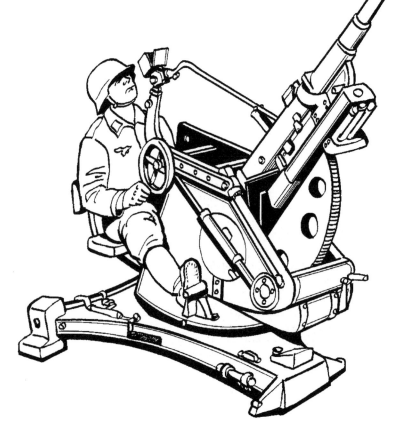

◀ 2cm Flak 30.

gun with manual elevation and traverse mechanisms. *Kanonier* 2 dialled the called target speed and distance onto the gun sight computer (when using the *Flakvisier* 35). *Kanonier* 3 dialled the target's heading and altitude change on the gun sight computer. *Kanonier* 4 fed ammunition to the gun. *Kanonier* 5 used the rangefinder and called out range to the target in 200m (220 yard) increments. The last crewman was a driver who took care of the towing equipment trailer, limber, vehicle or horse, but in combat he could also help the loader by bringing up ammunition.

The 2cm Flak 30 was widely sold all over Europe before the war, and remained in use in large numbers by all arms of the German military in all theatres of the Second World War. It was mounted on a great variety of self-propelled mounts, on vehicles, trains, submarines and ships.

2cm Flak 38

By the end of the 1930s, aircraft speeds had increased to the point where the Germans considered the 2cm Flak 30's rate of fire too slow to produce a reasonable chance of a hit or significant damage to a modern target. Furthermore, the gun's ammunition proved barely adequate in both muzzle velocity and explosive warhead content. It was also prone to feed jams. The system clearly required a redesign, but as Rheinmetall-Borsig had plenty to cope with, the project passed to the Mauser-Werke Company. Mauser's refinement, the light 2cm Flak 38 codenamed 'Erika', was designed in 1938 and entered Germany military service in early 1940.

The Flak 38 kept many of the features and components of the Flak 30, although the carriage required light modification, which was done by the firm Gustloff from Suhl. To keep design changes to a minimum, the ammunition and the 20-round ammunition boxes remained the same, but the gun was much improved compared to the Flak 30, as it was lighter and faster to operate, and featured a sight with a mechanical computing device of high quality and great

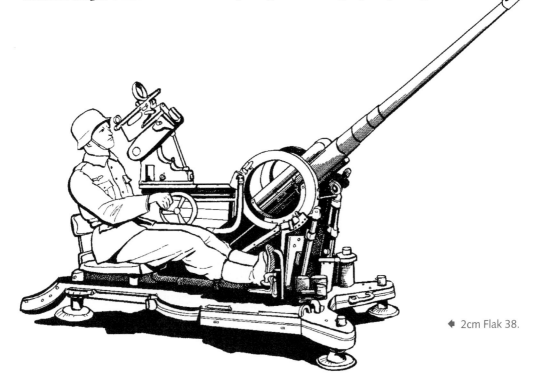

◀ 2cm Flak 38.

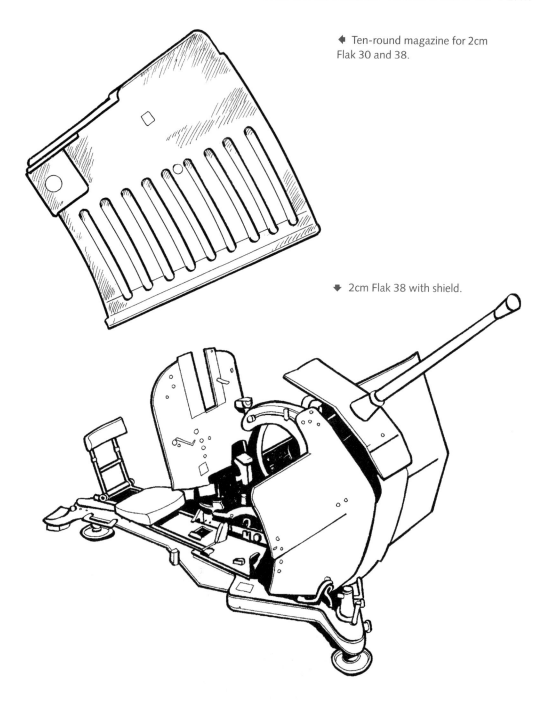

◀ Ten-round magazine for 2cm
Flak 30 and 38.

◀ 2cm Flak 38 with shield.

accuracy. The breech mechanism (bolt mechanism and spring return) was revised and the rate of fire was higher too, about 220 rounds per minute to a maximum ceiling of 2000m (6560ft). The Flak 38 had an overall length of 3.98m (157in), a weight in action of 420kg (16,564lbs), an elevation of −20 to +90 degrees and a traverse of 360 degrees.

The gun was transported on a two-wheeled trailer, designed so that it only took a few seconds to take the gun off and fire. The trailer could be towed by men, a horse or a light vehicle. In difficult terrain, the gun broke into six portable loads. It was fitted with a net to retrieve empty cases, and could feature a shield to protect the gunners on the battlefield. It was served by a crew of six or seven similar to the 2cm Flak 30. Both guns used the same ammunition and feed system. The 2cm Flak 38 was by far the most popular and most produced Second World War German Flak gun: about 18,000 examples were built during the conflict.

Gerät 239

In 1941 a modified lightweight version of the 2cm Flak 38 gun was produced by the Gustloff-Werke Company to match the special requirements of mountain units and paratroopers. Known as the 2cm-Gebirgsflak 38 or Gerät 239, this dual-purpose weapon had the same design as the 2cm Flak 38, but it featured a dramatically simplified mount using a lightweight tubular tripod that raised the entire gun off the ground, which had the side benefit of allowing it to be set up on more uneven ground. These changes reduced the overall weight of the gun to a mere 406kg (895lbs) in firing position. The 2cm mountain Flak 38 entered service in 1942, and was used both as an anti-tank and anti-aircraft weapon. However it was never a big success as its mount was too light for the gun and accuracy suffered as a result; by 1945 only 180 were in service.

⬇ 2cm-Gebirgsflak 38 (Gerät 239).

2cm Flakvierling 38

The development trend was always towards putting more lethal metal into the air, and this led to the production of the *Flakvierling* 38, which was without doubt the most feared of all anti-aircraft guns encountered by low-flying Allied aircrews. It was composed of four 2cm 38s mounted on a converted platform similar to that of the single gun but enlarged and strengthened. Often protected by a shield, this efficient and dreadful quadruple weapon was designed by Mauser for the Kriegsmarine in 1940 and was widely used by other arms of the German military. The four guns delivered a devastating 700–800 rounds per minute to a maximum effective ceiling of 2200m (6530ft), a formidable advantage as it could ensure more projectiles in the sky during a brief course of an engagement against low-flying enemy aircraft. It was also used just as effectively against ground targets.

Muzzle velocity was 900m/s (2953ft/s), elevation was −10 to +100 degrees and overall length was 4.33m (170.5in). The weapon was equipped with an electrical computing sight, often replaced by a simpler sight for economic reasons as the Second World War progressed. In action the gun weighed 1520kg (3352lbs), and was usually transported on a two- or four-wheeled trailer (*Sonderhänger* 52). In an emergency it was a matter of a few minutes to get the weapon ready for action.

◆ 2cm Flakvierling 38.

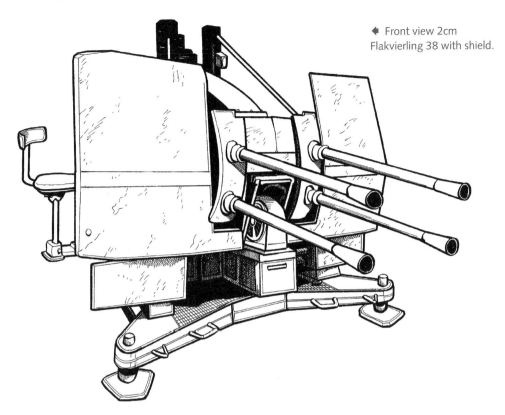

◀ Front view 2cm
Flakvierling 38 with shield.

It could fire from the trailer (only against ground targets), but a firm ground platform was preferred for accuracy. The mount had collapsing seats, folding handles, ammunition racks and a triangular base with a jack at each leg for levelling the gun. The tracker traversed and elevated the mount manually using two hand wheels.

The gun was fired by a set of two foot pedals – each of which fired two diametrically opposite Flak 38s – and could be operated either automatically or semi-automatically. As there were more guns to operate, the crew included a commander, a layer for bearing and elevation, a range-setter, four loaders and a range-taker (withdrawn after August 1944). The 2cm Flakvierling 38 could be towed behind a variety of half-tracks or trucks. It was also mounted onto half-tracks and tank chassis to produce mobile anti-aircraft vehicles (see Chapters 4 and 5). In Kriegsmarine use, it was fitted to boats and ships, and was also employed in fixed installations around ports, harbours and other strategic naval targets. It was also a common feature on Flak towers and trains, where it was mounted on a flatbed car or in an armoured turret.

3.7cm Flak 18

The 2cm was a good family of guns but larger and harder-hitting Flak weapons became necessary. Before and during the Second World War the Germans fielded four guns in the 3.7cm calibre. The 3.7cm Flak 18 gun was developed in 1934 by Rheinmetall-Borsig and Solothurn to increase punch with a heavier calibre of 3.7cm (1.45in). The Flak 18, codenamed 'Altvater' (old father) was little more than an enlarged version of the 2cm Flak 30; it had similar sight, accelerator and recoil

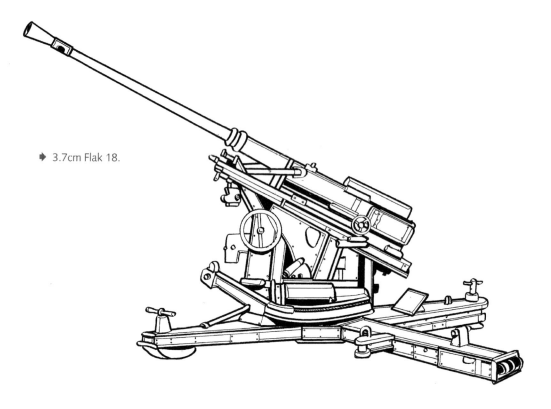

◆ 3.7cm Flak 18.

operation. There were, however, many teething problems when the gun was tested on manoeuvres held in 1935. It was mounted on a complicated, large, heavy, four-wheeled and expensive carriage. Traverse was slow, stoppages could occur, the sight used was complex, expensive and fragile and the gun demanded a crew of seven highly trained gunners. Because of these drawbacks, the 3.7cm Flak 18 was short-lived; only a few were built and development and production were stopped in late 1936, when a new improved design appeared.

3.7cm Flak 36 and 37

The improved 3.7cm Flak 36 entered service in 1937. The ballistics of the Flak 36 were the same as the Flak 18, but it was operated on a new three-legged mounting, and transported on a simpler, lighter and more efficient two-wheeled trailer –known as *Sonderhänger* 52 (Sd.Anh. 52), often towed by a standardised heavy car Horch Kfz 69/70.

In 1937, the design became the standard light anti-aircraft weapon, but it was further improved: the chamber was shortened to accommodate new ammunition (an 8-round magazine), and a clockwise-driven computing sight (the *Flakvisier* 40 produced by the firm Zeiss) was introduced. The new gun was designated 3.7cm Flak 37. In action it weighed 1550kg (3418lbs), it was magazine-fed, had a muzzle velocity of 820m/s (2690ft/s), was operated by barrel recoil and residual gas pressure, and could fire 80 rounds per minute to a maximum ceiling of about 4800m (15,750ft). Elevation was −8 to +85 degrees and traverse was the usual 360 degrees.

The 3.7cm 36/37 codenamed *Westerwald* became (together with the 2cm Flak 38) the German standard light Flak gun against low-flying aeroplanes during the

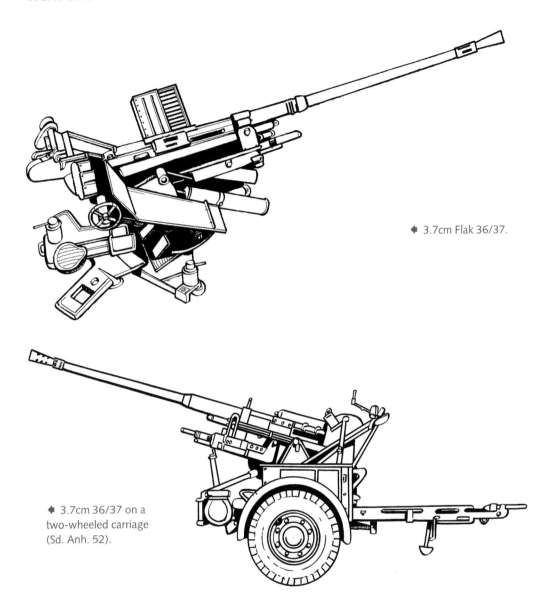

◆ 3.7cm Flak 36/37.

◆ 3.7cm 36/37 on a
two-wheeled carriage
(Sd. Anh. 52).

Second World War. It was fitted to a variety of self-propelled mounts, to Flak towers, trains, ships and submarines. By mid-1944, the Luftwaffe alone had 4211 Flak 36/37 guns in service.

3.7cm Flak 43

Externally the Flak 43 looked like the earlier 3.7cm models, but it was a much improved version, a design based on the Rheinmetall MK 103 automatic aircraft cannon. It had several changes intended to speed up manufacture: a new recoil mechanism, a new gas-operated breech mechanism and a simple sight (*Flakvisier* 43). The new gun, codenamed '*Scharzwald*' (Black Forest), continued to use existing 3.7cm ammunition, the barrel was almost the same and performance and data were similar to the 36/37, but the rifling was changed to a much steeper pitch, outsize

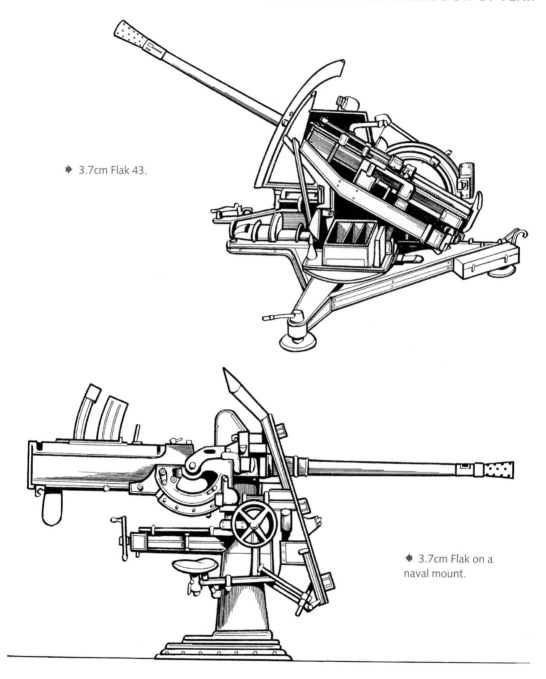

→ 3.7cm Flak 43.

◄ 3.7cm Flak on a
naval mount.

trunnions were positioned around the feed opening and the practical rate of fire was
increased (150–180 rounds per minute). The maximum vertical range was 4785m,
maximum horizontal range was 6490m, traverse and elevation speeds were higher,
and manufacturing time was shorter.

The 3.7cm Flak 43 gun was operated on a simplified three-legged mounting and
transported on a new trailer (the *Sonderhänger* 58), which subsequently brought
the weight in action down to 1219kg (2687.9lbs). Compared to its closest Allied
counterpart, the 40mm Bofors, the 3.7cm Flak 43 had over double the firing rate,

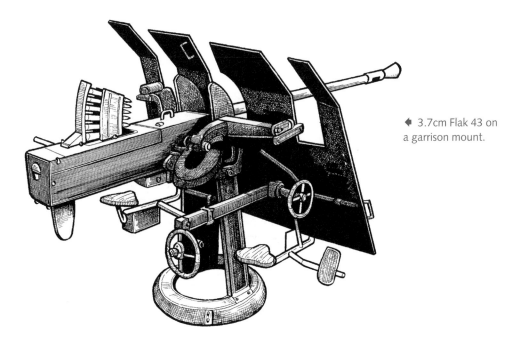

◀ 3.7cm Flak 43 on
a garrison mount.

could set up in much smaller spaces and was considerably lighter. Fortunately for
the Allied aircrews, it was put into production too late to have a decisive impact
on the outcome of the air war. In February 1945 there were 1032 Flak 43
guns in service.

3.7cm Flakzwilling 43

As Allied air power grew dramatically during the middle
period of the war, the 2cm quad-mount 38 proved to
have too little power and the 3.7cm was turned to as
its replacement. In order to increase firepower,
two 3.7cm Flak 43s were mounted one
above the other, not the usual side-by-
side configuration, on a heavier and

◀ Front view 3.7cm
Flakzwilling 43.

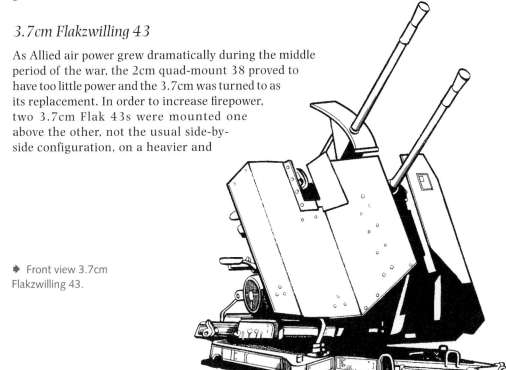

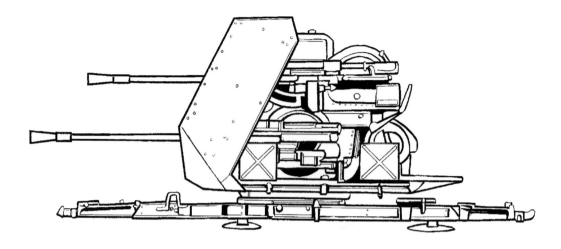

♠ Profile 3.7cm
Flakzwilling 43.

stronger mounting carried on a two-wheeled bogie trailer (*Sonderhänger* 106). The 3.7cm twin Flak 43 had a weight in action of 1248kg (2752lbs), a practical rate of fire of 180 rounds per minute, a traverse of 360 degrees, an elevation of −8 to +90 degrees and a maximum ceiling of 4800m (15,755ft). Although potentially a successful and powerful weapon, relatively few were produced, perhaps because of its height – which made it difficult to emplace – and because of political and administrative wrangling. Only about 390 units were in service in 1945, luckily for Allied aircrews. In 1944 a horizontal-mounted variant was experimented with, and it was also envisaged to produce a *Vierling* (quadruple) version, known as Gerät 341.

5cm Medium Flak 41

Experience showed the Germans that there was a middle zone where planes were too low and moving too fast to allow heavy guns to engage them but too high for small calibre weapons. This led to an attempt to produce intermediate Flak guns of 5cm (1.9in) calibre. To fill the gap between the light 2cm and heavy 8.8cm anti-aircraft artillery, in 1936 the German Army commissioned the Rheinmetall Company to develop a medium Flak gun. The result was the 5cm Flak 41. The weapon had a calibre of 5cm (1.97in), an overall length of 8.55m (337 inches), a weight in action of 3100kg (6836lbs), an elevation of −10 to +90 degrees, a traverse of 360 degrees, a practical rate of fire of 130 rounds per minute and an effective ceiling of 5600m (18,374ft). The gun was automatic, gas-operated, fed by five-round clips, mounted on a four-wheel carriage for travelling (*Sonderhänger* 204) and on a triangular platform for firing.

   Introduced in 1941, 50 units were produced for troop trials. The 5cm Flak 41 looked good but it proved to have major faults, including inaccuracy due to a complicated sight, excessive recoil, excessive vibrations when firing and poor travelling stability. A major problem was the ammunition. Despite its 5cm calibre, it was rather underpowered and on firing produced a prodigious amount of muzzle blast and flash that distracted the aimer, even in broad daylight. The carriage proved rather bulky and awkward to handle in action, and despite having been designed with fast targets in mind, the traversing mechanism was underpowered and too slow.

◀ 5cm Flak 41.

In action the Flak 41 had a crew of seven men. Loading the ammunition was no easy task for it was fed into the gun in five-round clips that were difficult to handle. Though designed for use against aircraft targets, the Flak 41 was also provided with special armour-piercing projectiles for use against tanks, but this AP round appears to have been little used as the Flak 41 was one of the few German weapons that was not selected for mounting on a self-propelled carriage. The gun was not further developed and never produced.

There was another project, the 5cm Flak 214 codenamed '*Neckartal*', developed by the Mauser Company, consisting of a batch of discarded 5cm Pak 38 anti-tank guns converted to an aeroplane weapon and Flak role. None were ever produced, and the 5cm programme was one of the biggest failures of the German gun industry.

Another attempt by Rheinmetall-Borsig to produce a medium anti-aircraft gun was the 5.5cm Flak Gerät 58 codenamed '*Stammgericht*'. This was a slightly enlarged version of the 5cm Flak 41, but a quite modern design with the gun, differential recoil, predictor, displacement corrector and radar in one cohesive high velocity weapon system using stamped sheet-metal components in order to simplify production. By early 1945 three prototypes were made, but the end of the war stopped the development of this promising programme.

FOREIGN LIGHT FLAK GUNS

In addition to German-designed and built weapons, captured anti-aircraft machine guns and anti-aircraft fast-firing cannons were widely used by the Germans, particularly after 1940 when large arsenals fell into their hands.

40mm Bofors m/36

The Swedish 40mm m/36 L/60, often referred to simply as the Bofors gun, was one of the most famous and ubiquitous medium weight anti-aircraft systems of the Second World War. Designed in 1929, the gun had a reputation for reliability and accuracy, and thus was purchased by the US, Britain and many European nations. A small number, largely British captured, were in service in the German Army, and known as 4cm Flak 28. The Bofors fired a 2lb shell fixed in clips of four rounds, it

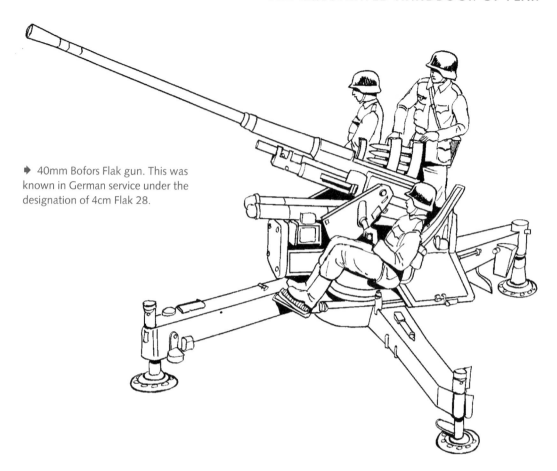

◆ 40mm Bofors Flak gun. This was
known in German service under the
designation of 4cm Flak 28.

had a maximum ceiling of 20,000 feet (pragmatic upper limit was about 12,500
feet) and a rate of 120 rounds per minute. It could be mounted on a four-wheeled
carriage for land operation and was also mounted on ships.

Cannone da 76/45 C.A.

Based on the British Vickers 3-inch gun, the Italian Army 76/45 had a calibre of
76.2mm (3in), an elevation of −5 to +80 degrees, a traverse of 360 degrees and a
maximum effective ceiling of 6405m (21,000ft). Generally mounted on a pedestal it
could be used as a static coastal gun as well as a anti-aircraft gun. Although already
obsolete at the start of the war in 1939, some 76/45 C.A. guns were taken over by
the German Army after 1943 under the designation 7.62cm Flak 266/3 (i).

Cannone-Mitragliera da 20/65 modello 35

Designed by the Italian locomotive works company Ernesto Breda from Brescia, this
gas-operated gun with a calibre of 20mm (0.78in) was intended for use against both
aircraft and tanks. It came into Italian Army service in 1935, and served throughout
the Second World War. It used a rather complicated mount and was served by a crew
of three or four. It had a weight in action of 307.35kg (677lbs), a length of 1.30m
(51.2in), an elevation of −10 to +80 degrees, a traverse of 360 degrees, a maximum
effective ceiling of 2500m (8200ft) and a practical rate of fire of 120 rounds per
minute. Ammunition was fed from a 12-round magazine. The gun could be towed

◀ Italian Cannone da
76/45 C.A.

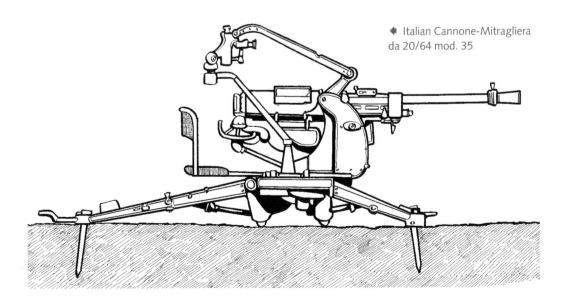

◀ Italian Cannone-Mitragliera
da 20/64 mod. 35

by a light vehicle, and could be broken into four pack loads for use in mountainous terrain. After 1943, the 20/65 modello 35 was taken over by the Germans under the designation 2cm Breda (i).

20mm Oerlikon

The light 20mm Oerlikon anti-aircraft gun was one of the most valued anti-aircraft guns in Allied use. Made in Switzerland, it was sold all over the world. It was a simple blowback heavy machine gun, which could be mounted on aircraft, tanks (e.g. on the Skink tank and on the anti-aircraft Crusader), ships (on cargo, warships and landing craft) or on a ground mounting. The gun alone – without mounting – weighed 66.75kg (147.15lbs) and was 2.21m (87in) in length. Served by a crew of three, it was fed by a drum-shaped magazine with a capacity of 60 rounds. The rate of fire was 650 rounds per minute to a maximum range of 1100m (3600ft). The 20mm Oerlikon was not a common light Flak gun in German service on the battlefield, but a number were used for training purposes. The German versions were British captured or purchased in Switzerland.

⬥ 20mm Oerlikon anti-aircraft gun.

HEAVY FLAK GUNS

Heavy Flak artillery consisted of long-range guns firing against high-flying aircraft, particularly strategic bombers. Flak artillery's task was to shoot down enemy planes, but also to signal their position to friendly fighters/interceptors by means of flares, and to hinder their action by forcing them up to an altitude from which they could not bomb with accuracy or were forced into taking evasive action that prevented any bombing at all.

Heavy Flak guns required a high muzzle velocity to cut down the flight time of the projectile, leading to excessive barrel wear and short accuracy life. Ammunition used by German heavy anti-aircraft guns included high explosive shells fitted with time fuzes. These exploded after a chosen time interval for which the fuze could be set. The shell fragments were projected outwards from the burst at high velocity and this produced a certain lethal area, larger or smaller according to the size of the round. The Germans, however, were unable to develop a workable proximity-fuzed shell. In 1943 controlled-fragmentation rounds were introduced for the 8.8 and 10.5cm shells. These rounds, far more effective against Allied heavy bombers than the regular high explosive rounds, had grooves cut on the inside face of the casings, so that when the charge detonated the case broke up into a smaller number of larger fragments.

During the Second World War the Germans developed the incendiary shrapnel. This was a thin-walled projectile containing numerous small pellets. When the shell exploded the pellets were blown outwards and forwards, piercing the skin of any nearby aeroplane, injuring the crew, starting fires in the fuel tanks and exploding ammunition and bombs on board.

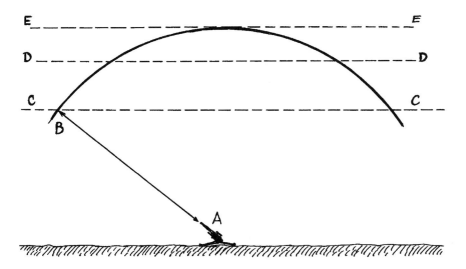

◆ AB is the gun's range. CC is the effective ceiling at which the gun gets its best capability and can engage an enemy aircraft. DD is the practical ceiling, the longest setting of time fuze a lucky shot can hit the target. EE is the maximum ceiling, the height at which (ignoring everything except gravity) the gun can propel a shell until it becomes motionless and falls back to earth. The maximum ceiling is in practice never reached by a gun in service because it rarely points vertically, and the running time of the shell's time fuze expires and the projectile explodes before reaching that altitude.

Obviously anything thrown into the air comes back down because of gravity. Shells falling back to earth were a serious hazard, especially in densely populated areas. Therefore self destruction devices in the form of adjustable time fuzes were installed in heavy Flak shells making sure that, should they miss their target, they would explode in the air and would not return to earth.

The Germans had excellent heavy guns, notably the types 8.8cm, 10.5cm and 12.8cm. After 1940, they also utilised a number of heavy anti-aircraft guns captured from defeated nations, but the demands of war soon spoiled all pre-1939 arrangements. When it came to forecasting the future, the Luftwaffe was no more visionary than any other comparable body. The appearance of new aeroplanes, new bombs and new tactics, and the frequency and ever increasing scale of Allied attacks on Germany led to sudden demands on designers to develop powerful solutions. A sudden flurry of activity in the anti-aircraft business took place, and the military's demands on the armament industry were always the same: improve the performance of weapons, increase their range and velocity, but do not augment weight.

7.5cm Flak L/60

During the 1920s the Treaty of Versailles prevented Germany's Reichswehr from producing or possessing modern weapons. In order to circumvent this interdiction, the Krupp Company made secret arrangement with the Swedish Bofors Company for a design team to work in Sweden on the development of new guns. One product of this clandestine partnership was the 7.5cm L/60 anti-aircraft gun. It had a calibre of 7.5cm (2.95in), a length of 4.5m (177in), a weight in action of 3140kg (6924lbs), an elevation of −5 to +85 degrees, a traverse of 360 degrees, a maximum ceiling of 9km (29,539ft) and a muzzle velocity of 850m/s (2789ft/s). The gun was

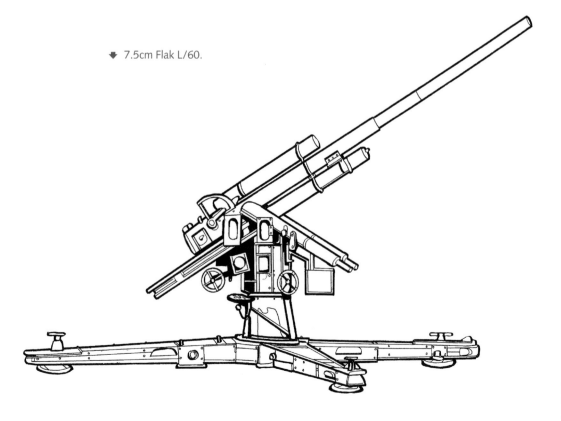

◆ 7.5cm Flak L/60.

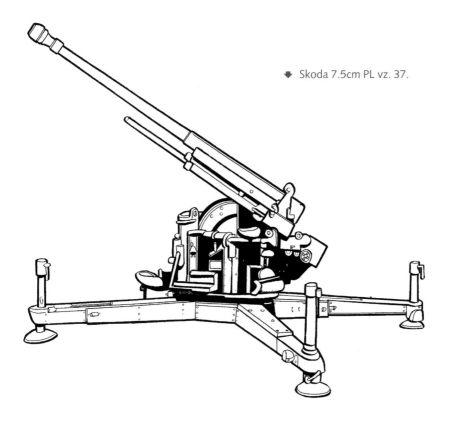

⬇ Skoda 7.5cm PL vz. 37.

transported on a four-wheeled trailer and operated and fired on a cruciform mount. In 1930, the gun was ready and tested, but the German War Office rejected it as it did not meet the performance and requirements they wanted. Nevertheless Krupp produced the weapon, and sold it to Spain and Brazil. In 1939, a batch of undelivered L/60s was taken over by the German Navy and used as a coastal and Flak weapon. The Krupp Flak L/60 incorporated many features which were eventually employed in the design of the formidable 8.8cm series.

Skoda 7.5cm PL vz. 37

Designed in 1937 by the Czech Skoda Company, the PL vz. 37 entered service with the Czechoslovakian Army in the same year. It had a calibre of 75mm (2.95in), a length of 3.65m (143.7in), a weight (emplaced) of 2800kg (6174lbs), an elevation from 0 to +85 degrees, a traverse of 360 degrees, a muzzle velocity of 775m/s (2543ft/s) and a maximum ceiling of 9200m (30,185ft). The gun, fitted with a muzzle brake, was transported on a four-wheeled trailer and operated on a cruciform platform. After the annexation of Czechoslovakia in 1938, the PL vz.37 went into service in the German Army as the 7.5cm Flak M.37 (t). Some were used by the Italians under the designation Cannone da 75/49.

Russian 85mm anti-aircraft gun model 1939

The 85mm, entering Soviet Army service in 1939, was one of the most successful of Russian guns for it was still in worldwide use in the early 1970s. It had a calibre of 85mm (3.34in), a weight in action of 3057kg (6740lbs), an elevation of −2 to +82 degrees, a traverse of 360 degrees, a muzzle velocity of 800m/s (2625ft/s) and

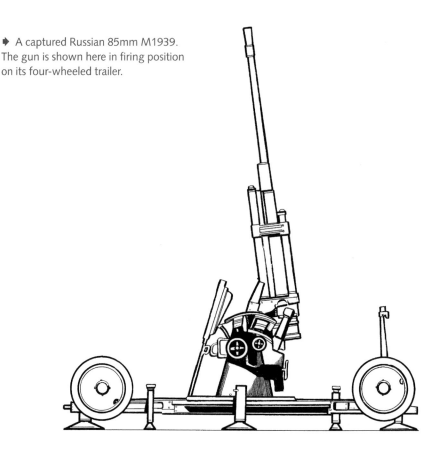

♦ A captured Russian 85mm M1939.
The gun is shown here in firing position
on its four-wheeled trailer.

a maximum ceiling of 7620m (25,000ft). In 1941 a number of these guns were
captured and passed into German service under the designation 8.5/8.8cm Flak
M.39 (r).

8.8cm Flak model 18, 36 and 37

When the 7.7cm L/60 model was rejected by the German War Office, the Krupp
team, working in partnership with Bofors in Sweden, developed another more
powerful Flak gun with a superior calibre of 8.8cm (3.46in). The result of their work
was undoubtedly the most famous German heavy Flak gun of all: the legendary
'*Acht-komma-acht Zentimeter*' ('eight-comma-eight centimetre').

In the early 1930s, the new design, known as 8.8cm Flak 18, was brought
back to Germany where it could be mass-produced on production lines, at car
manufacturers or tractor factories, without the need for specialised equipment. After
the seizure of power by Hitler in January 1933, the 8.8cm *Flugabwehrkanone* 18
entered production by the Krupp Company, and was issued to the German military
in contravention of the Versailles Treaty. The gun, soon in full production, was an
immediate success.

The 8.8cm Flak 18 had a length of 4930m (194.1in), an elevation of −3 to +85
degrees, a traverse of 360 degrees and a muzzle velocity of 820m/s (2690ft/s). A
simple but ingenious semi-automatic loading system ejected fired rounds, allowing

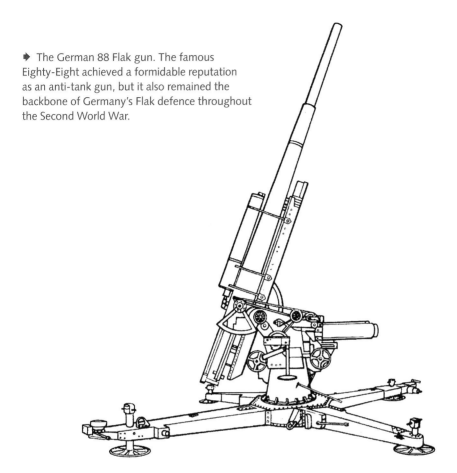

◆ The German 88 Flak gun. The famous
Eighty-Eight achieved a formidable reputation
as an anti-tank gun, but it also remained the
backbone of Germany's Flak defence throughout
the Second World War.

it to be reloaded by operating a single handle and inserting a new shell. This
resulted in excellent rate of fire of 15–20 rounds per minute to a maximum ceiling
of 8000m (26,250ft). In firing position, the gun weighed 5150kg (11355.75lbs),
which meant that only a powerful vehicle could move it on the field. The 8.8cm was
transported on a four-wheeled trailer known as *Sonderhänger* 201, very often hauled
by a specialised *Zugkraftwagen* SdKfz 7 (halftrack prime mover). The halftrack also
carried the crew, with other attendant vehicles carrying predictors, range finders
and communication and observation equipment, and also extra ammunition. In an
emergency the gun could be fired from the trailer, but only against ground targets.
When regularly firing the wheels were dismounted and the gun was set on folding
four-legged cruciform outriggers resting on screw-jacks for stability. Since the 8.8cm
was rather conspicuous because of its height, it was vulnerable on the battlefield.
Whenever possible, therefore, it was dug in so that only the barrel appeared over
the top of the embankment. Naturally local conditions and frequent moves did not
always permit the time to devise effective concealment.

   The gun was crewed by eleven men: the gun commander; tractor driver; layer for
elevation; layer for line traversing; loader; four ammunition handlers; fuze setter
operator; and fuze setter/round handler. With a rate of fire at about 15 rounds per
minute, the crew was kept busy in combat. If a member of the team was injured or
killed, another crewman stood in for their role, which in the case of ammunition
handlers meant redoubling their efforts to keep up with supplying rounds. The

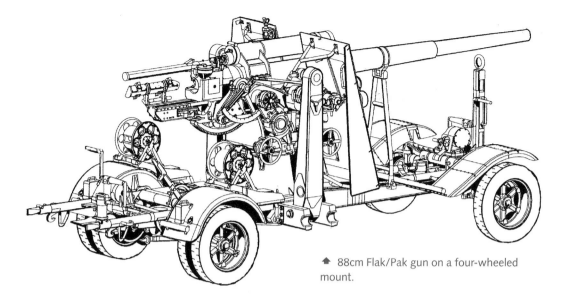

▲ 88cm Flak/Pak gun on a four-wheeled
mount.

8.8cm model 18 first saw combat with the Condor Legion during the Spanish Civil
War, where it was fitted with a shield for the protection of the crew, and extra sights
for firing at ground targets.

In 1936, a slightly improved version of the model 18 entered service, known as
the 8.8cm Flak 36. It differed in two main features: firstly the construction of the
barrel, redesigned by Rheinmetall, included three removable liners. These could
be changed when worn instead of changing the whole barrel, thus enabling a
change to be made in the field if necessary, and also making the barrel cheaper.
Another advantage was that small manufacturers could produce the barrel in
short sections, thus simplifying mass production.

Secondly, the model 36 was fitted on a new and heavier trailer (*Sonderhänger*
202) with double-tyred wheels mounted on two identical and interchangeable
bogies. The gun was towed with the gun pointing to the rear, allowing it to be set
up much more quickly, simply by dropping the base while still mounted on the
wheels. This was useful to the troops as the basic concept of *Blitzkrieg* was fast
moving operations.

Apart from these two major points and other minor details (notably the shield
protecting the crew and improvements made to the levelling arrangements), the
model 36 and 18 were very similar.

Another variant appeared in 1939, the 8.8cm Flak model 37 codenamed
'*Rauschgeld*'. This had a revised data transmission system, which lent itself
exclusively to the anti-aircraft role, and additional instrumentation to allow the gun
layers to more easily follow directions from the single director. The model 37 also
used a simpler and lighter trailer design.

In the Flak role, the 88 model 18 and 36 was a very good weapon, certainly
better than average, but the design really made its reputation in the Pak role (Pak,
as previously mentioned, being short for *Panzerabwehrkanone*, anti-tank gun),
particularly during the North African campaign of 1941–42. It could fire a wide
range of ammunition including high explosive against aircraft and personnel, and
AP 40 armour piercing rounds, with which it could penetrate over 150mm of
armour at a range of about 2km. It was thus an unparalleled anti-tank gun during
the early years of the Second World War, being the most widely used and one of

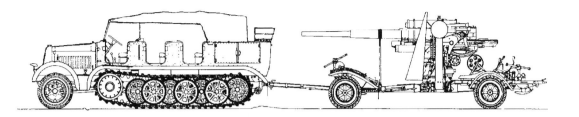

⬆ *Zugkraftwagen* (halftrack) type SdKfz 7
towing an 8.8cm Flak gun.

⬇ 8.8cm crew.

the most feared tank destroyers, and was still formidable against all but the heaviest
tanks up until 1945. The 88 had few rivals until the end of the war, and was a multi-
purpose weapon, used as a Flak gun, an anti-tank gun, a howitzer for long range
bombardment (and destruction of concrete fortifications) and even as a coastal
defence gun. It was widely employed for several self-propelled mountings, both Pak
and Flak, and also emplaced on trains and ships.

Many parts of the three models were interchangeable; it was not uncommon to
find a Flak 37 barrel on a Flak 18 carriage. The three models of the 88 series were
the mainstay of the German artillery, and remained in combat service on all fronts
throughout the Second World War. In August 1944 there were nearly 11,000 model

◆ 8.8cm on a cruciform mount.

18, 36 and 37 guns in service, most of them employed as Flak guns. Some were used by the Italians under the designation Cannone da 88/56 C.A.

The success of the 88 series as an anti-tank gun was so remarkable that it led to the development of a separate line of anti-tank guns, known as Pak 88, and as the main armament for tanks such as the Panzerkampfwagen VI (SdKfz 181) Tiger, the self-propelled tank destroyer *Nashorn*, and the tank destroyer *Elefant*.

There is no doubt that the 88 was an effective gun, but it must also be said that it was skilfully publicised and magnified into an all-conquering super weapon, which it certainly was not. The legend of the 88 as a Pak gun probably came from the fact that the Germans had plenty of them at a time when the Allies had little or nothing comparable. As a Flak gun it was no better than its contemporaries, and was of a fairly conventional design. As already said, with a height of 2.41m (92.2in) it had a very high profile, which made it easy to spot on the battlefield.

8.8cm Flak 41

Despite its success the '88' 18/36/37 fell behind the improving performances of later Second World War aircraft. As early as 1939, the Luftwaffe anticipated the increase in speed and height of bombers, and drew specifications for a new gun, intended from the start for use in both Pak and Flak roles. The result was a new design by Rheinmetall-Borsig, known originally as Gerät 37, which was eventually (in 1941) designated 8.8cm Flak 41 codenamed '*Eisenerz*' (iron ore).

Only the 8.8cm calibre remained; the other features of the Flak 41 – barrel, ammunition and mounting – were new designs. The gun was longer with the barrel in three changeable sections with a sleeve, a jacket and a locking collar to hold everything together; the ballistics were greatly improved; the cartridge case held a more powerful charge; the firing circuits were separated for Flak and Pak use; and the carriage used a turntable-mounted chassis to which the gun was attached by trunnions behind the breech. By using a turntable on a four-legged platform, instead of the usual pedestal mounting, the result was a low silhouette, which could be easily concealed, an important feature in a Pak role. The 8.8cm model 41 had an overall length of 9658m (380in), a weight in action of 7840kg (17,287lbs), an elevation of −3 to +90 degrees and a traverse of 360 degrees. With a muzzle velocity of 1000m/s (3280ft/s), it could fire a 9.40kg (20.69lb) high explosive shell to a maximum range of 15,000m (49,215ft). Improvements to the loading system raised the firing rate to 20 rounds per minute.

The Flak 41 was an impressive weapon with formidable potential but the early production models were riddled with teething problems, mainly owing to the complexity of the gun's systems and the sheer number of new and untried features: it was prone to problems with ammunition, and cases often jammed on extraction after firing.

The first 8.8cm Flak 41s were not issued to the troops until 1943. The gun was rarely used in the anti-tank role, but it proved to be an outstanding anti-aircraft weapon. However, it never fully recovered from its early mechanical troubles and always required a great deal of skilled maintenance. In February 1944 there were only 279 in use. This low production number was due to the complexity and costs of the gun, but also due to the excellent design of the earlier and unrivalled 8.8 Flak 18/36/37.

A final adaptation, designated 8.8cm Flak 37/41, consisted of the Flak 41 gun mounted on the carriage of the 8.8cm Flak 37. Only thirteen were produced. In spite of all its troubles the 8.8cm Flak 41 was a good weapon, and some units were still employed by the Czechoslovakian Army until the early 1960s.

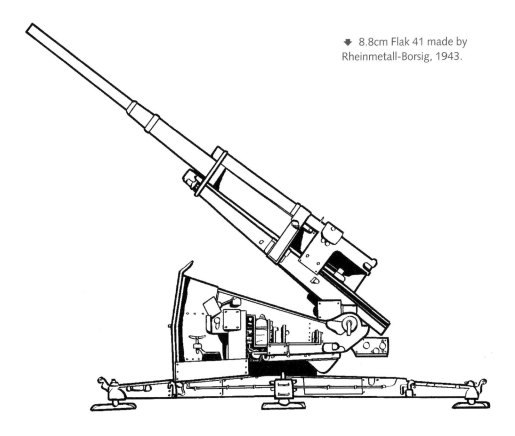

➧ 8.8cm Flak 41 made by Rheinmetall-Borsig, 1943.

10.5cm Flak 38/39

This heavy gun, provisionally named the Gerät 38, was approved in 1933 for higher altitudes than those possible with the 8.8cm series, namely up to 9450m (31,000ft). Designed by Rheinmetall, and entering service in 1937, it was designated 10.5cm Flak 38 (codenamed '*Regenbegen*'). It resembled a scaled-up 8.8cm Flak 18, but there were many technical differences, notably the electrical firing and power-control system, the semi-automatic loading mechanism, and sectioned barrel with a calibre of 10.5cm (4.13in).

The gun rested on a compact four-legged platform, it had an overall length of 10,310m (405.9in), a height of 2.9m (114in), an elevation of −3 to +85 degrees, a traverse of 360 degrees, a maximum ceiling of 12,800m (42,000ft) and a muzzle velocity of 880m/s (2886ft/s). The design was slightly improved in 1939, resulting in a variant designated 10.5cm Flak 39. The breech was horizontally sliding and semi-automatic allowing an increased rate of fire.

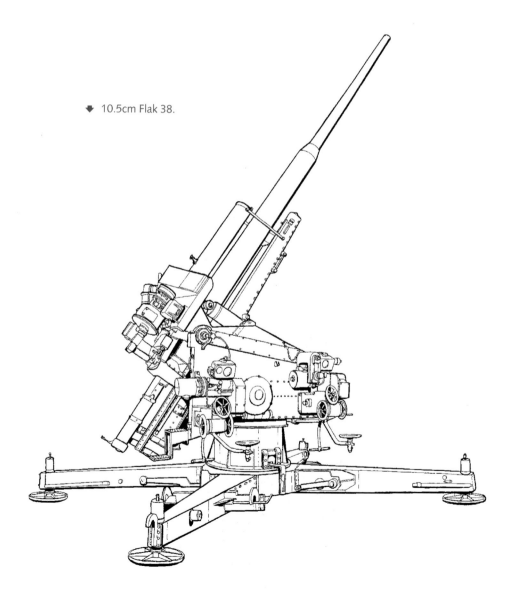

◆ 10.5cm Flak 38.

Operated by a crew of 10 or 12 men, the gun fired several types of ammunition: high explosive with anti-aircraft time fuze; high explosive shell with percussion fuze; and armour piercing with ballistic cap. The 10.5cm Flak 38/39, though reliable and well made, was not without its disadvantages. In a mobile configuration, it took 15–20 minutes of hard work to bring it in and out of action. Its excessive complete weight of 10,224kg (22,544lbs or 10.06 tons) made it difficult to transport by road and operate in the field. It was thus much better suited for use in the defence of Germany in static batteries mounted either in permanent emplacements or on railway carriages so that batteries could be rapidly moved where they were most needed. The 10.5cm was therefore the backbone of German static defences, also being mounted in twin mount on special Flak towers in major cities.

In 1944 there were 1025 heavy 10.5cm Flak 38/39 used in a mobile role mounted on trailers, 877 were fixed on static emplacements, and 116 were mounted on railroad trucks. By the end of the war, several developments were made for improving its performances (e.g. new barrel, muzzle-squeeze attachments, sabot projectiles and 'Peenemünde' arrow shells), but none came to fruition before the end of the Second World War.

12.8cm Flak 40

By 1936, the Luftwaffe Flak artillery authorities decided that an even larger piece would be needed in the near future, and new specifications were drawn up resulting in the heaviest German Flak gun of the Second World War. Designed by Rheinmetall-Borsig under the designation Gerät 40, it passed its tests with flying

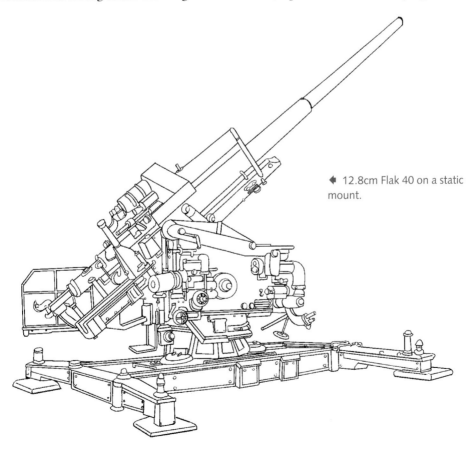

◀ 12.8cm Flak 40 on a static mount.

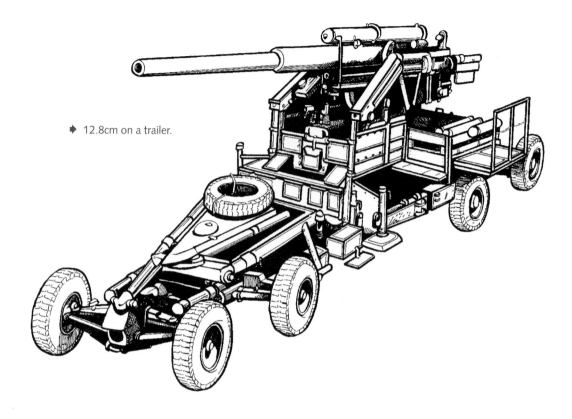

➡ 12.8cm on a trailer.

colours in 1937. Entering service in 1942, it was actually a scaled-up 10.5cm
Flak 38/39. The 12.8cm Flak 40, codenamed '*Havelland*,' had a calibre of 12.8cm
(5.04in), an overall length of 15m (590.9in), a height of 3965m (156in), a weight
in action of 27,000kg (59,535lbs, 26.58 tons), an elevation of −3 to +88 degrees,
a traverse of 360 degrees, a rate of fire of 12 rounds per minute, a muzzle velocity of
880m/s (2887ft/s) and a maximum ceiling of 14,800m (48,559ft). Compared with
the 8.8cm, the 12.8cm used a powder charge four times as great, which resulted
in a shell flight time only one-third as long. This made aiming against fast-moving
targets much easier.

In spite of its size and weight, the new weapon was originally intended to be
transported on a special firing platform placed on an eight-wheel trailer designed
by the Meiler Company. But being much too cumbersome and heavy, only six were
produced in this configuration; the rest were used in static emplacements (about
450 units) and on railway flat cars (about 200 units), its pedestal being then bolted
down in concrete or metal.

12.8cm Flakzwilling 40

The heavy 12.8cm Flak 40 also existed as *Flakzwilling* (a two-barrelled twin
configuration known as Gerät 44 codenamed '*Innsbruck*') placed side-by-side with
mirror loading arrangements on an enlarged cradle. The 12.8cm Flakzwilling
40 was produced by Hanomag in Hannover and 34 of these powerful units were
installed on top of concrete *Flaktürme* (large anti-aircraft towers) in the most
important cities and industrial areas of the Third Reich, notably Berlin, Vienna

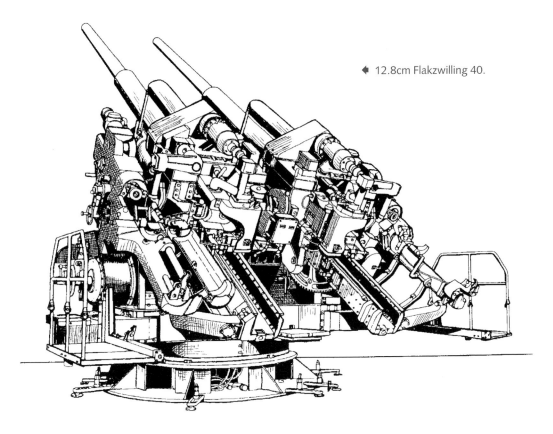

◀ 12.8cm Flakzwilling 40.

and Hamburg. In this role, operated by a crew of 10 or 12, the 12.8cm Flak 40 proved highly effective with a rate of fire of 24 rounds per minute. Although it never replaced the 88, the 12.8cm was one of the best, largest and most effective heavy anti-aircraft guns of its era. There was also a version with improved performance and longer barrel, known as 12.8cm Flak 45, but this was never put into production.

SUPER HEAVY FLAK GUNS

Super heavy anti-aircraft guns (*Uberschwere Flakgeschütze*) had calibres of 15cm and above. In May 1938 Rheinmetall proposed an enlarged version of the 12.8cm. This big gun, known as Gerät 50, was to be transported in three loads: gun, mounting and platform.

In September 1938 Krupp presented its design, a large Flak gun with a new form of barrel rifling, and a massive 10-round magazine attached to the breech in order to speed up loading and increase the rate of fire. There were even larger projects with calibres of 21cm and 24cm, the Gerät 80 by Krupp and Gerät 85 by Rheinmetall. It is doubtful whether such monster Flak guns with exaggerated ballistic demands would have ever been practical and cost-effective.

None of these projects got further than artist's impressions and general arrangement drawings. In September 1943, the Luftwaffe cancelled all contract on Flak guns above 12.8cm calibre, in order to concentrate efforts and production capacity on existing models.

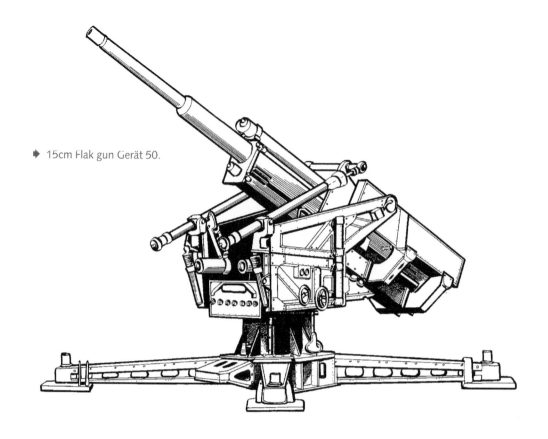

◆　15cm Flak gun Gerät 50.

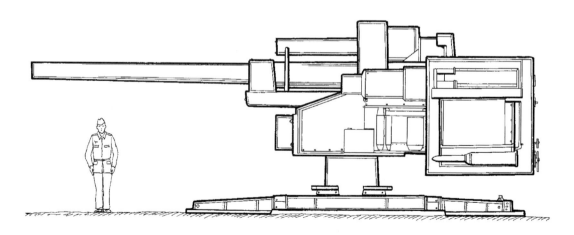

◆　Project by Rheinmetall for a 15cm Flak gun.

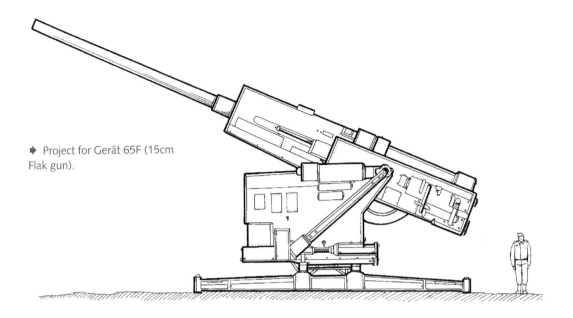

◆ Project for Gerät 65F (15cm Flak gun).

EXPERIMENTAL FLAK GUNS

When the Allied armies invaded Germany at the end of the Second World War they were followed by investigating teams of scientists and engineers whose task it was to examine test centres and research establishments. During that process a number of projects for far-fetched and wildly experimental Flak weapons came to light.

Electric Gun

In 1943 an electrical engineer called Otto Muck, a consultant to Siemens, put forward the idea of projecting a missile by using electric energy. There would be a large barrel 100m (328ft) in length installed in a shaft sunk in the ground near Lille in northern France and pointed at London. This would fire a 15cm fin-stabilised shell weighing 200kg (450lbs) to a range of 250km (155 miles), thus able to bombard the British capital at a rate of 500,000 projectiles a month. The power estimated was 100,000 kW demanding a power plant using 54,000 tons of coal each month. His project was forwarded by the Ministry of Armament and Ammunition to eminent scientists and serious engineers who soon realised out that Muck's basic assumptions were wrong. Even if this gun had been feasible, it would have involved such large expense and demanded so much electrical energy that the project was doomed from the start. Besides, by the time Muck presented his project, the V2 rocket was almost ready for operational service.

Sound Cannon

Designed by Dr Richard Wallauschek, the Sound Cannon would have used powerful air waves consisted of large paraboloid reflectors, the final version of which had a diameter over 3m. The dishes were connected to a chamber composed of several sub-unit firing tubes whose function was to allow a mixture of methane and oxygen into the combustion chamber, where the two gases were ignited in a cyclical series of explosions. Each explosion initiated the next by producing a reflected, high-intensity shockwave, and so creating a very high amplitude sound beam. This high and strong note of unbearable intensity was emitted at pressures in excess of 1000 milibars about 50m away, a level of pressure above the limits that humans can endure. At such a range, half a minute of exposure would be enough to be lethal. Even at longer range the effect would be formidable and the victim would be incapacitated for some time afterwards. No operational or physiological tests were ever carried out. It was suggested, however, that laboratory animals were used to prove the basic soundness of the concept. The cannon was never deployed for its intended purpose.

Sun Cannon

This was a large sun-reflector intended for use against hostile aircraft – only on sunny days, of course. Nothing was known about any test results or operational use for this bizarre weapon.

Vortex Gun

The vortex or whirlpool gun was designed and built by an Austrian scientist named Dr Zimmermeyer at an experimental institute at Lofer in the Tyrol. It was basically a mortar barrel of a large calibre sunk into the ground. The shells, containing coal dust and a slow-burning explosive in the centre, were intended to expel hot gases to create an artificial whirlwind or tornado which would hopefully upset the stability of enemy planes, make crews lose control and thus crash the aircraft. It was not known whether the pressure of the tornado would have been powerful enough to cause frame failure in aircraft caught in the air stream, but the pressure and turbulence on the wings might have been strong enough to cause substantial damage. This idea had already been envisaged in 1913 by Captain F.W. Barron of the British Royal Artillery. Dr Zippermeyer's whirlpool gun worked in theory, but it would have been unable to produce enough energy to reach the height at which Allied bombers flew, and the gun was never used in practice.

Wind Cannon

The Wind Cannon was developed by a factory in Stuttgart during the war. It was a strange device consisted of a large angled barrel like a bent arm resting in alarge cradle that would eject a jet of compressed air against enemy aircraft. The cannon worked by the ignition of mixtures of hydrogen and oxygen. The powerful explosion triggered off a rapidly ejected projectile of compressed air and water vapour, which, like a solid shot of air, was as effective as a small shell. Experimental trials of the cannon at Hillersleben demonstrated that a 25mm-thick wooden board could be smashed at a distance of 200m, proving that a powerful region of compressed and high-velocity air could be deployed with sufficient force to inflict some damage. The cannon was installed on a bridge over the Elbe, but with no significant results, as one might suspect. The wind cannon was an interesting experiment but a practical failure.

GROUND-TO-AIR MISSILES

Rocket Technology

The Luftwaffe Flak was well aware of the rapid improvements in aircraft performance, and from the time of its creation in 1935, authorities were preparing to deal with the bombers of the future. In some cases, however, their solutions demanded ballistics that were difficult to achieve, and sometimes the performance of Allied aircraft in 1944 advanced so rapidly that regular guns became obsolete before they were actually built. It was therefore decided that conventional gunnery could no longer cope with the air war with which Germany was confronted, and more effort went into developing a variety of unconventional ground-to-air projectiles. As a result, a totally new weapon entered the German Flak artillery by the middle of 1944: the guided missile.

Rocket artillery has a long history dating back to mediaeval China, but by the beginning of the twentieth century this type of weapon had been largely overlooked. During the Second World War the full potential of rockets became apparent. Every major belligerent power made some progress in that field, but it was the Germans who made the greatest advances.

Basically a rocket missile is an unmanned self-propelled spacecraft, which carries a destructive load. It consists of an airframe with or without wings and fins, housing a motor, fuel tanks for solid or liquid fuel, a control system, guidance device and warhead. The essence of a rocket, in contrast to a projectile fired from a conventional gun, is that it contains its own propellant. The method of propulsion is based on Newton's Third Law of Motion: 'To every action there is an equal and opposite reaction.' A rocket produces hot gases by combustion and allows them to escape at high speed through a back-facing vent producing a forward thrust. The advantage of this is that the rocket exercises no back thrust or recoil upon the frame which launches it. It therefore requires no heavy device to discharge it, only a relatively simple launching frame to hold and guide it during the initial phase of its flight. This can be a platform, a pad and pedestal for vertical launching, or a ramp or rail for inclined launching. Additional booster rockets can be attached to the body of the missile – to give a high initial launch speed – that are then jettisoned after burnout. The initial disadvantage of rocketry lay in inaccuracy, particularly in the German Flak sphere where targets were high-flying aeroplanes. For that purpose efficient methods of guiding a rocket to its target were developed.

German rocket development started in the early 1930s under the control of the Army Weapons Department, established near Berlin. This expertise, however, was given only low priority by the Nazis and it was not until the last phase of the Second World War that the Third Reich concerned itself with the problem of increasing the effectiveness of guided rockets in an anti-aircraft role. It was only by 1944 (at which time the war was already effectively lost), that the Germans accelerated their efforts and developed a sophisticated experimental missile programme.

Radio-controlled rocket-powered missiles for anti-aircraft use were developed in response to a demand for weapons that could destroy high-flying Allied bombers. The intention was to deploy batteries of these missiles to defend German population and industrial centres. In spite of considerable achievements, Germany's programme of technological and scientific development was, however, characterised by chaotic organisation. The Luftwaffe's requirements changed frequently and often drastically, resulting in a vast number of prototypes designed only to be abandoned, wasting time, effort, materials and money.

There was no superior office or one single agency to coordinate the efforts of research, industry, armed forces and manufacturers. When the Third Reich started to collapse, German technologists and scientists were put under great pressure to develop war-winning and secret retaliation weapons, culminating in the design of the flying bomb V1 and the supersonic rocket V2. But they frequently saw their – often remarkable – achievements come to nothing through a lack of vision at the top. Indeed anti-intellectualism was a pronounced feature of the ideology of Hitler's National Socialism. Besides, because of Nazi anti-Semitism, universities, laboratories, scientific institutes and research centres had been purged of their 'non-Aryan' and Jewish members after the seizure of power in 1933, depriving Germany of many of her most productive brains. Personal rivalries between the service chiefs only made matters worse.

In spite of a combination of apathy, conservatism, outright ignorance and contradictory requirements, together with Hitler's maniacal preference for conventional offensive weapons, the achievements of German technologists in the domain of rocketry were astonishing, as they succeeded in gaining a lead in the field. They spent little energy and time on simple free-flight projectiles but instead developed sophisticated surface-to-air designs, one or two of which actually entered service in limited numbers by the end of the war. Fortunately, German overall military situation by that time was so bad that they were unable to fully exploit their advance, the old story of 'too little, too late'. Had these revolutionary weapons been fully developed, completed and made operational in time, they would have been formidable additions to the Reich's air defence, and they might even have had an important effect upon the course of the war. As it was, their role was negligible. By the end of the Second World War it was clear, however, that a new era was dawning, and new weapons were necessary as the performance of aircraft continued to improve. German designs were without doubt the precursors of modern guided missiles such as the American Seacat, Hawk, Terrier I and Nike-Hercules, and the British Thunderbird.

Messerschmitt Enzian

The ground-to-air missile *Enzian* ('Gentian'), designed by Dr Konrad and Dr Wurster of Messerschmitt, was based on the Messerschmitt Me 163 Komet single-seat rocket fighter. The radio-guided anti-aircraft missile's wings, fuselage and tail unit were made of wood and coating. It was launched from a short steep-angled ramp supported by a cruciform platform – in fact a converted 8.8cm gun mount. The *Enzian* existed in several experimental versions known as E1, E2, E3, E3B, E4 and E5 with slightly different dimensions, performances and weights due to various power plants used. The *Enzian* E4, for example, was powered by a Konrad DVK rocket engine with 2000kg thrust, had a speed of 1000kmph (556mph), a flight time of 70 seconds, an effective ceiling of 16,155m (53,000ft) and a range of 24,500m (80,360ft). It carried 300kg (661lbs) of high explosive detonated by an infra-red proximity fuze. It weighed 1800kg (3960lbs), had a length of 3750mm (12ft 3 5/8in), a wingspan of 915mm (3ft 1/8in) and a maximum diameter of 915mm (3ft 1/8in). Development began in 1943, and at least 60 units at various stage of development were built, of which ten were flown at Karlshagen in April 1944. It was also envisaged to use it as a ground-to-ground and even as an anti-tank weapon. Despite considerable research and work, the missile never progressed past the testing stage.

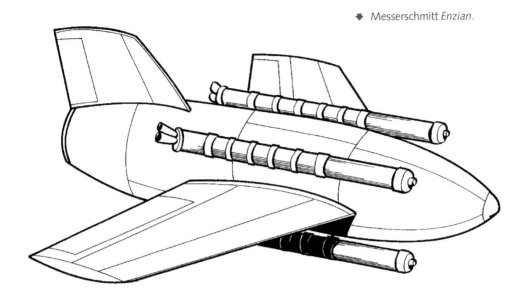

⬇ Messerschmitt *Enzian*.

Henschel Hs 117 Schmetterling

The Hs 117 *Schmetterling* (butterfly), sometimes called the V3, was designed by Dipl. Ing. Henrici and Professor Herbert Wagner from the Henschel Aircraft Company. Based on the Henschel Hs 293 glide bomb, development began in 1941, but the device was given low priority by the Luftwaffe for years on the grounds that it was a defensive weapon. The concept was revived in late 1943 as a possible response to the increasing Allied air attacks on Germany.

The *Schmetterling* was a mid-wing bomb-shaped monoplane with a length of 4.29m (14ft), a diameter of 350mm (13.77in) and a wingspan of 2m (6ft 7in). The wings were made of coated wood, and the fuselage and tail unit were made of a light riveted alloy. It carried a 25kg (55lb) warhead of high explosive detonated either by impact or by a Fuchs (Fox) proximity fuze. The missile was propelled by a liquid-fuel rocket engine (Walter HWK 109-729 with 375kg of thrust) and two Schmidding 109-553 solid-fuel boost rockets (each developing 1750kg of thrust) assisting launching and discarded after a few seconds of flight. It had a speed of 756kmph (416mph), a flight time of 33–57 seconds, an effective ceiling of 10km (32,800ft) and a maximum range of 32km (20 miles). Operational weight with accelerator rockets and the warhead was 440kg (970lbs).

The Hs 117 was vertically launched from a special carriage, and radio controlled with the FuG 203 or FuG 230 guiding system, the two ground crew operators keeping both missile and target in view from a special tracking station fitted with a joystick with 18 channels in order to avoid jamming. It was also planned to drop the *Schmetterling* from a twin-engined Heinkel He 111 bomber, and promising tests were carried out in the period May–November 1944. Due to intensive Allied bombing attacks on the factories where the missiles were produced, the *Schmetterling* scheme was never brought into operational service and abandoned in February 1945.

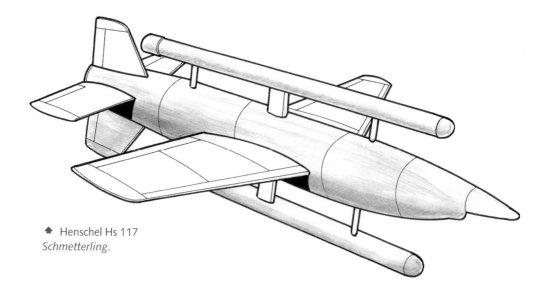

⬆ Henschel Hs 117
Schmetterling.

Rheintochter R-I and R-III

The anti-aircraft missile *Rheintochter* ('Daughter of the Rhine') was developed by
the Rheinmetall-Borsig Company from November 1942 onwards. It existed in two
slightly different versions (R-I and R-III). In August 1943 the test unit R-I was
completed, but the Luftwaffe turned it down due to its low altitude ceiling, and work
on the improved R-III started. The fuselage, made of coating of light alloy, had a
length of 4300mm (14ft 1 1/5in) and the wings were made of wood with a span of
2928mm (9ft 7in). Maximum diameter was 335mm (1ft 1/8in).

The version R-III was powered by two releasable solid fuel rockets developing
7000kg of thrust each and a Konrad rocket engine using liquid propellant
delivering 2180kg of thrust. The missile had a maximum speed of 756kmph
(416mph), a flight time of about one minute, an effective ceiling of 10km
(32,800ft) and range of 32km (17.7 miles). Version R-I carried a load of 150kg
(330lbs) of high explosive and R-III 100kg (220lbs), which was detonated by a
Kranich acoustic proximity fuze.

Rheintochter was launched from a converted 8.8cm gun carriage and controlled
through radio command optical tracking (flares attached to the fins) and convergent
radar beam, the operator using a joystick device. It seems that a few R-IIIs were
fired at the Belgian port of Antwerp in late December 1944. However, after a lot
of work and 82 test launchings, of which only four failed, the *Rheintochter* scheme
was abandoned in February 1945, the main reason being that it could not equal
the altitude performance of the *Enzian* and *Schmetterling* projects, and that it was
considered unlikely to be completed in time to have any effect on the outcome of the
war. There was a project for a variant, known as *Fernraket Rh.Z. 61/9 Rheinbote*, with
a length of 11m, a range of 220km, carrying a 20kg explosive warhead.

EMW C2 Wasserfall

The surface-to-air missile *Wasserfall* (waterfall) borrowed several features of the
contemporary A4 (V2) missile; in fact it was essentially a scaled-down V2. Design
by Dr Ing. Haase, development by the Elektro Mechanische Werk Company (EMW)
started at the Peenemünde test centre in 1942, and the first firing tests were carried

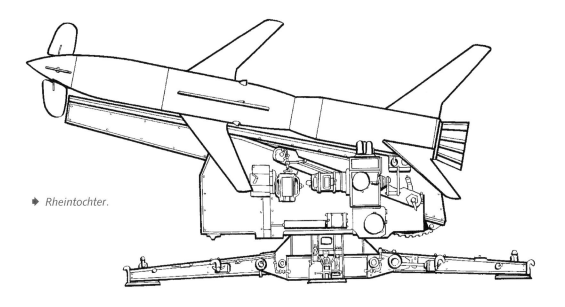

◆ *Rheintochter.*

◆ *Wasserfall.*

out across the Baltic Sea in February 1944, during which the
Wasserfall reached an altitude of 23,000ft. By July 1944 seven
more missiles had been made by Arado and Henschel, tested and
fired. Development stopped in February 1945 without any of
them being ever engaged against Allied aircrafts.

The *Wasserfall* was a cigar-shaped rocket with a length of
7.45m (24ft 5.25in) and a maximum diameter of 720mm
(2ft 4 and 3/8in); it was fitted with small wings with a span of
1584mm (5ft 1/8in). It was powered by an EMW rocket engine
developing 8000kg of thrust, fuelled by Visol, SV-Stoff and
pressurised compressed nitrogen. It had a maximum speed of
2772kmph (1496mph), a ceiling of 20km (12.5 miles) and a
range of 26,400km (87,120ft).

The missile carried a 235kg (516lb) high explosive warhead
detonated by a codified radio impulse and proximity fuze. To
make sure that the missile would explode in the air and not fall
back to the ground, it was fitted with a self-destroying system
comprising an explosive charge of 90kg (198lbs).

Wasserfall was vertically launched from a pad like the V2.
A plan was made to design a smaller version from *Wasserfall*,
codenamed *Taifun* (typhoon), which was intended to have
a tremendous speed of 4500kmph. The German *Wasserfall*
project led to the development of the post-war American
missile Nike.

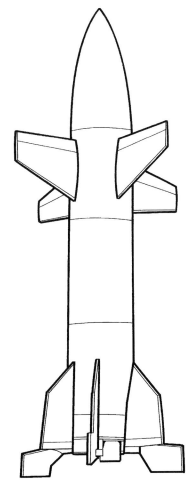

Feuerlilie F25 and F55

The anti-aircraft missile codenamed 'Fire Lilly' was designed by the Research Control Section of the German Air Ministry, using aerodynamics developed by Dr G. Braun and A. Busemann. *Feuerlilie* was also based on experience gained by a test gliding bomb codenamed FK 2200 Hecht (pike). *Feuerlilie* existed in two different versions.

Feuerlilie F25 had a cylindrical fuselage with a total length of 2.1m (6ft 10.7in), mid-fuselage mounted swept-back wings with a span of 1.15m (3ft 9.25in) and a tail unit with a single fin and high-mounted tail plane. It was powered by a Rheinmetall 109-505 solid diglycol fuelled rocket engine developing 500kg (1100lbs) of thrust, and had a maximum speed of 840kmph (522mph). The device was launched from an inclined ramp, and controlled by radio link. The F25 made it first test flight in April 1943 at Peenemünde.

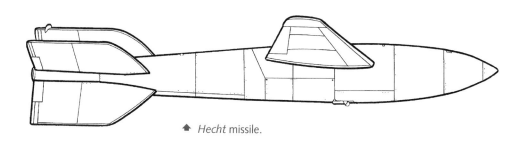

↟ *Hecht* missile.

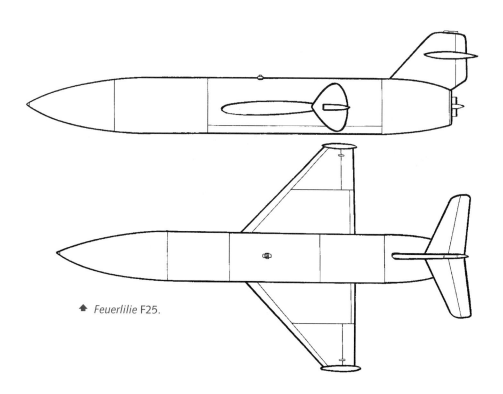

↟ *Feuerlilie* F25.

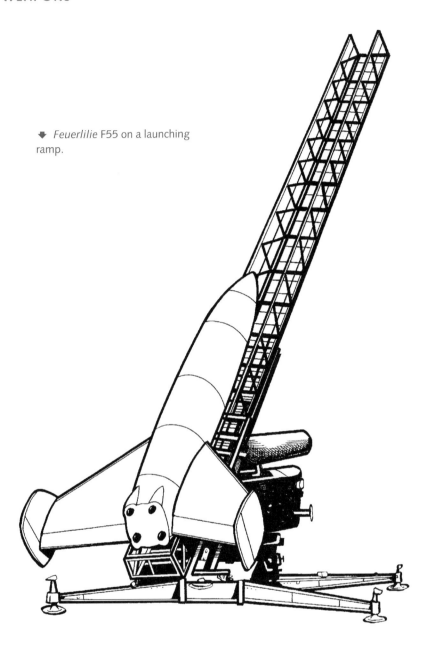

◆ *Feuerlilie* F55 on a launching ramp.

Feuerlilie F55, a new tailless design intended for supersonic speed, had a length of 4.8m (15ft 9in), and wings mounted to the rear of the fuselage with a span of 2.5m (8ft 2.5in). F55 was powered by a liquid-propellant rocket engine designed by Dr Conrad developing 6350kg (13,970lbs) of thrust. In May 1944, the F55, fitted with four solid-propellant Rheinmetall 109-505 rocket engines was successfully tested and flew to a supersonic speed of Mach 1.25, about 1500kmph (932mph). The end of the war prevented further development of this promising rocket system.

Föhn

Föhn (warm and dry wind blowing in spring in the Alps, also meaning 'thaw' in German) was a multiple anti-aircraft rocket launcher firing 7.3cm high explosive projectiles. The device, transported on a trailer, was composed of a pedestal and a simple framework of racks holding 35 spin-stabilised rockets each carrying a 280kg high explosive warhead detonated by a fuze mounted in the nose; each was fitted with a self-destruction charge ensuring that it did not fall back down unexploded. No further information is available.

Zeppelin Flakmine V7 Feuerball

The surface-to-air anti-aircraft V7 *Feuerball* (fireball) was composed of a conical central body with a total height of 2.5m storing fuel and an explosive charge of 250 or 500kg. It was powered by four rotating Pabst ramjet engines mounted on a rotor with a diameter of 7m, acting like a giant eight-bladed propeller (actually the same system as that working the Focke-Wulf Fw VTOL fighter *Triebflügel*). The whole

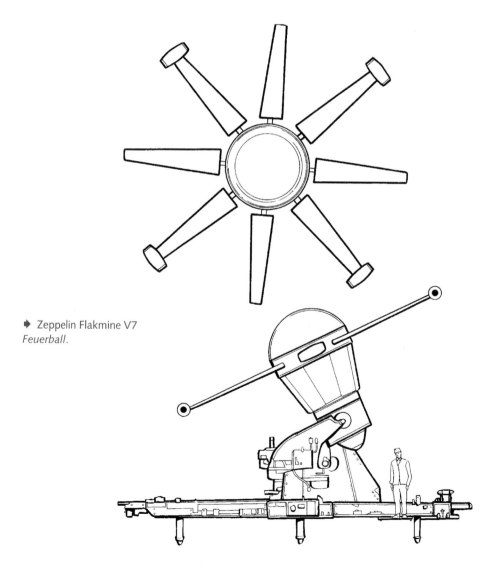

➡ Zeppelin Flakmine V7
Feuerball.

device weighed about 2000kg. Since ramjets do not operate at slow speeds, the rotor had probably to be driven at take-off by small rocket booster engines fitted to each ramjet pod. Launched from a cruciform platform, the Flakmine *Feuerball* was to be detonated in the middle of an Allied bomber formation by means of infrared beam, radar or acoustic fuze. Due to the enormous gyroscopic force created by a rotor that size, it is doubtful whether the device could have been made workable. The project was never developed.

Fliegerfaust

The concept of the effective anti-tank *Panzerfaust* and *Panzerschreck* was developed for a one-man portable anti-aircraft weapon called *Fliegerfaust* (literally 'aeroplane fist') also known as *Luftfaust* (air fist). The *Fliegerfaust*, designed by the Hugo Schneider AG of Peizig, existed in two versions. Version A had four 2cm calibre barrels. Version B was composed of a bundle of nine 2cm calibre barrels set together into a portable device about 1.70m long with a weight of 6.5kg. It had a fore handgrip, a pistol-like electrical firing grip and a simple optical sight for aiming. For firing the weapon was shouldered like a bazooka, the shooter pressed the trigger and first a salvo of five small rockets were fired, the remaining four being fired one second later. The

◀ *Fliegerfaust* and a bundle of ammunition.

◀ Firing a *Fliergerfaust*.

high-explosive projectile was developed from the standard 2cm Flak shell to which an advanced electrical detonating system was added.

The projectiles would have left the barrel with a velocity of 300 metres/second, and the maximum ceiling was 500 metres. After firing the weapon would be quickly re-loaded by introducing a bundle of nine fresh rockets in the barrels at the rear end of the weapon. The *Fliegerfaust* would have been a formidable weapon as it would have given a small fighting team (say one shooter, three or four ammunition carriers/loaders, and a few riflemen for close-range protection) tremendous firepower. Although it had a very short range and its projectiles would have dispersed in a large area, the weapon could possibly have been engaged as much against low flying aircraft as against ground targets, perhaps with devastating effects. Fortunately the *Fliegerfaust* was developed too late to see combat service at the front. At the beginning of 1945, some 10,000 of them were ordered, but only a few prototypes were ever built, none of which ever reached combat troops in the field, although a 1945 photograph of the Hotel Adlon in central Berlin clearly shows at least three expended *Fliegerfaust* Bs lying in the rubble.

BALLOONS

Balloon barrages (*Sperrballone*) were found at many of the most important areas in Germany and her occupied territories, as well as at relatively isolated, vulnerable locations, such as individual factories or harbours. The unmanned tethered barrage balloon, resembling fan-tailed goldfish, acted as physical obstacle. It was simply a large bag of lighter-than-air gas (often hydrogen) attached to a steel cable anchored to the ground in order to deny low-level airspace to enemy aircraft. It was both ingenious and simple, providing three major benefits: it forced aircraft to higher

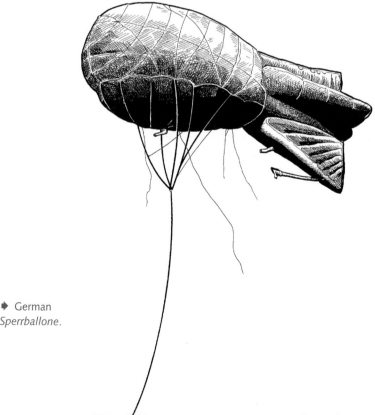

➧ German
Sperrballone.

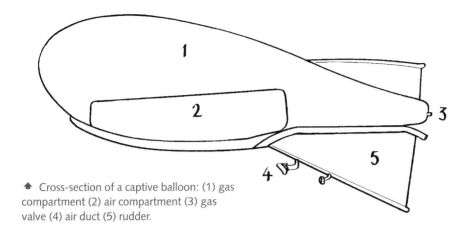

Cross-section of a captive balloon: (1) gas compartment (2) air compartment (3) gas valve (4) air duct (5) rudder.

altitudes, thereby decreasing surprise and bombing accuracy; it enhanced ground-based air defences and the ability of fighters to acquire targets, since intruding aircraft were limited in altitude and direction; and the cable presented a definite mental and material hazard to pilots. Indeed both the balloon itself and the cable it was attached to formed a dangerous obstacle impeding dive-bombers and strafing runs from fighter aircraft and ground attackers.

The first few thousand feet from the ground were taken care of by these obstacles, which could remain permanently in position. In practice, the height below which enemy pilots would not fly when they saw a balloon barrage was usually well above the level of the top of the balloons. At the speeds at which Second World War air combat took place, a second would have brought them down to the position where they might become entangled in the cables. To avoid a fatal collision, Allied airmen were forced to fly high, which reduced the accuracy of their attacks and placed them at a higher altitude, which was more favourable for certain Flak weapons. Indeed, strategically placed barrage balloons could be used to channel attacking aircraft towards Flak artillery just like barbed wire channelled infantry towards machine guns. On the other hand, barrage balloons were limited in their direct success at bringing down enemy aeroplanes, being immobile and passive weapons. The Germans learned from experience that captive balloon barrages were not well suited to protect small, isolated targets. They found that such a barrage was vulnerable to hostile fighter planes, and served its purpose only in areas where anti-aircraft guns and friendly fighters could protect it.

Barrage balloon units were part of the *Luftsperrwaffe* (Air Barrage Arm), which was a branch of the Air Force. The personnel wore the uniform of the German Luftwaffe Flak artillery. The organisation of barrage balloon units varied in different places because of different needs. Usually the standard barrage balloon unit was the battalion, consisting of 3 batteries each manning about 16 balloons. In the early years of the war, the smallest unit consisted of a motorised squad of 12 men, each squad equipped with 2 balloons – one for manning and one in reserve. The Germans developed two main sizes and types, notably with a capacity of 77m³ (2718ft³) and 200m³ (7062ft³). An average balloon was 62 feet long with a maximum diameter of 25 feet. Tethered by a steel cable, they could be raised or lowered by means of a winch. Their height could be regulated and stabilised, and a rudder kept the nose into the wind. The average height at which balloons were flown was 6000–8000 feet, some as low as 4500 feet. Balloons flown at 11,000–12,000 feet were reported but operation at high levels involved longer and thus weaker cables, which consequently reduced defensive value. Flown either in isolation or more commonly in dense groups, barrages usually formed an irregular belt about 0.6 miles wide and about 1.75 miles from the outer edge of the strategic area. The plan for a barrage was coordinated with light and medium calibre anti-aircraft gun defence, which protected the larger gaps in the belt. Balloons were launched from both fixed and mobile sites (i.e. the backs of modified vehicles), and they could be attached to ships as well. The principal manufacturer of German balloons was the firm Riedinger at Augsburg. When this factory was attacked and severely damaged by an Allied air raid in the end of February 1944, production was largely disrupted.

The use of balloons was not without disadvantages. They were slow to be put into action and they clearly indicated the location of a target. They could be destroyed by a single burst of a machine-gun firing incendiary rounds, by bad weather or strong winds, and they could break from their anchor causing extensive damage (e.g. to high tension electricity cables). The use of the barrage balloon was thus totally abandoned after the Second World War, but the terrorist attack on New York on 11 September 2001 has revived interest in the technology, since they represent a cheap, reliable and easily deployable method to protect sensitive static targets against air attack.

SMOKE SCREENING

Another passive weapon used by the Germans was smoke screening: the release of dense clouds of artificial smoke in order to mask the exact location of military, economic and industrial targets. Smoke has been used in warfare throughout history to conceal tactical movement on the battlefield and as a hindrance to good shooting, a primitive method being to burn damp straw upwind. The advances in chemistry and artillery design since the end of the nineteenth century made the quicker and more reliable smoke shell available. The Germans had special *Nebeltruppen* ('fog troops'), which were trained for this kind of warfare.

The use of smokescreens had a considerable protective value particularly against enemy day bombing attacks. In addition, decoy smokescreens were also effectively employed upon a number of occasions to protect nearby targets such as battleships, docks, naval installations, oil refineries, important blast furnaces, factories, canals and harbours. Certain German cities were protected by extensive smokescreen systems. On several occasions, Allied pilots reported dark-grey smokescreens over Berlin, 20–30 miles long and 2 miles wide. Most commonly deployed in a canister, smokescreens were often put up immediately upon the sounding of an air raid warning, and within about 20 minutes the target was completely covered in smoke, sometimes so dense and thick that visibility on the ground extended for only a few yards. Smoke screening was, of course, always subject to the vagaries of wind and weather. On some days a smokescreen could be highly effective, and on others it would be quickly blown away.

A frequently used device was the Smoke Generator 41 type, consisting of a 40- to 55-gallon steel drum fitted externally with a stopcock and a steel projection tube. It contained 20 gallons of a chlorosulfonic acid and sulphur trioxide mixture, which was expelled by means of a cylinder of compressed air contained within the generator drum. Alongside the generator, a similar drum of smoke acid was provided for recharging. By this meant a smokescreen could be maintained at full strength for two hours. The smoke came from the generator in the form of a liquid, which immediately vaporised. It had the colour of tobacco smoke and was almost odourless and harmless, but irritating to the throat. Another generator consisted of two canisters, one containing a mixture of chlorosulfonic acid and sulphur trioxide, and the other compressed air for atomising the smoke acid. This type of equipment provided an uninterrupted generation of smoke for about four hours. Other chemical substances used included white phosphorous (WP), which ignited in contact with the air, and instantly produced a cloud of dense white smoke, which dissipated rather quickly. Another was hexachlorethane (HCE), which took time to develop but built up a long lasting and thick screen. The generators were scattered around the target either in groups of several or at intervals of roughly 75 yards.

When the Allies started to use radar to direct their bombers, the smoke generators lost a great deal of their effectiveness. In some cases, the Germans resorted to the corner reflector, a device made of metal, which when floated in sufficient numbers on a stretch of water (e.g. a basin or a river), could change the outline of the coastline on the radar screens. This only worked in bad weather, as on a clear day the corner reflectors could not deceive bomber crews.

Smoke screening was often combined with various methods of camouflage for disguising targets. Painted dazzle patterns were used to soften the edges of buildings to make them blend with their surroundings, and reduce the shadows they cast on the ground. Camouflage nets and layers of earth and debris were placed on roofs to give the impression of piles of rubble. Decoy factories, fake bridges and railway tracks were built in order to deceive Allied bomber crews. It should be pointed out however, that the sophisticated German camouflage produced fewer benefits than expected. One inescapable fact about cities, buildings and factories is that they can never totally be hidden from air reconnaissance. Besides, Allied intelligence services did not just rely on air reconnaissance for information on potential targets, getting much of their information from spies and Resistance informers. The Photographic Reconnaissance Unit (PRU), equipped with fast planes (Spitfire, Mosquito and Lightning), regularly flew recce missions above enemy territories, taking pictures, mapping German progress step by step and evaluating the results of previous attacks. The gathering of intelligence, photographic coverage by the PRU and a comprehensive evaluation service played an essential role, contributing a great deal to the success of the Allies in the air war over Germany.

3

EQUIPMENT

AIR DEFENCE

Possessing effective anti-aircraft guns was one thing, but using them with accuracy was a horse of a different colour. Early Flak guns were sometimes successful, but none of them were very effective, since they were designed by men with rather optimistic ideas, basing their fire control systems on 'guess, point, fire and pray'. In anti-aircraft warfare the problem was not one of penetrating (as in anti-tank warfare) but one of hitting the relatively unarmoured, rapidly flying target. Flak fire only obtained results if the projectiles reached their target or exploded in its close vicinity. Flak fire had to have a flat trajectory to be as precise as possible and a high velocity to punch the target. Firing accuracy was only possible by making a precise calculation of the lead for hitting small, highly manoeuvrable and fast aircraft moving in three dimensions.

As can easily be imagined, Flak fire was a complicated task demanding accurate calculations and rapidity. Air attack (acquisition of ground targets, navigation and bombing) and air defence (detection of intruders and firing at them) was a particular kind of warfare waged between small groups of highly trained fighting men (Allied pilots versus German gunners and also Luftwaffe interception airmen), a deadly game of hide-and-seek. It was also a terrible contest between the courage and endurance of professionals manipulating sophisticated detection systems and complex weapons designed by competing scientists. The whole affair involved the skill and judgement of commanders and staff planners, often exercising control and command at long distance. Expertise in expensive electronics and communication systems was at least as crucial as combat flying skills. Success ultimately went to the side which was able to track the movements of the adversary and read his signals while keeping its own secret. The German Flak was backed by a very advanced optical industry developed by many talented scientists, such as optician Carl Zeiss (1816–1888), physicist Ernst Abbe (1840–1905), and chemist and glassmaker Otto Schott (1851–1935) to name just a few.

FLAK FIRE CONTROL

Generalities

Time was of the essence for every Flak gun crew. A few minutes, even seconds, could make the difference between a hit or a miss, even life and death. Early warning systems such as radar proved helpful later on in the war, but even then it still took time from detecting a target and getting the message through to the gunner. Time was precious, the more so as the target could change its speed and altitude, or divert from its original course. In short, optical instruments remained the eyes of the Flak troops during the entire conflict. Optical equipment used by the Flak crews can be separated into three different categories: gun sights, spotting binoculars and rangefinders.

A gun sight is an optical device that establishes an optical line or axis for the purpose of aiming a weapon. The axis line runs from the observer's eye, through a suitable mark in the instrument, to the target. Used to assist aim by guiding the eye and aligning it with a weapon to be pointed, gun sights range from the most basic crosshair or reticle to extremely elaborate pieces of optical machinery, even for smaller guns. As the war progressed, several gun sights for a single type of gun were developed, keeping pace with demand and technical achievements. In general, one can say that as wide angle glass techniques evolved, the enlargements of the direct aiming sights grew bigger, giving the user a better chance to hit a target from a greater distance. This evolution was of the essence, as when suddenly confronted with a *Tiefflieger* – an aircraft approaching fast at low altitude – the gun sight was all that stood between the gun crew and death.

The Germans use three main methods of fire control, namely: continuously pointed fire, with director control; predicted concentration fire by plotting; and barrage fire. In continuously pointed fire, operators for each battery independently followed the target through telescopes. Its altitude was inserted from a range finder, and the necessary calculations were made mechanically by the director, for aiming the gun at a point in space where the shell and the aeroplane would arrive simultaneously provided the aeroplane did not change the course, altitude or speed on which the director based his prediction. Appropriate evasive action therefore consisted of changes in course and height, at intervals determined by the necessary time for prediction of aim and flight of the shell. Due to the longer time of flight of shells, and the shorter period during which the gun could engage, the effectiveness of this type of fire decreased rather rapidly at higher altitudes. The effective ceiling for this type of fire was lower by about 6000 feet than the maximum fuze range of the shell.

Predicted concentration fire was less effective than continuously pointed fire. This was used when darkness or cloud prevented visual control, or when radar information was of low quality. For this type of fire, a plot of the aircraft's course was made in a central control room, and as soon as the intruder's course on its bombing approach could be predicted, necessary data were calculated for a future point of its arrival in the sky. Each gun battery, utilising the basic data, made its own computation for this predicted point and each battery fired a salvo so timed that rounds shot by all batteries burst simultaneously at the predicted point. Sometimes second and third salvos were fired immediately on the same data. This method required that the aircraft be flying reasonably straight and level for about 90 seconds before reaching the predicted point. Evasive action was indicated up to the actual beginning of the bombing approach, which was as short as consistent with accuracy of bombing. Subsequent concentrations against bomber formations passing through the same predicted point might be fired in a much shorter time since the initial plotting had already been done.

Finally, barrage fire, as the name indicates, depended on the placing of a barrier across the probable course of the aircraft. This was the least effective and the most wasteful type of Flak fire. It was used when darkness or cloud prevented the use of continuously pointed fire or when good data was not available on the exact position and altitude of enemy bombers. A geographical or fixed barrage was fired by all guns within range into a certain sky volume or box, usually just outside the expected bomb release line of the aircraft. If the barrage was properly placed, the aircraft had to fly through the bursts in order to bomb the objective. Enemy aircrews therefore tried to make sure that gunners were kept uncertain, up to the last possible moment, as to the intended objective and the direction of the bombing approach. Before fire started, detection of target was done by means of sound locators, searchlights and radar later in the war (see below).

Summing up the complicated Flak fire techniques, one can say that in order to shoot down a high-flying aeroplane successfully, Flak gunners had to know three parameters: altitude, direction and speed of the target. If direction could be guessed (although a pilot could always carry out evasive manoeuvres), distance, speed and altitude were given by a range finder, predictors and rapid calculation devices. Knowing the altitude enabled the gunner to determine the time when the shell had to explode. Knowing direction and speed of the target enabled him to give the gun a correct angle of fire. A plane moving at 360kmph travelled about 3km in 30 seconds, therefore Flak gunners did not aim at the target itself but anticipated its movement taking account of its speed and other important factors such as their own gun velocity, ammunition used and various ballistic and atmospheric data such as wind velocity.

At a time when computer, microwave, infrared or laser technology were unknown or in their infancy, Flak fire still relied on optical, electrical and manual methods, as well as trigonometrical tables, slide-rules, pencils and paper. Preparation was effected and transmitted to batteries by command and fire control posts (known as *Befehlstelle*, *Feuerleitstelle* or *Feuerleitstände*). The fire control stations were manned by skilled personnel operating sophisticated and efficient instruments. These included the *Kommandogerät* (for calculating firing data transmitted to the gunners by means of an electric indicator), *Entfernungsmessgerät* (range finder for measuring distance to the target) and a *Hilfskommandogerät* for auxiliary calculations. These sophisticated devices, however, did not in any way operate like a modern computer. In today's parlance they were 'analog' systems using or generating electrical currents and voltages that were proportional to the information they represented. Loading and firing orders were transmitted by telephone from the commanding officer to the gun crews.

In theory, the problem of anti-aircraft fire was a simple matter of three-dimensional geometry provided some figures were known, particularly the speed, course and altitude of the target, the velocity of the shell and the wind speed. If the target was within range, anti-aircraft artillery could not miss, but in practice many thousands of shells were of course fired for every one that scored a hit. Calculations were made with the assumptions that the target would maintain a constant course, height and speed. The higher and faster the aircraft was flying and the longer the time of flight of the shell, the less likely were the assumptions to be justified. The likelihood of a direct hit was obviously always very low. As the Second World War progressed, Allied bombers became more powerful, better protected and were able to fly faster and higher. As a result the war ended with the Allied bombers just ahead of the German anti-aircraft artillery.

Range Finders

Originally the Flak troops depended on inverted image range finders, a system that was developed during the First World War. In this type, the single ocular displayed two images of the same object, one image being inverted to the other normally positioned image. By turning a knob, mirrors inside the range finder were moved in such a way that the images were moved until they mirrored each other. The range was then readily readable from a scale. This method was time consuming,

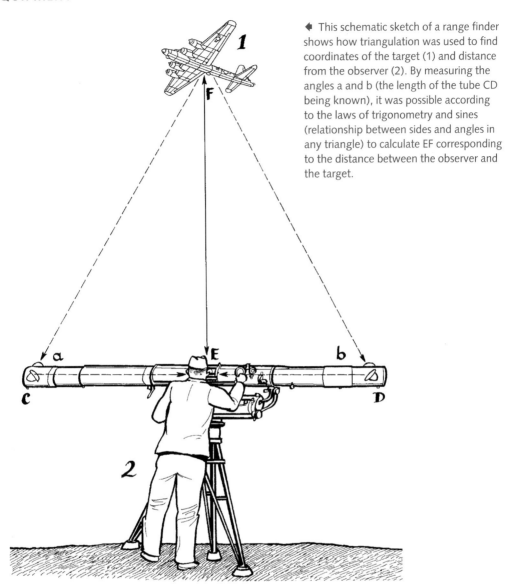

This schematic sketch of a range finder shows how triangulation was used to find coordinates of the target (1) and distance from the observer (2). By measuring the angles a and b (the length of the tube CD being known), it was possible according to the laws of trigonometry and sines (relationship between sides and angles in any triangle) to calculate EF corresponding to the distance between the observer and the target.

and proved inadequate particularly when following small, fast-moving targets. The system was replaced by stereoscopic (two oculars) range finders when these became available in the mid-thirties.

The coincidence optical range finder (also called the stereoscopic range finder or parallax range finder) was one of the many optical instruments designed during the Second World War. Before the widespread use of radar technology to determine accurate distances between weapons and their targets, range finders using mechanical and optical principles were used for all sorts of military ranging, including land, naval and anti-aircraft artillery. Human eyes can judge distances because each eye sees a slightly different view of an object against a background. However, human stereo vision is limited to distances of less than about 90m (300ft) because the eyes are fairly close together. The coincidence range finder was designed to overcome this limitation and increase the distance between

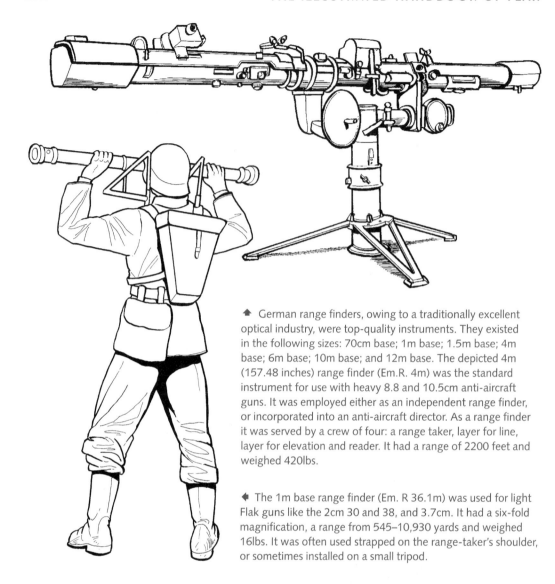

✦ German range finders, owing to a traditionally excellent optical industry, were top-quality instruments. They existed in the following sizes: 70cm base; 1m base; 1.5m base; 4m base; 6m base; 10m base; and 12m base. The depicted 4m (157.48 inches) range finder (Em.R. 4m) was the standard instrument for use with heavy 8.8 and 10.5cm anti-aircraft guns. It was employed either as an independent range finder, or incorporated into an anti-aircraft director. As a range finder it was served by a crew of four: a range taker, layer for line, layer for elevation and reader. It had a range of 2200 feet and weighed 420lbs.

◀ The 1m base range finder (Em. R 36.1m) was used for light Flak guns like the 2cm 30 and 38, and 3.7cm. It had a six-fold magnification, a range from 545–10,930 yards and weighed 16lbs. It was often used strapped on the range-taker's shoulder, or sometimes installed on a small tripod.

◆ Portable *Entfernungmessgerät* (range finder). This coincidence optical range finder (*Entfernungsmesser* 14 nr 500S) consisted of a cylinder about 1m in length and 10cm in diameter. Standing on a tripod or carried by the operator, it had objective lens with rotating covers at each end, an eyepiece at the centre and a thumbwheel adjustment at the right side. This instrument was used to determine the distance to an object with the use of mirrors and lenses.

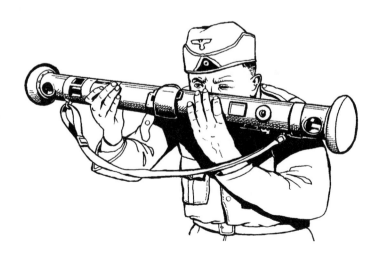

the eyes. Basically it consisted of a long tube on whose ends were mounted two lenses facing forward, and of an operator eye-piece in the centre of the tube. The lenses reflected the scene from two different viewpoints to the central eye-piece. By overlapping the images and adjusting one of the mirrors, the images viewed could be made to coincide exactly. The length of the tube was known, and the angle by which the mirror needed to be moved could be calculated or read out on an adjustable roller geared to a scale, indicating the distance to the object/target being observed. For magnification, telescopes were used in the system instead of simple mirrors and lenses.

Predictors

In the 1930s the concept of a central post was accepted as the only workable method of Flak fire control, and all advanced countries developed devices which could mechanically predict future height and position of a target as well as range and fuze length, and could instantly pass this data to gunners. The German *Kommandogerät* (stereoscopic director or predictor) was a fire-control instrument that combined into one device a 4m-base Zeiss stereoscopic height and range finder, and a fire director. Several types were employed, for example the Model 36 used with the 8.8cm Flak gun, and the Model 40 used with the 10.5cm Flak gun. The stages in the production of the firing data in the Model 36 were as follows: first the height and range finder furnished present azimuth (angle between a reference plane and a point), angle of sight and slant range to the target, termed 'initial data'. Second, the rate of change, obtained by continuously feeding this

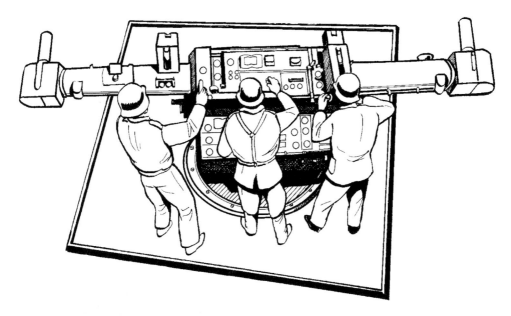

⬆ *Kommandogerät* (stereoscopic director or predictor). The method used was based upon the principle that in similar triangles homologous sides are proportional. This means that, for a right-angled triangle, the ratio of adjacent side length to opposite side length is constant. By using a reticle with marks of a known angular spacing, the principle of similar triangles can be used to find either the distance to objects of known size or the size of objects at a known distance. In either case, the known parameter is used, in conjunction with the angular measurement, to derive the length of the other side.

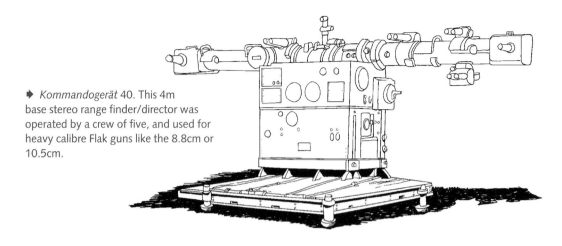

◆ *Kommandogerät* 40. This 4m base stereo range finder/director was operated by a crew of five, and used for heavy calibre Flak guns like the 8.8cm or 10.5cm.

data into the predictor, provided the horizontal ground speed and the course angle of the target, termed 'intermediate data'. Third the combination of initial and intermediate data provided the vertical and lateral deflection and range correction to determine the future position of the target. From this combination, the gun data was obtained by mechanical computation within the predictor. The gun data thus obtained (in terms of firing azimuth, quadrant elevation and fuze for the shells) were normally transmitted electrically to the guns by means of receiver dials fitted with concentric circles.

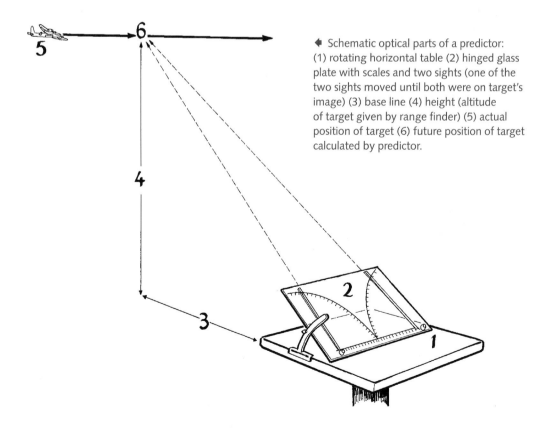

◀ Schematic optical parts of a predictor: (1) rotating horizontal table (2) hinged glass plate with scales and two sights (one of the two sights moved until both were on target's image) (3) base line (4) height (altitude of target given by range finder) (5) actual position of target (6) future position of target calculated by predictor.

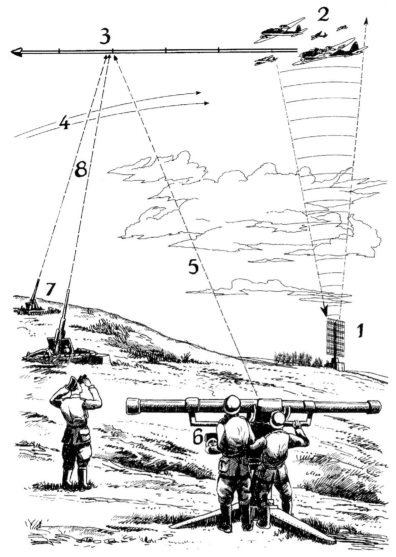

◀ Schematic diagram showing how Flak fire control worked: (1) detection of intruders by sound locator or spotters, later by radar (2) actual position of target (3) future position of target worked out by predictor (for example a plane flying at a speed of 180 miles per hour, moves at 264 feet per second) (4) known wind velocity to which predictor was set (5) distance and height calculated by range finder and predictor (6) predictor/range finder (7) Flak batteries (8) path of shells aiming at future position of target (fuze setting indicated by predictor).

The *Kommandohilfsgerät* (auxiliary fire director) was an instrument used for auxiliary purposes, and operated on the principle of calculation of the rates of change of angular velocity. A separate 4m-base stereoscopic height and range finder provided the present slant range to the target. By following the target continuously for azimuth and elevation, and by setting in range continuously, the rates of change of azimuth, elevation and slant range were obtained. These, multiplied by time of flight, gave the lateral and vertical deflections and a correction for range. These corrections, applied to the present data, provided future data which were corrected for abnormal ballistic conditions, dead time and drift, which were then passed to the guns as gun azimuth, quadrant elevation and fuze. Data were quickly transmitted to the guns by telephone.

The theodolite was basically an optical instrument that consisted of a telescope placed on a mount, free to rotate about its vertical and horizontal axes. The telescope was fitted with graduated circles that could be read out through magnifying lenses. It was used to determine and measure horizontal and vertical

➡ A theodolite, used to correct Flak fire.

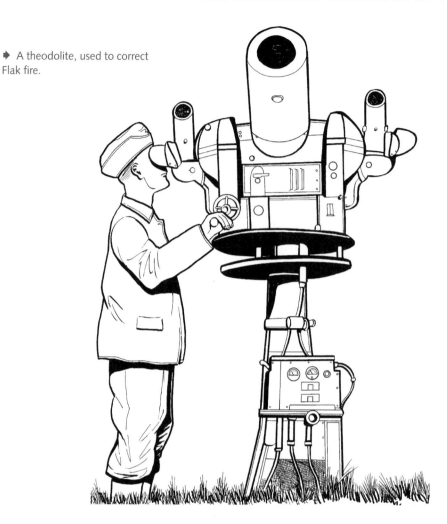

➡ Peilgerät.

angles, enabling the observer to bring correction to Flak fire. A number of other optical devices were also used, such as the *Peilgerät*, in order to bring additional data to Flak firing. Today these techniques have been replaced with computers, microwave, infrared or laser range-finding methods.

SEARCHLIGHTS

Generalities

A searchlight is an apparatus fitted with reflectors for projecting a powerful beam of light of approximately parallel rays in a particular direction, usually devised so that it can be swivelled about. Searchlights, at least in military use, were employed to illuminate a battlefield, and more generally to detect and track enemy aircraft at night. During the First World War, searchlights had been occasionally used to locate hostile aircraft, but they were not sufficiently numerous or coordinated with air defence to cause enemy pilots much concern. They also had too short a range and lacked intensity. They were occasionally used to create 'artificial moonlight' to enhance opportunities for night attacks. After the end of the First World War the German development of searchlights was effectively stopped by the Treaty of Versailles, but resumed in 1927. The Germans placed great reliance on searchlights, which were later deployed in very large numbers in Flak-defended areas. They were also occasionally used for propaganda and set decoration: in 1934, during the Nazi Party rally at Nuremberg, the architect Albert Speer had the idea of using 130 searchlights; at night they created a vast illuminated space with the beams forming the pillars of a gigantic cathedral of light. Searchlights also have a long history in show business, being used at movie premieres, in films and theatre plays; the waving searchlight beams are still to be seen in the logo of the 20th Century Fox movie studio.

At the outset of the Second World War, searchlights were combined with sound locators (acoustic direction finders), with the direction finders guiding the searchlights to the right part of the sky where they swept until they found the target. Later in the war searchlights were radar directed. Spacing of searchlights varied considerably, but in heavily defended areas about 1500 yards was a common average. Once a locator had locked onto an aerial target, the idea was for both lights and guns to be trained on the aircraft (via the height and distance data received from the locator) so it could be simultaneously illuminated and then fired at and possibly destroyed or at least damaged enough to prevent it carrying out its bombing mission.

Searchlights were also useful because they hid targets from view and counteracted the effect of parachute flares by concentrating a cone of light over them. They also tended to impede accurate navigation of Allied planes. They subjected aircrews to considerable strain en route to and from their objectives, and could dazzle pilots on the approach lanes to their targets and blind bombardiers using optical bombsights. They were also used to assist night-fighters to find and approach their targets unobserved.

Searchlights were occasionally used tactically in ground battles. During the Ardennes offensive in the winter of 1944, the Germans shone searchlights on low clouds in order to give light to advancing troops. Another occasion was during the battle for Berlin in April 1945 when 143 Soviet searchlights tried to blind General Henrici's defence when Russian forces crossed the Neisse river.

The searchlight was based around extremely high power carbon arc lamps. Basically, a carbon arc lamp works by hooking two carbon rods to a source of electricity. With the other ends of the rods spaced at the right distance, electrical current flows through an 'arc' of vaporising carbon creating an intense white light. The luminous intensity emitted by a searchlight is measured in candela (cd) chosen in the visible spectrum near green, corresponding to a wavelength of about 555 nanometres.

German Second World War searchlights came in three main categories defined by the diameter of their glass reflector: 60cm, 150cm and 200cm. In September 1940 – excluding units emplaced at naval facilities – Germany had 2540 searchlights (60cm and 150cm). During the war this number grew rapidly. By February 1944 the Quartermaster General of the Luftwaffe General Staff reported that stocks of floodlights were as follows. 60cm: 6376 units; 150cm: 7311 units; 150cm

◆ 150cm searchlight.

quadruple floodlight: 61 units; 200cm: 2262 units; and thus a grand total of 13,748 units. A few obsolete 110cm searchlights and captured French 200cm and 240cm searchlights were also employed.

Searchlights were transported on trailers and put in action in special open emplacements where wheels were dismounted and the devices were placed on screw-jacks. They also could be placed on trains, trucks and ships. Fragile and expensive devices, they were often stored in concrete bunker-garages (see Chapter 5) and rolled out for action.

The wartime use of searchlights had several drawbacks. They were extremely expensive to build and to operate (each searchlight battery had to be provided with its own power plant) and they were very fragile to transport and operate. At night they were themselves clear targets that could be destroyed by low-flying aircraft, and they indicated from a distance where Flak batteries were deployed and in consequence where the target was located. After 1945, due to the remarkable development of radar and electronic techniques, searchlights became totally obsolete, at least in the military anti-aircraft ground-to-air role.

Searchlight Directors

The German Army, and especially its Flak arm, mainly relied on spotting binoculars until radar techniques were developed. A large number of binocular types were engineered and produced for military purposes. However, one model was especially noteworthy. Lacking advanced electronic means of enemy aeroplane detection, Flak troops were almost entirely dependent on visual methods for finding, identifying and ranging their targets. In order to improve their searching efficiency at night, the use of searchlights was adopted. Their use was to be limited to the shortest time period possible as roaming the skies would only give away the lights' positions, making them sitting ducks for Allied pilots. The answer was found in the development of the *Scheinwerfer-Richtungsweiser* 35 (searchlight director), which in the event became the most produced military telescope.

Using a ten power objective in combination with an 80mm objective lens, this telescope (*Doppelfernrohr* DF 10 x 80) proved an excellent instrument for searchlight tactics. The searchlight director used the sound of the aircraft engine to crudely aim his wide field, high luminous binocular. Once a plane or a formation of planes was caught in the binocular's reticle (or reticule), the observer read position and elevation from the bearing circles on the binocular's mount and shouted it to the searchlight crews. These in turn lit their apparatus, thereby catching the planes in columns of blinding light, making them an easier prey for the gun crews. If all went well, the Allied crews had no time to react. The *Scheinwerfer-Richtungsweiser* 35 was such a success that it continued to be the eye of the Flakwaffe and even the entire German Army for the remainder of the war, outlasting the searchlights themselves.

Whether large or small calibre guns were concerned, mobile Flak batteries or fixed positions, large or small rangefinders, the 10 x 80 was there to service them in detection, identification and directing. The device was placed in a searchlight control station located several hundred feet away from a searchlight battery so that the controllers could see illuminated aircraft better, as the light beam was so bright that vision would be adversely effected if the control station and its operators set up too close to the searchlight; all that would be visible would be the cone of illuminated atmospheric particles in the path of the beam. The controllers were situated far from the light for safety reasons, since searchlights made easy targets.

The binocular searchlight director evolved over the years. Filters changed, lens coating was applied, scopes for the 8.8cm gun were developed and a change was made from aluminium models to steel versions. The culminating point was the

◆ The *Scheinwerfer-Richtungsweiser*
35 (Scheinw.Riw. in short, also
called *Flakglas*, searchlight director)
was designed in 1935 by the Busch
Company. It was the standard
instrument used by Luftwaffe and Heer
Flak to coordinate the operation of
searchlights.

development of German heavy infrared scopes for night vision at the end of the
war. This experimental device, in combination with a giant infrared lamp, known
as the *Beobachtungsgerät* 241, was carried on vehicles such as the armoured
halftrack SdKfz 251/20 Uhu, and was intended to support Panther tanks operating
at night. By the end of the war the Germans had a considerable advantage in
night vision devices. The introduction of genuine night sights based on infrared
transmission was only in its infancy in 1945, but the Germans appeared to have
developed 'passive' systems in which the use of infrared radiation relied on the
natural emission of infrared beams from the target itself, for example, a tank engine
exhaust, or the heat of the human body. In spite of the many experimental devices
produced, including *Obi* (detecting bomber plane exhaust), *Donau* 60 (detecting
ship funnels for coastal artillery fire), *Spanner* (fitted to fighter aircraft to enable
them to home-in on bombers at night), and *Vampire* (rifle sight), few practical
results were achieved in combat.

60cm Searchlight

Developed in the late 1930s, with a 60cm diameter parabolic glass reflector, this searchlight was powered by an 8kW generator. The lamp output was rated at 135 million candelas, and it had a detection range of about 5km for targets travelling at an altitude of 1500m; with the beam dispersed this reduced to about 3.2km. It required a crew of three and could be transported using a single axle Special Trailer model 51. Typical tactics were to sweep the searchlight in an S-shaped pattern along the target's expected course with the beam dispersed; once the target was detected it was then tracked using the focused beam. The 60cm searchlights were not powerful enough to reach the Allied bomber streams later in the war, so they were typically employed in tandem with with 2cm and 3.7cm low-level flak guns.

150cm Searchlight

Developed in the late 1930s the Flak Searchlight 34 and 37 used 150cm diameter parabolic glass reflectors with an output of 990 million candelas. The system was powered by a 24kW generator, based around a 51 horsepower (38kW) 8 cylinder engine giving a current of 200 amperes at 110 volts. The searchlight was attached to the generator by a cable 200m long. The system had a detection range of about 8km for targets at an altitude of 4000–5000m. The system could be made mobile using two sets of Special Trailer 104 units, one for the searchlight and one for

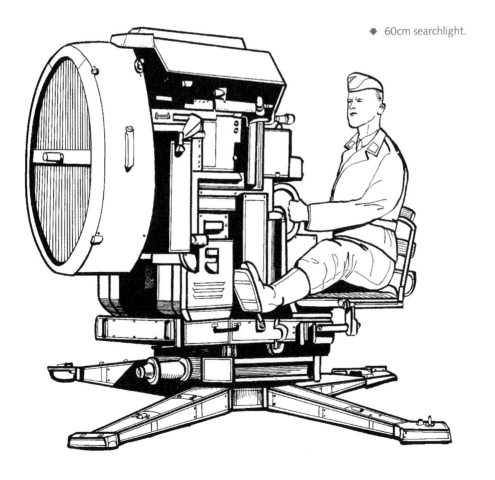

⬇ 60cm searchlight.

the generator. It required a crew of seven to operate. The searchlight could be traversed through 360 degrees and elevated from −12 degrees through the vertical to −12 degrees on the other side. Early war tactics for searchlight deployment had the searchlights forward of the Flak guns in a 'zone of preparation', laid out in a grid with 5km between each light. Sound locators deployed with the searchlights helped them find targets; later these were replaced with radar systems. Sixty-one special fixed quadruple 150cm mounts were produced in an effort to extend the range of the 150cm searchlights but these proved unsuccessful.

200cm Searchlight

In order to reach bombers flying at increasingly higher altitudes, more powerful searchlights were needed. In 1943 the first 200cm Scheinwerfer-43 searchlights with a power of 2.7 billion Hefner candlepower (2.4 gigacandela) were delivered to troops in the field. Powered by a 120kW generator, it could detect targets at distances of up to 13km. Typically the 200cm searchlight was employed in the centre of a triangle of three 150cm searchlights. The smaller searchlights deployed at a distance of about 2.5km from the larger central 'master' searchlight. The master searchlight would find the target, and the 150cm lights would cone the target providing a solid triangulation.

TARGET DETECTION

Sound Locators

Before radar technology was developed, the practical means of detecting aeroplanes at a distance was by listening to the noise of their engines with the aid of large sound locators. The *Horchgerät* or *Ringtricherichtungshörer* (RRH, acoustic monitoring device) was a mobile and orientable device featuring an acoustic horn (much more accurate and sensitive than the human ear) mounted on a trailer for detecting sound made by plane propellers; it had a range of 5–12km depending on weather and wind direction. The size of the horn served to gather in more of the sound and it thus increased the range of detection. The sound was not always electrically amplified and early systems were acoustically coupled to the operators' ears by tubes like those of a stethoscope. As the operators pointed this large hearing device, their direction and elevation movement would generate electric signals that could be sent to a control station using a fire-control system. This was used to transmit the desired angular information to searchlights, guns and sights. This kind of primitive device was good only at determining direction and little else. The sound locator was a cumbersome system, it was barely effective when tracking the engine noises from a single aircraft, and if more aeroplanes were present in its area, the device became swamped and provided little usable information.

Radar Technology

The original term for radar was RDF (Radio Direction Finding); another term used was Radio Location. The word Radar (an acronym from for *Radio Detection And Ranging*) was coined in the US and was soon universally adopted. In German, radar is called *Funkmeßgerät* (literally 'wave measuring device', FuMG).

Radar is a detection method based on the broadcast of strong and short radio impulses. Waves are reflected if they meet a solid metallic flying or navigating body. By measuring the time from the departure of the impulse until the return of the

echo one may calculate the distance between the radar station and the target. Radar thus detects and determines with precision the existence and position of a target. In addition radar indicates its speed and movement by measuring and analysing the constantly changing differences between the transmitted frequency and the return of the echo. This data can be obtained day or night, up to hundreds of kilometres (depending of course upon the strength of the device) and in any weather, since radar is little affected by climatic conditions. Second World War radar techniques were, however, rather primitive and limited to the detection of aircraft and ships, the clutter from objects on the ground making it an unlikely tool for ground warfare. Since 1945 great strides have been made in this domain.

The radar principle rests on studies made by the German scientist Heinrich Hertz in 1887 and on the research of several other physicists. The method was experimented with and developed under conditions of great secrecy during the 1920s and 1930s and was finally greatly improved and used with success during the Battle of Britain in 1940. The radar sets used during the Second World War – compared to modern devices – were complex, primitive and cumbersome instruments. Each device included a powerful, very high frequency microwave generator, a highly sensitive receiver catching back echoing beams, sophisticated devices translating radio waves into visual form on a round screen, scanners, primitive computers and various precise calculating instruments. Waves were sent off and received back by means of a large aerial. The shapes of German aerials depended on the frequency that was used. They were either constructed as a rectangular flat metal frame or a parabolic round dish. Radar also had naval

▲ This sound locator, used for Flak searchlight teams for initial aiming at night, had a crew of three: the traverse aimer was perched on the left seat, the elevator aimer on the right seat and the calculator in the middle.

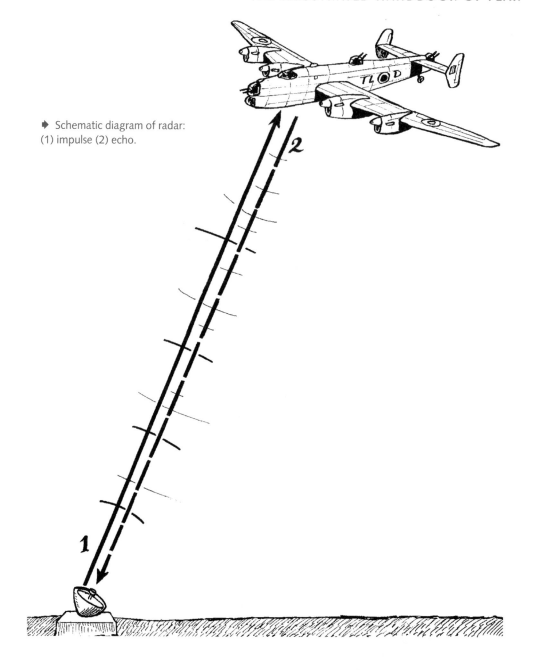

◆ Schematic diagram of radar:
(1) impulse (2) echo.

applications developed by the Allies to detect submerged submarines: ASDIC (apparently Allied Submarine Detection Investigation Committee, though there is some debate about the acronym) and SONAR (Sound Navigation And Ranging).

German Radar Systems

During the first years of the war, the Germans did not fully appreciate the tactical possibilities of radar and for a time the Allies' radar development was well ahead of the Germans'. However, they made tremendous efforts to match Allied technical progress and to overcome the various tactical problems resulting from the Allied superiority. Electro-magnetic detection became widely used from the second half of 1942, when the Kriegsmarine and Luftwaffe – learning from their unhappy experience in the Battle of Britain – installed many radar stations forming a wide chain through northern Europe. Codenamed *Himmelbett* ('bedtester'), this network covered the entire Atlantic coast from Kirkenes in northern Norway to the Spanish border. Along the shores of Holland, Belgium and northwest France there was a major radio station every ten miles, backed by a dense and comprehensive system. Obviously radar stations were always placed at sites offering a good and wide reception: advanced shore points, capes, promontories, islands and hills. The Luftwaffe developed this cover to a high pitch of efficiency as part of the air defence of the Reich and the German Navy strengthened it with an additional series of stations for the detection of shipping. In theory this screen could not be pierced for the network was capable of picking up ships at a range of 25–30 miles offshore, and any sizeable force of aircraft south of the line of the Bristol Channel to the Wash.

The Kammhuber Line was the name given to the German night air defence system established in July 1940 by Colonel Josef Kammhuber (1896–1986). The first

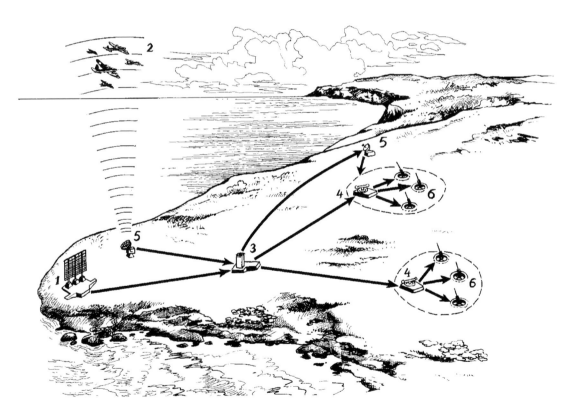

♠ German Flak was efficient because of a good organisation based on rapid communication. Early warning radars (1) detected intruders (2) and gave alarm to regional command posts (3). There data were analysed and, when the number of planes, as well as altitude, speed and direction were calculated and when possible targets were determined, information was passed through and orders were issued to local Flak fire-leading stations (4), which – with the help of predictors and close range radars (5) – coordinated and directed anti-aircraft guns batteries (6).

version of the line consisted of a series of radar stations with overlapping coverage, layered three deep from Denmark to the middle of France, each covering a zone about 32km long (north-south) and 20km wide (east-west).

German ground radar fell into two main categories: Small Würzburg designed for Flak control, but also used for height finding in the aircraft reporting service, as well as larger Würzburg-Riese primarily used for aircraft interception control; and early warning set (Freya, Mammut or Wassermann) for long range detection. These various types of ground radar equipment played a large part in the German system of air raid warning, control of Flak fire and direction of fighter interception. The fighters used were usually the Dornier Do 17, Junkers Ju 88 or Messerschmitt Bf 110.

Many devices were developed by the Allies to limit or nullify the effectiveness of the German equipment (notably Window), but at the same time the Germans developed numerous countermeasures. This arms race in radar led to extremely rapid development of new techniques and equipment on both sides

FLAK CONTROL RADAR

FuMG 62 Würzburg

The *Würzburg* radar (FuMG 62) was the primary ground-based gun laying radar for both the Luftwaffe and the German Army. Initial development took place in 1934 before the war, entering service in 1940. Eventually over 4000 Würzburgs of various models were produced by the Telefunken Company. The system was based on a klystron microwave tube operating in the range of 54–53cm (553–566 MHz) – an extremely short wavelength for the time – with a pulse length of 2 microseconds, a

⬇ Radar *Würzburg* FuMG 62.

➡ *Würzburg* radar.

peak power of 7–11kW and a PRF of 3750 Hz. It had a maximum range of about 29km (18 miles), and was accurate to about 25km. Würzburg used a 3m paraboloid dish antenna mounted on a wheeled trailer, which could be folded along the horizontal midline for transport. Several versions of the basic Würzburg system were deployed over the course of the war. The first, *Würzburg A*, was operated manually and required the operators to pinpoint the target by maintaining a maximum signal on their oscilloscope display. An experimental *Würzburg B* added an infrared detector for fine tuning, but in general these devices proved to be unusable and production was discontinued.

Würzburg C featured lobe switching to improve aiming accuracy. The C model was aimed by sending the signal out of one of two slightly off-centre feed horns in the middle of the antenna, the signal being switched rapidly between the two horns. The *Würzburg D*, introduced in late 1941, added a conical scanning system, using an offset receiver feed that spun at 25 Hz, leading to much improved accuracy on the order of 2 degrees in azimuth and 3 degrees in elevation. About 4000 *Würzburg* FuMG 62s were produced during the Second World War, making it the standard radar system of the German Flak forces.

◆ *Würzburg* on trailer.

FuMG 65 Würzburg-Riese

The *Würzburg D* model was, however, not accurate enough for the direct laying of Flak guns. In order to provide radar systems with much greater accuracy, the FuMG 65 *Würzburg-Riese* ('Giant Würzburg') was developed. Based on the same basic circuitry as the FuMG 62 D model, the new version featured a much larger antenna (7.4m in diameter), known as *Nashorn* (Rhinoceros), and a more powerful transmitter with a range of up to 70km (44 miles). Azimuth accuracy was 0.2 degrees and elevation was 0.1 degrees, more than enough for direct gun-laying. The system was now too large and too heavy (total weight was around 18 tons) to be carried on a truck trailer, and was instead adapted for operation in a cabin, housing the crew and the instrument, placed on a pivot shaft which in turn rested on a concrete base. The whole device could also be emplaced on a railway carriage, the *Würzburg-Riese-E* FuMG-E, of which 1500 were produced during the war. The naval designation of the Luftwaffe FuMG 64 *Würzburg-Riese* was FuMO 64, adapted and used by the Kriegsmarine for naval and coastal operations. The improved variant, *Würzburg-Riese Gigant*, was a planned enlarged version with a 160kW transmitter, which never entered production.

FuMG 64 Mannheim

Designed in 1942, radar Mannheim was intended for Flak fire. It had a 3m wide dish attached to a frame and two crossbeams fixed on a rectangular rotating box, which was set on a pivot shaft on a cross platform. This was often placed in a circular earthwork pit with a diameter of about 8m and a breastwork approximately 1.9m high, offering not only protection for the device and crew against shrapnel, but also preventing interference, reflection and waves bouncing back from the ground leading to errors in elevation angles. Radar Mannheim was transported on a two-axle trailer (type *Sonderhänger* Sd.Ah 204) with the pivot shaft lowered and segments of the reflector folded in toward the centre of the dish. It had improved optical and electrical plotting options, a mechanical horizontal range and elevation computer. Distance accuracy was 10–15m at a range of 25–35km, with the azimuth and vertical accuracy at 0.15 degrees. There was

◀ Radar *Würzburg-Riese* FuMG 65.

an improved version, known as the FuMG 77 *Marbach/Rotterheim* with a 4.5m dish and more elaborate electrical ranging components giving a range of about 27–30km. This radar was only produced in limited numbers. In 1944, other improved devices for air surveillance and precise location plotting Flak fire were designed: the FuMG 74 *Kulmbach* and FuMG 76 *Marbach*, together forming the so-called Egerland System. They operated the 9cm wave length, had a 4.5m dish reflector and a range of about 30–50km. Both *Kulmbach* and *Marbach*, however, never left the prototype stage.

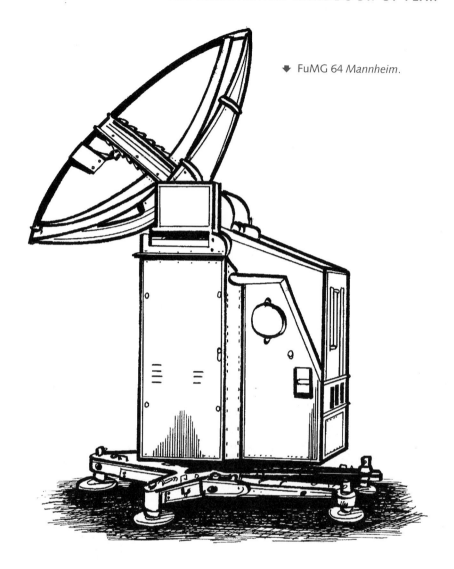

➥ FuMG 64 *Mannheim*.

EARLY WARNING RADAR

Freya

Freya was an early warning radar, often used in concert with the primary German gun laying radar, Würzburg, finding targets at long ranges and then handing them off to the Würzburg for tracking. First tests of what would become Freya were conducted in early 1937, with initial delivery of an operational radar to the Kriegsmarine in 1938. The Freya radar was operating in the 1.2m wavelength and was able to use smaller antennas and also offered better resolution. Later in the war Freya operated in the band from 2.5–2.3m/120 to 130 MHz, with a pulse width of 3 microseconds, a peak power output of 15–20kW and a pulse repetition frequency of 500 Hz. However it had a maximum range of only 160km (100 miles) and could not accurately determine altitude, but it was a fully steerable and semi-mobile system. Freya came in several variants (such as FuMG 43, FuMG 451 and FuMG

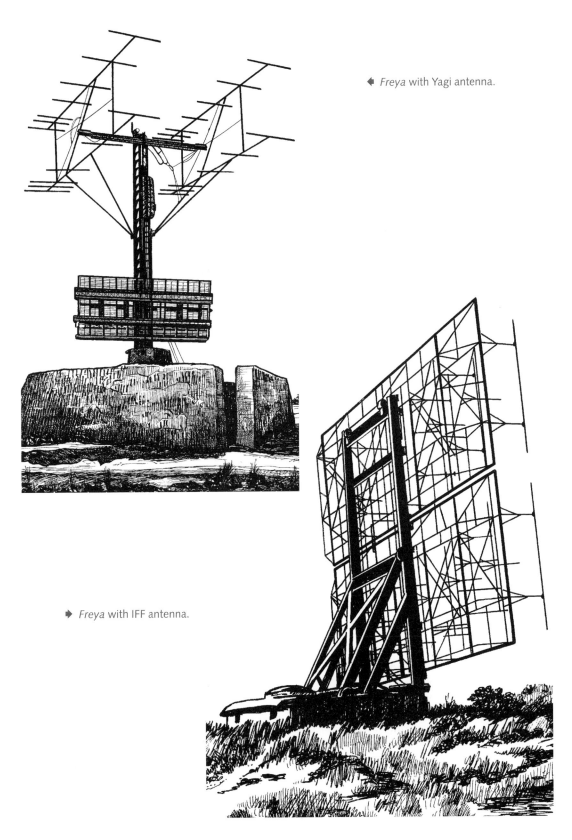

Freya with Yagi antenna.

Freya with IFF antenna.

◆ Radar *Freya* (Kriegsmarine version called *Seetakt*).

321) using various systems of antenna according to wavelengths (Yagi, Fahrstuhl Radattel, IFF). A naval version operating on a slightly different wavelength was also developed and was used on battleships of the Kriegsmarine under the designation FuMG 328 *Seetakt*.

Wassermann

Right after the outbreak of the Second World War, an order was issued for an early warning radar system with a greater range than that of Freya. The *Funkmeßgerät* FuMG 402 Wassermann radar, designed and produced by the Siemens Company in 1942, was an early warning device with a range of about 200km. Basically it was composed of a strong 30–40m mast (with tension cables running from the top to the ground to provide stability) supporting a flat vertical rectangular metal antenna – actually four Freya antennas set up vertically on top of each other. This framework could be as high as 30–37m high and 13.5–21m in width. The mast (a metal tube approximately 4m in diameter) and thus the aerial fixed to it, were placed on a concrete base that could rotate owing to a large toothed gear drive. The whole device could thus fully rotate giving a 360 degree angle of action. Several improved variants (notably FuMG 402 Mark I to V with various shapes of masts, some as high as 51m, and with improved electronics) were produced during the war. Two special Luftwaffe bunkers were designed to house radar Wassermann: types L480 and L486 (see Chapter 5).

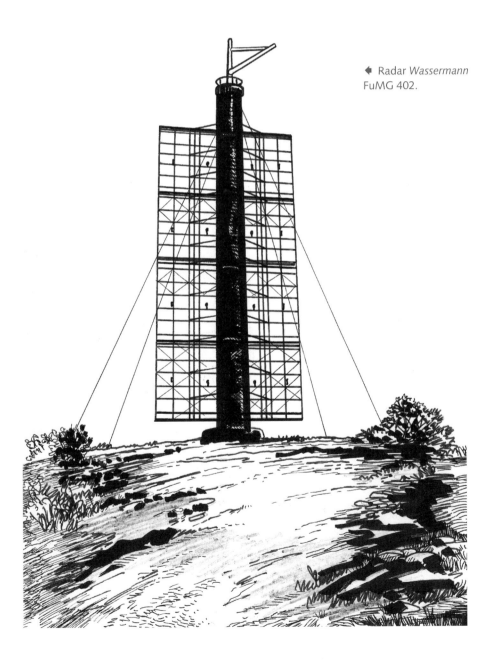

◀ Radar *Wassermann* FuMG 402.

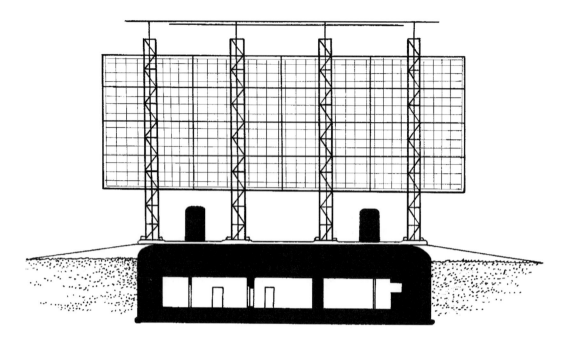

Mammut

Funkmeßgerät FuMG 51 *Mammut* (Mammoth), designed and produced by the Telefunken Company, was an early warning instrument with a range of 200–300km. Its aerial, weighing some 150 tons, was a large flat vertical frame 15m high and 30m wide (in fact eight Freya antennas). The aerial was fixed (it could not rotate) and searching in space was made by means of electronic compensators giving a directional angle of 120 degrees forwards and 120 degrees backwards. The upper section acted as the transmitter and the lower section as the receiver. The huge aerial was attached to four treillis masts in a row fixed on the roof of two specially Luftwaffe designed bunkers (types L485-1 and L485-2) in which crews operated the equipment. It should be noted that the navy bunker type V143 was simultaneously designed for the same Mammut radar. Mammut radars were usually placed in coastal regions in occupied Europe (France, Belgium, the Netherlands, Denmark and Norway).

SIGNAL SERVICE

A comprehensive and efficient air signal service in aerial warfare was vital to the German military effort. Neither offensive nor defensive air operations could be conducted without a complete network of signal communications, or without radio, teletype and telephone equipment for the direction and control of Flak fire. So vital was the role of the *Luftnachrichtenwesen* (German Air Force Signal Service) that it has a greater proportionate wartime expansion than any other arm of the Luftwaffe with an estimated personnel strength of 175,000–200,000. Its functions included: the transmission of all information, orders and communications necessary for the operation and functioning of the Luftwaffe Flak, if possible both by landline and by wireless; the establishment and supervision of all navigational aids to aircraft; the manning of observation and radar posts in connection with air defence; control of air traffic, air safety and rescue services; and the interception and jamming of enemy signals. To handle its multiple duties, a flexible and efficient organisation was developed, consisting of many self-contained specialist units placed under the command of the *Generalnachrichtenführer der Luftwaffe* (Director General of Signal Communications, one of the departments of the German Air Ministry).

During 1941 and early 1942, the German Air Force fighter and Flak organisation was concerned mainly with defence of targets in occupied countries such as northern France and the Lowlands). The bulk of aerial combat was taking place in the relatively small area over those countries and over the English Channel, and the existing warning system, consisting of a coastal radar belt and visual observers, was adequate. But the greater depth of penetration by Allied bombers in 1943 required that the German Air Force protect targets in Germany as well as in occupied territory, and the defensive problem thus became infinitely more complex. Additional radar posts, observation stations and Flak batteries were required. German anti-aircraft artillery and detection equipment had to be placed in tactically favourable positions, and they were forced to enlarge the scope of their activities to cover all areas subject to attack. Such developments naturally led to considerable changes in the Luftwaffe air defence organisation and the methods of Flak control. The liberation of France, Belgium and the southern part of the Netherlands in 1944 further complicated the defensive problem by depriving the Luftwaffe of a large and efficient part of its early warning system, of Flak batteries as well as of many excellent airfields at a time when the weight of the Allied air assault was increasing.

4

MOBILE FLAK

NAVAL MOBILE FLAK UNITS

The *Marineflak* batteries could be mobile, set up on *Kriegsfischkutters* (KFK, armed civilian patrol boats), *Vorpostenboote* (patrol boats) and *Flak-Boote* (anti-aircraft gunships). These gunboats – which could be either specially designed for the purpose or converted (requisitioned) civilian fishing boats – or armed trawlers, made patrols, escorted convoys and defended ports and installations. Patrol boats, organised in *Hafenschutzflotillen* (Harbour Protection Flotillas) were the workhorses in the costal operations of the Kriegsmarine. Used for patrol duty, escort or submarine hunting, they were used in all coastal zones where the Kriegsmarine was operating. Equipped with anti-aircraft guns of various kinds and numbers, they could harm enemy planes but were outgunned if they encountered destroyers or bigger warships.

◆ German Flak boat.

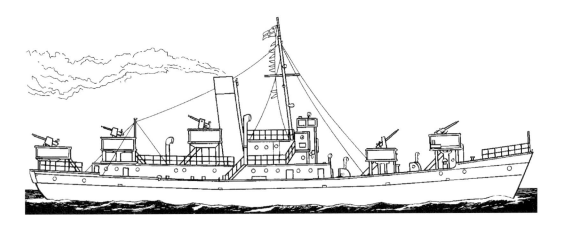

Originally developed for Operation *Sealion* (Germany's planned but never carried out invasion of England in 1940), the so-called *Siebelfähre* (Siebel ferries) designed by aircraft builder Fritz Siebel (then commissioned a colonel in the Luftwaffe), was a shallow-draft catamaran landing craft operated by the Wehrmacht. The craft was composed of two heavy bridging pontoons (or two barges) spaced 6m apart in a catamaran arrangement connected by steel crossbeams. On top of these a broad deck was installed and in the centre, mounted on a pyramid-shaped truss-work, were two end-to-end aircraft or truck engines. The craft served a variety of roles (transport, gunboat, convoy escort, minelayer) in the Mediterranean, Baltic and Black Seas as well as along the English Channel. The Siebel ferry pontoons were also used as Flakships as their flat bottoms, squared off fronts and wide decks constituted an exceptionally stable gun platform, onto which the Luftwaffe mounted various Flak pieces.

◆ *Vorpostenboot* (patrol boat).

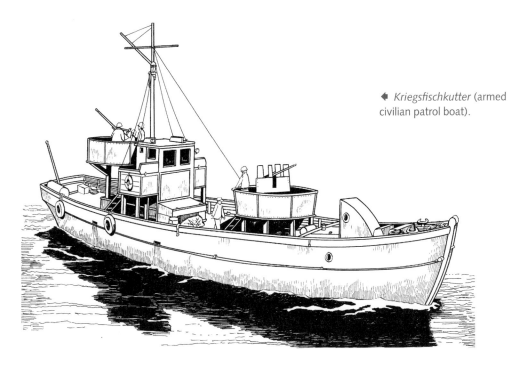

◆ *Kriegsfischkutter* (armed civilian patrol boat).

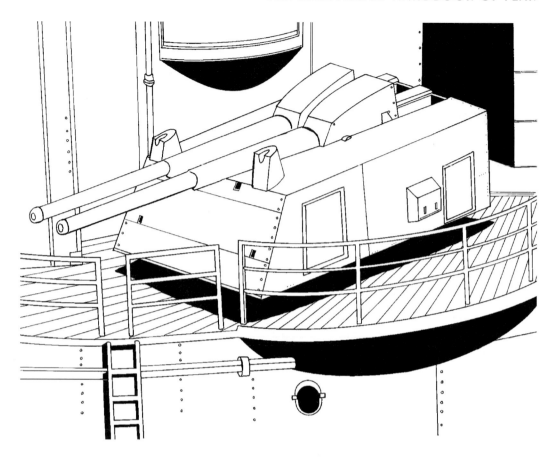

↑ Twin anti-aircraft 10.5cm Flak gun on a warship.

Foreign captured and German discarded warships were also converted to the role of floating anti-aircraft battery. The *Niode*, the ex-Dutch warship *Gelderland* launched in 1899, had a crew of 300, and was armed with 14 10.5cm Flak guns, 8 3.7cm Flak guns and 16 2cm Flak guns; she was used to protect the minesweeper base of Ijmuiden in the Netherlands. Another example was the *Hansa*, which was armed with 8 3.7cm guns and 30 2cm Flak guns. The battleship *Tordenskjold*, a 3858-ton coast defence battleship, was built in England. Launched in 1897, she served in the Norwegian Navy until captured during the German invasion in April 1940. She was taken over by the German Navy, converted to an anti-aircraft ship and renamed *Nymphe*. Bombed and beached in May 1945, she was scrapped in 1948. The battleship *Tirpitz*, after being damaged in 1943, was moved to Tromso in Norway to act as a stationary coastal defence and anti-aircraft battery; she was armed with 16 10.5cm, 16 3.7cm and 70 2cm Flak guns.

Even submarines were modified to be Flak gunboats. Four VIIC U-boats (U-441, U-256, U-621, and U-953) were modified to be surface escorts for attack U-boats operating from the French Atlantic bases. They had greatly increased anti-aircraft firepower with two 2cm quadruple Flakvierling mounts and the experimental 3.7cm automatic gun installed on the decks. A battery of 8.6cm line-carrying anti-aircraft rockets was also tested, but this idea proved unworkable. At times, two additional single 2cm guns were also mounted. The modified U-boats became operational in June 1943 and at first appeared to be successful against the surprised Allied crews, until the RAF developed counter-measures. When the Allies began calling in surface hunters to assist the aircraft, the Flak U-boats were withdrawn (in November 1943) and converted back into fighting submarine vessels.

RAILWAY MOUNTS

The military use of railway has been around almost from the birth of the technology. It has three main modes: transportation; armoured trains; and railway artillery.

Transport

The first and most obvious military use of railway was troop and supply transport. Instead of marching, large armies with supplies, cavalry and artillery could now be moved quite rapidly. As early as 1846 the Prussians were able to concentrate a whole army corps of 12,000 men at Krakow, and some troops were moved by rail to Schleswig-Holstein during the war against Denmark in 1848–1850. The Austrian Empire used the railroad in 1850 for the ponderous movement of 75,000 men, 8000 horses and 1000 vehicles from Vienna and Hungary to the Silesian border. Military transport by rail also played a role in the Crimean War in 1854–1855, in the campaign of Italy in 1859, in the Austro-Prussian War of 1866, but it was left to the American Civil War (1861–1865) to demonstrate that the railway had become a major strategic asset, allowing for example General Sherman's amazing campaign from Chattanooga down into Georgia. During the two world wars, military railway transport was in action behind every one of the widely scattered battlefronts, justifying a predominant place in the war programmes of all belligerents.

Armoured Trains

An even more specific use of railway by the military was the development of armoured trains (in German *Eisenbahn Panzerzug* abbreviated as Eis. Pz-Zug). Heavily armed and armoured rolling fortresses had been used by most combatants in one form or another since the invention of rail travel. During the First World War Britain and France had produced several, and Germany built them to cover their supply lines through the long expanses of Poland and eastern Russia. The Soviets made good use of armoured trains during the Civil War of 1917–1922. The Russian example was followed by Poland, Czechoslovakia and Austria in the inter-war period.

There was a staggering array of armoured train variants built during the Second World War, mounting a variety of armament, from light anti-aircraft guns up to disembodied tank turrets and howitzers. By 1940, the German disposed of several Panzer trains, including improvised armoured convoys and foreign material pressed into German service. The equipment and crews of these trains varied, from boxcars armoured in a makeshift way with sandbags and light weapons to elaborate mobile forts with thick armour and considerable firepower.

Railway Artillery

Artillery mounted on railway carriages (in German *Eisenbahnartillerie* shortened as E-Art) was another military use of railway that first appeared during the American Civil War. This innovation was a heavy mortar protected by armour emplaced on a

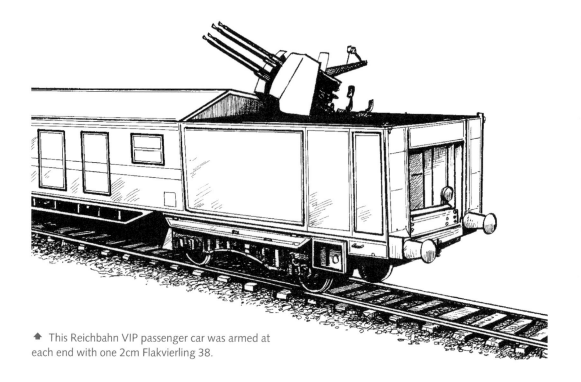

✦ This Reichbahn VIP passenger car was armed at
each end with one 2cm Flakvierling 38.

◆ Heavy 12.8cm Flak gun mounted
on a flat car.

flat car. If early railway artillery consisted of a normal field gun flung on the nearest flat car or on a gondola, this method was developed by all major industrial powers in the last years of the nineteenth century. Heavy cannons were progressively placed on special carriages with a standard fitting gauge, carefully designed suspension and specific pieces of equipment. Britain and the US used railway artillery mostly as mobile coast defence units; in contrast the French and the Germans deployed theirs as heavy front-line artillery. Railway mounted artillery, widely used during the First World War, presented many advantages: it consisted of heavy guns with a long range that could not be transported on roads, they had a formidable fire-power allowing them to fire far behind enemy lines from a relatively safe distance, and a great mobility owing to the dense European railway network. The Germans had a good experience with long-range guns. In 1918 they had built the so-called Paris Guns – extraordinary guns with a range of 75 miles, which fired on the capital of France with the intention to launch a terror bombardment and break the morale of the French.

With the Nazi accession to power in January 1933, and open rearmament launched in 1935, railway guns got the go-ahead and huge long range cannons were ordered from Krupp of Essen, and Hannoverische Machinenfabrik AG (in short Hanomag) from Hanover reflecting Hitler's love for gigantic and prestigious weapons.

During the Second World War, military supply convoys, VIP passenger cars, railway artillery and armoured trains always included *Flakwagen* (flat wagons) carrying anti-aircraft MGs as well a light and heavy Flak guns. As the air war above Germany escalated, specific anti-aircraft artillery mounted on trains was created,

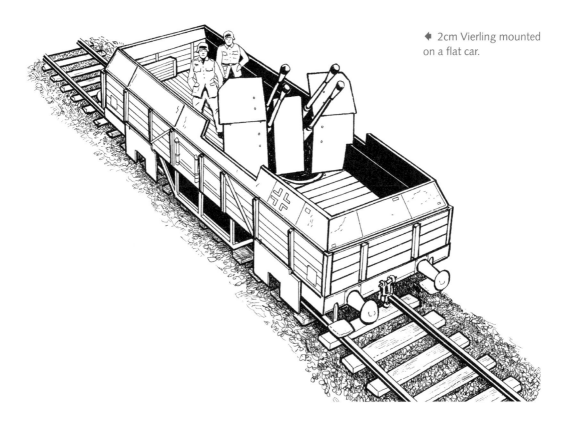

◀ 2cm Vierling mounted on a flat car.

known as *Eisenbahn-Flak*, allowing mobility to Flak batteries. Converted passenger coaches and roofed freight cars with part of the roof removed were often used instead of freight cars, a measure probably dictated by the need to economise on specially constructed cars.

There were several standardised *Geschützwagen* (gun carriages) especially adapted to Flak defence: *Geschützwagen* I and II were intended to carry 2cm, 3.7cm or quad 2cm guns; *Geschützwagen* III and IV carried 8.8cm, 10.5cm and 12.8cm guns, which were fitted with armoured sides that could be folded down when in action creating a larger working platform for the crew, and movable outriggers arms, which could be deployed for stability when firing. Safety fences on all four sides of the gun insured that it was not fired below the safety angle. These measures made it impossible for the gun to strike obstructions such as tunnels, signal posts or other trains. Other safety measures included the posting of look-outs to prevent firing which might damage telegraph wires, signal posts, tunnels or other obstructions, and a complete prohibition of firing on electrified lines with overhead cables.

In addition there were armoured passenger cars for the crews, and other carriages carrying field kitchens, supplies, ammunition, power plants, searchlights, range finders, radars and other related equipment. In practice the allotment of Flak cars varied considerably. Examples of trains were as follows: engine, 5 passenger coaches, 5 box cars, Flak car, 12 box cars, 5 flat cars, 3 box cars, 8 flat cars; or engine, 4 passenger coaches, 14 flat cars, Flak car, 25 box cars. When the train stopped, the guns might be moved from the cars and deployed on the ground so as to give a better field of fire. The decision to do this naturally depended on the probable length of the halt.

The powerfully armed, self-supported and mobile Flak trains fulfilled several distinctive tasks. They defended strategic railroad tracks, important junctions and stations, bridges, tunnels and marshalling yards. They enabled the transport of heavy guns and ponderous equipment, which otherwise were complicated or even impossible to move by road. They enabled the rapid allocation of Flak firepower in strategic areas with little anti-aircraft defence (for example a newly conquered region), and could be used to reinforce Flak fire in vulnerable industrial centres.

⬇ Armoured Flak railway car.

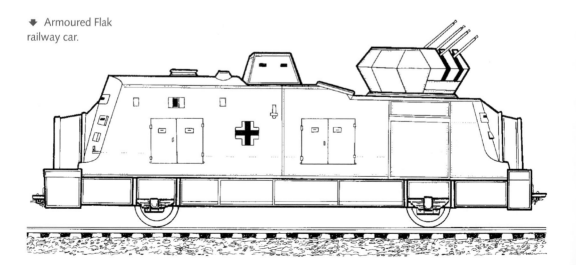

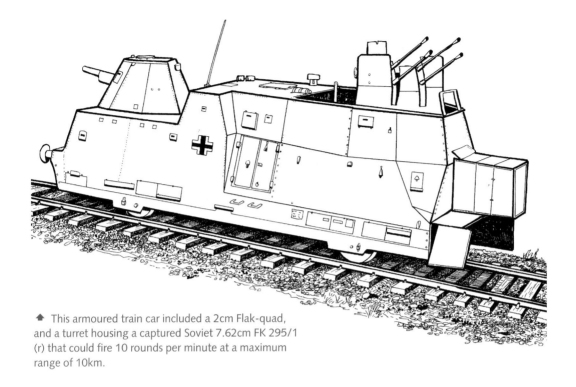

◆ This armoured train car included a 2cm Flak-quad, and a turret housing a captured Soviet 7.62cm FK 295/1 (r) that could fire 10 rounds per minute at a maximum range of 10km.

◆ Known as *Betonröhren Flakwagen 2-fach mit Flak*, this armoured car was composed of two cylindrical concrete pits housing various types of light Flak guns, and a command post in the middle. There was a variant with only one concrete pit placed in the middle of the car.

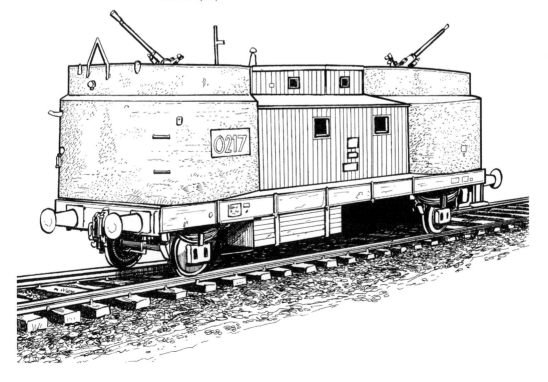

Railway Flak units were organised into regiments, battalions and batteries; the precise composition of the units is not known. It is believed that the regimental organisation formed a pool from which units might be drawn as the necessity arose, either for mobile defence or train protection. The formation most frequently met with was the battery, which in mobile defence probably moved and operated as a self-sufficient unit. In the case of train protection, the battery headquarters presumably administered detachments allocated to different trains. Although railway Flak units were part of the German Air Force and were administered through Luftwaffe channels, train protection detachments were operationally subordinate to the transport authorities. Flak guns provided for the protection of military trains might in certain circumstances be manned by army personnel.

Railway heavy artillery, armoured trains and mobile Flak gun batteries presented, however, serious drawbacks. They were constrained to going where the rail went, and the lay out of the railroad tracks did not necessarily fit the development of the battle and thus greatly limited their use. In the Soviet Union there was another problem: Russia did not use the normal European gauge (1435m) but a broad gauge of 1524m. Therefore only captured trains could be used, or German trains had to be adapted to fit the Russian gauge. Germany was obliged to construct two special gauge conversion yards on the German-Soviet border, one at Malaszevica (Brest-Litovsk) and the other in Przemsyl.

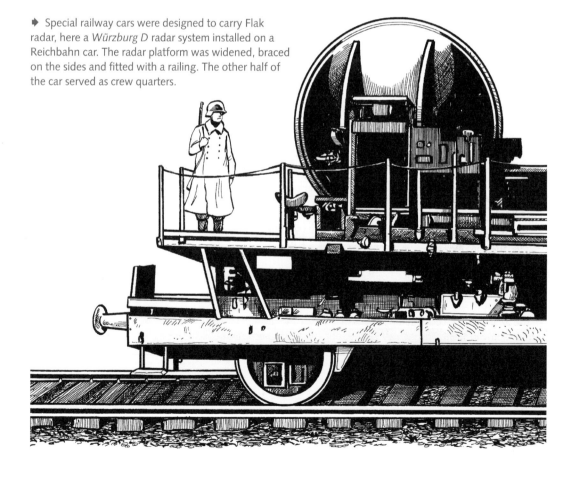

◆ Special railway cars were designed to carry Flak radar, here a *Würzburg D* radar system installed on a Reichbahn car. The radar platform was widened, braced on the sides and fitted with a railing. The other half of the car served as crew quarters.

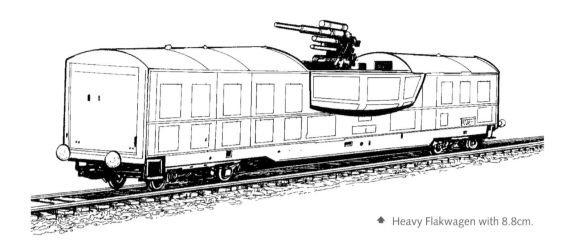

↟ Heavy Flakwagen with 8.8cm.

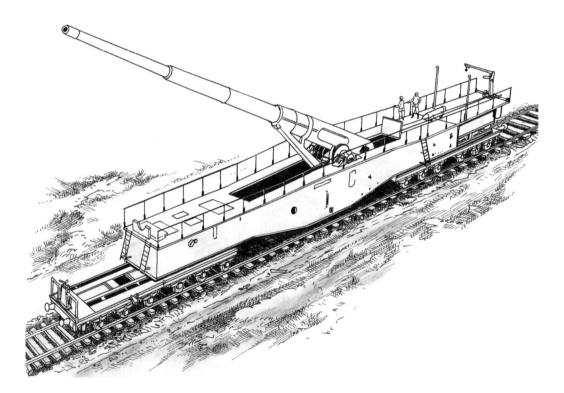

↟ The 28cm K5 (E), designed by the Krupp Company in the early 1930s, was accepted for service in the German Army in 1936. The 28cm K5 (E) was the best workaday railway gun ever built, and formed the backbone of the German *Einsenbahnartillerie* (railway artillery). The deep-groove barrel was 21,539m (70.08 feet) long and fired a 255.5kg (563.38lb) high explosive ribbed shell. The K5 gun was placed on a 29m long carriage, a simple box-girder assembly carried on two six axle bogies, with the front bogie slung so as to allow the front of the box-girder to be swung across it for aiming the gun. For large angles the whole weapon was mounted on a special portable turntable built at the end of a short spur of track laid at the desired firing point. For firing a crew of ten was required, but transport, installation and maintenance demanded hundreds of soldiers. The 28cm K5 (E) railway gun was also called *Schlanke Bertha* ('Slim Bertha', referred to as 'Anzio Annie' by the Allies in Italy).

Railway super-guns were built at considerably high expense, and – if firepower was remarkable and range considerable – rate of fire was rather low; moreover they could not engage specific targets with any great accuracy. Railway guns and armoured trains were heavy and therefore slow, they might be easily ambushed in unsafe territories, and they were dangerously exposed, especially to aerial attack. To immobilise or slow them down, it only took one destroyed bridge or stretch of track. One sabotaged rail-switch might cause a derailment. Because of these disadvantages, railway artillery and armoured trains were already obsolete during the Second World War. All German railway military material was discarded and scrapped after 1945.

CAR AND TRUCK MOUNTS

The growth of Allied air power and the decline of the Luftwaffe forced the Germans to defend not only fixed installations but also transport columns from air attack. The German Army soon came to realise that car- or truck-drawn anti-aircraft guns were at a disadvantage due to their limited mobility, their reliance on prepared firing positions and the delay in their being put into action. To limit these drawbacks, the Wehrmacht developed Flak weapons no longer towed but mounted on the rear of cars and trucks.

⬥ Standardised Horch/Ford with 2cm Flak gun. This vehicle, known as *schwerer Einheits Personenkraftwagen* (s.EpKw, heavy standardised car) was introduced in 1938. Originally intended as a personnel carrier for six soldiers (including the driver), it was used as staff car, personnel carrier, light artillery tractor, ambulance and command or radio car. Some models were employed as *Selbstfahrlafette* (mobile artillery or self-propelled gun) carrying a Flak gun on an open platform. The side rails round the open platform were covered by light wire mesh and opened sideways when the weapon was cleared for action.

⬥ 2cm Flak 38 mounted on an Opel Blitz. The 4 x 2 Opel Blitz LKW 3.6-36S 3-ton truck was the mainstay of German transport, and its production was continued well past the end of the war forming the mainstay of post-war German commercial civilian transport. Designed in 1938 by Opel (then the German subsidiary of General Motors), the Blitz was a very successful truck. Some 100,000 of them were produced and engaged on all fronts in numerous versions including troop carrier, field kitchen, cargo truck, ambulance, radio truck, fuel tanker, mobile laboratory, fire brigade truck, mobile cipher office, cistern, workshop-carrier, and half-track variant designated Opel-*Maultier* (mule). Another version included an armoured cab and a platform designed to take a light anti-aircraft gun; the vehicle was then transformed into a light *Selbstfahrlafette* (self-propelled-gun) and called Opel Blitz 3t mit 2cm Flak 38; ammunitions for the gun were usually transported in a two-wheeled trailer towed by the truck.

Mobile Flak was primarily used to protect moving vulnerable targets like truck convoys or larger units like Panzer formations or infantry divisions on the move. The intention was for the battery commanders to place their guns in such a way as to prevent the attacking aircraft from crossing the line of bomb release or from strafing (engaging ground targets with its guns), or alternatively, if this was not possible, to distract the attacking aircraft so that it missed its target.

If a self-propelled Flak gun was intended to remain in the same position for an extended period of time, a small wall of earth, wood, stones or other suitable materials was erected around it. If it was soft-skinned like a truck, the entire vehicle was often dug in so only the gun and the top of the truck's cab were above ground. Of course, one always took every possible advantage of cover offered by the terrain features, including, hills, valleys, vegetation and buildings.

In practice any heavy car or truck could be used as a Flak weapon-carrier, so only a few specific examples will be examined below. Note in the following section that Kfz is the abbreviation for *Kraftfahrzeug* (motor vehicle). The Kfz ordnance number was attributed by the *Heereswaffenamt* (the Army Ordnance Office, often referred to as the *Waffenamt*). If the whole vehicle was of a special design, created by the Army itself, it was given an SdKfz ordnance number (*Sonderkraftfahrzeug* meaning special purpose motor vehicle). The allocation of Kfz and SdKfz numbers helped to distinguish vehicles in the ordnance vocabulary; it was used for labelling

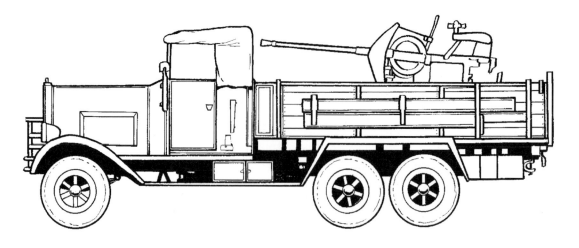

✦ 2cm Flak 38 mounted on a Henschel 33D. The 6 x 4 Henschel 33 medium cross-country truck, designed in 1934, was one of the most long-lived models of the early 1930s. This versatile vehicle existed in several conversions including troop or cargo carrier, radio truck, gas decontamination vehicle for personnel, fire truck with pump and water tank containing 2500 litres and self-propelled light anti-aircraft gun.

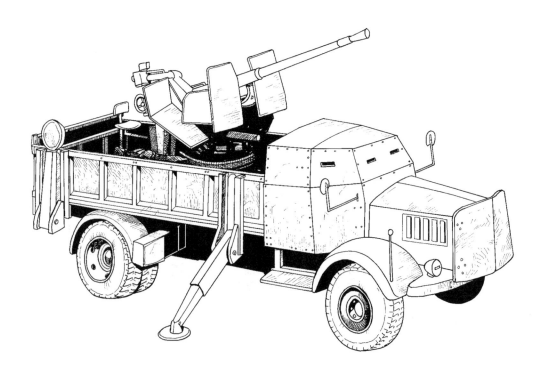

✦ 3.7cm Flak 36/37 on armoured Daimler-Benz L 4500A truck. Appearing in 1938, the Mercedes-Benz L4500 was in the load class 3.5–5 tons. A few L4500As were converted to self-propelled anti-aircraft guns with a *Kabinenpanzerung* (enclosed armoured cab), armed with various weapons, usually a 2cm Flakvierling or a 3.7cm Flak 36 or 37-gun mount on a flat bed body. Ammunition was carried in a standardised *Anhänger* (trailer).

all working drawings and spare parts lists peculiar to that type of vehicle. As already mentioned in Chapter 1, Flak guns mounted on vehicles could also be used as anti-tank weapons, a dual role (Pak/Flak) that often proved of great importance on the battlefield.

The *Leichter Truppen-Luftschutz Kraftwagen* (Kfz 4) was a Stoewer 4 x 4 light personnel car fitted with a special mount at the rear of the vehicle armed with a *Zwillingslafette* composed of twin MG 34 or two MG 42 machine guns. The *Selbsfahrlafette auf E-Fahrgestell s.Pkw* was a 4 x 4 Auto Union medium personnel car armed with a 2cm Flak 30 gun. The *Schweres Truppen-Luftschutz Kraftwagen* (Kfz 70) was a 6 x 4 light truck Krupp L2H 143 with a rear compartment arranged to house a 2cm Flak 30 gun protected by a shield.

Many other combinations were, of course, possible. For example 2cm and 3.7cm Flak guns were mounted on the chassis of an Auto Union 4x4, Standardised Horch/ Ford heavy cars, the Henschel 33D or Krupp L2H143 medium truck, Opel Blitz light trucks or Mercedes-Benz 4500 heavy trucks. In fact any heavy car or truck could be converted to a mobile anti-aircraft vehicle. Even the small KdF Volkswagen K1 Typ 82 *Kübelwagen* (the mass-produced military version of the 1936 sedan Volkswagen 'Beetle', to a certain extent comparable to the legendary US jeep) could be fitted with a machine gun for use in an anti-aircraft role.

However, it should also be noted that, although the Wehrmacht was mechanisation-conscious, Second World War German forces always suffered from motor vehicle shortages, as automotive production could never keep pace with the

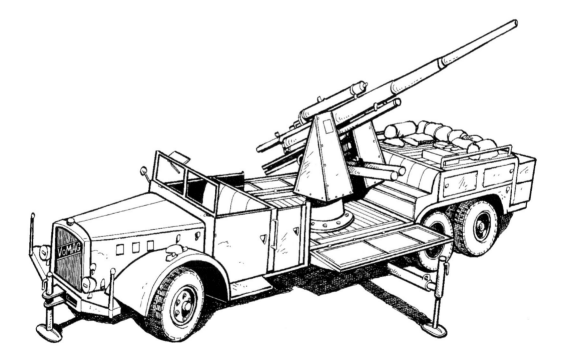

◆ 8.8cm mounted on a Vomag truck. The acronym 'Vomag' stands for *Vogtländische Maschinenfabrik AG* (engine works company) in Plauen. Up to the Second World War it was the second largest manufacturer of commercial motor vehicles (trucks, buses and later also tanks) in the German market. Twenty units of the 9-tons heavy truck Vomag 6L were built as 8.8cm Flak mount and allotted to the motorised 1st Battalion of Flak Regiment 42.

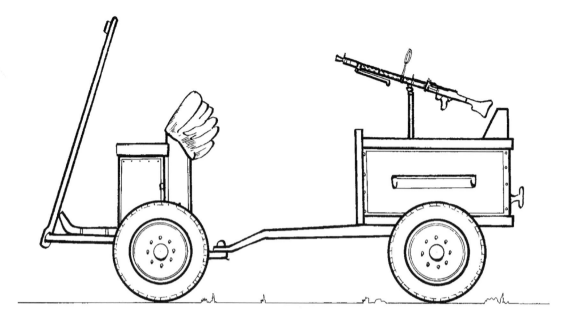

◆ MG Flakwagen 36.

◆ MG Wagen 08.

expansion of the army and the extent of the war fronts. Another critical problem was Germany's petrol supplies which had to be imported and parcelled out carefully between the various arms of the services. It seems difficult to reconcile this situation with the Blitzkrieg image, but only the elite armoured and Waffen SS divisions were fully motorised. In fact the bulk of the German Army used legwork, bicycles and horsepower. Until 1945 horse-drawn wagons were universally used for artillery, transport and heavy loads, some wagons being especially designed, standardised and used to carry infantry support and anti-aircraft machine guns like the MG Wagen 08 and the Flak MG Wagen 36.

HALF-TRACK MOUNTS

Horse-drawn wagons, motorcars and trucks were totally dependant on roads
and tracks suitable for motor vehicles. So to increase cross-country capability,
Flak guns were also mounted on halftracks. A half-track is a vehicle with regular
wheels on the front for steering, and caterpillar tracks on the back to propel the
vehicle and carry most of the load. The purpose of this combination is to produce a
vehicle with the cross-country capabilities of a tank and the handling of a regular
wheeled vehicle.

◆ Demag SdKfz 10/4 with 2cm Flak 30. The *Leichte Selbsfahrlafette SdKfz 10/4* was
composed of a converted 1-ton semi-tracked tractor SdKfz 10 armed with a 2cm Flak 30 gun.
Because the armoured sides had to be dropped when in action to facilitate all-round traverse,
this combination gave poor protection to the crew and gun. Therefore a modified version
was issued, the *Leichte Selbsfahrlafette SdKfz 10/5*, better armed with a 2cm Flak 38 gun
protected by an armoured cabin.

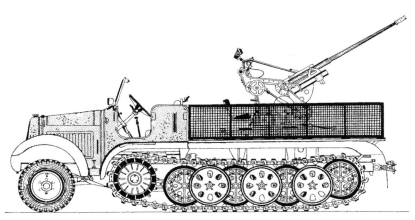

◀ The self-propelled
Flak gun SdKfz 6/1
was composed of
a medium 5-ton
halftrack carrying
a 2cm Flak 30. The
SdKfz 6/2 was a
variant armed with a
3.7cm Flak 36 gun.

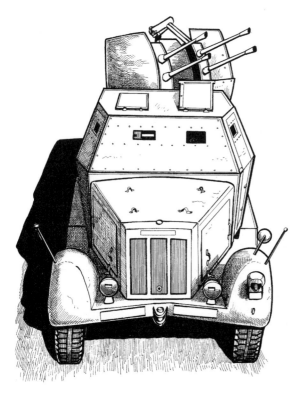

▲ 8-ton SdKfz 7/1. The *Mittlerer Zugkraftwagen SdKfz 7/1* was introduced in late 1941; the equipment consisted of a medium semi-tracked 8-ton tractor converted to carry the 2cm Flakvierling 38. The sides had to be lowered to permit an all-round traverse. Late production vehicles in this series were equipped with an armoured cab.

◀ Front view SdKfz 7/1.

⬥ *Flakpanzerwagen* SdKfz 251/17. The halftrack SdKfz 251 was the armoured variant of the light 3-ton SdKfz 11. Produced by the Hanomag and Büssing-NAG companies, the SdKfz 251 was intended to be an armoured personnel carrier, but eventually conversions included no less than 22 combat variants. The SdKfz 251/17, produced in limited numbers, was armed with a 3.7cm Flak 43 gun. The weapon was protected with a shield, and positioned behind the driver's compartment; it had a crew of 4 or 6. The variant SdKfz 251/21 was another Flak armoured vehicle, with a mount of three 1.5cm Mauser MG 151 heavy machine guns capable of firing 750 rounds per minute each, or three 2cm automatic rapid-fire anti-aircraft guns; the weapons were electrically operated and the vehicle electrical supply could be used. The heavy machine guns were protected with a shield. The vehicle carried 3000 rounds in readiness, and it had folding sides providing room for weapon and crew.

⬥ The variant *Mittlerer Zugfraftwagen SdKfz 7/2* was an 8-ton halftrack SdKfz 7 armed with a 3.7cm Flak 36 gun.

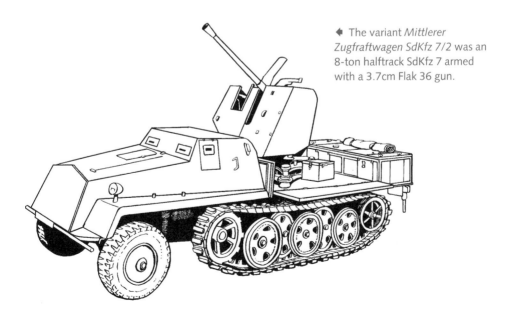

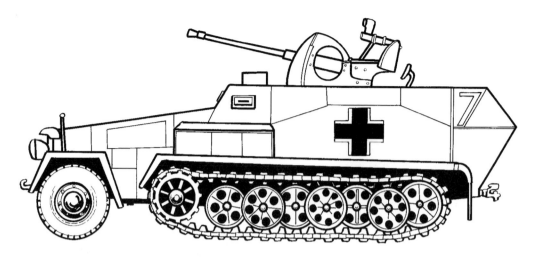

♠ *Flakpanzerwagen* SdKfz 251/17 (variant).

♠ The *Flakzugkraftwagen* 18-t, issued in 1940, consisted of a heavy 8.8cm Flak type 18 or model 37 (Sf) gun mounted on a Daimler-Benz 18-tons SdKfz 9 halftrack. The famous 88 was removed from its pedestal from the four-legged anti-aircraft mounting and bolted to the chassis of the converted semi-tracked vehicle. Jacks were attached to its sides to increase stability when firing. A three-sided shield was added to protect the gunners, and armour was applied around the engine and the driver's cabin. Fifteen armoured SdKfz 9s with 88 Flak guns were built in early 1940, and originally intended to protect moving columns. In a secondary role they could also be used as tank destroyers and assault guns to attack fortified positions with direct fire. In 1941–42 a plan was launched to build 112 more but the concept was abandoned as it soon appeared that a full-tracked, fully armoured vehicle was a more effective prospect.

♠ SWS with 3.7cm Flak 43. The development of the *Schwere Wehrmachtsschlepper* (German Army heavy tractor) began in 1942 as a replacement for the 5-ton half-track truck (SdKfz. 6). Approximately 1000 vehicles were built and were mainly used with a platform superstructure as a supply vehicle for the troops. By the end of the Second World War dozens of vehicles were also equipped as a self-propelled mount for the 3.7cm Flak 43 gun. In addition to the additional protective armour for the engine and driver's cab, these vehicles had a reinforced chassis to bear the weight of the anti-aircraft gun and ammunition.

♠ The French Citroen-Kegresse P 14 half-track. The twin 13.2mm Hotschkiss anti-aircraft machine gun was mounted on this half-track, as well as on the Somua MCG half-track and 6x6 truck Lorraine 28. A few were captured by the Germans after the French were defeated in June 1940 and were used as Flak training vehicles.

Before and during the Second World War the Germans developed three main categories of half-tracks depending on the load to be towed: *leichter Zugkraftwagen* (light half-tracks) including the light 1-t SdKfz 10 (built by Demag), and the light 3-t SdKfz 11 (Hansa-Lloyd-Goliath); *mittlerer Zugkraftwagen* (medium half-tracks) including the medium 5-t SdKfz 6 (Büssing-NAG) and the medium 8-t SdKfz 7 (Krauss-Maffei); and *schwerer Zugkraftwagen* (heavy half-tracks) including the heavy 12-t SdKfz 8 (Daimler-Benz) and the super heavy 18-t SdKfz 9 (FAMO).

Half-tracks were originally designed as artillery tractors towing light, medium or heavy guns in the forefront of the battle, but were not intended as vehicles from which to fight. Under the pressures of war, this soon changed and half-tracks were adapted to a multitude of combat roles. Instead of towing guns, which reduced mobility and cross-country capability, halftracks were converted into weapon-carriers equipped, for example, with smoke generators, flame-throwers, heavy mortars, rocket launchers, and of course anti-aircraft guns. Weapons were installed at the rear of the chassis, ready to be operated at very short notice, and the vehicle's cabin itself was often fitted with protective armour.

TANK MOUNTS

The concept of *Flakpanzer* consisted of a tank with the turret removed and replaced with an anti-aircraft gun protected by an armoured shield or plates, or emplaced in a fully rotating turret. During the early stage of the Second World War the Germans realised the necessity of introducing specialised vehicles into their Panzer division structure to amplify their anti-tank (Pak) and anti-aircraft (Flak) capabilities. It was difficult for the tractor and horse-drawn equipment to keep pace with the 'lightning' advance of tanks, and they were also at a great disadvantage when it came to protection. The first Flakpanzer 38 (t) based on the chassis of the Czech 38 (t) tank appeared in 1940 with a small calibre Flak gun.

◀ *Oberfeldwebel* (Staff Sergeant), Panzer troop. This Staff Sergeant of the motorised anti-aircraft artillery wears the two-piece tropical Panzer uniform designed in 1941–42 for the *Deutsches Afrika Korps* (DAK, German African Corps) in Northern Africa. The dull olive-khaki uniform was intended to be practical yet also to convey the elite status of the Panzerwaffe. It consisted of a lightweight four-pocked jacket and long, loose trousers with a large pocket on the left thigh, gathered by tapes over brown laced boots. The uniform, worn with a shirt and tie, included various headgear: forage cap; peaked cap; soft peaked cap; or regular army steel helmet. It was practical being especially designed for men operating in confined spaces. This man is equipped with goggles, binoculars, a leather *Meldtasche* M1935 (report/map case) and pistol in a holster attached to a service belt.

◆ This Flakpanzer crewman *c.*1944 wears the distinctive reed green Panzer drill uniform introduced in mid-1942 as working dress and hot weather combat dress. It included a *Panzer Feldjacke*, a short hip-length, double-breasted, tight-fitting jacket, often with a large pocket on the left chest; it had no other external pockets as they could snag inside the vehicle. The *Feldhose* (trousers) were green, full length and slightly baggy with a large pocket on the left thigh.

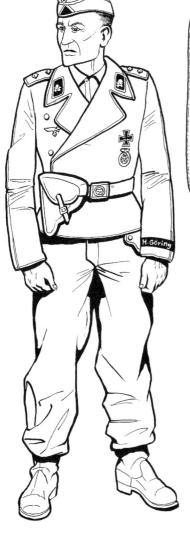

◀ Tank crewman of the Hermann Göring Division. The collar patches were the most eye-catching feature since they displayed a white metal *Totenkopf* (death's head) in a black rectangular cloth badge.

As the war proceeded, and particularly with the experience gained on the Eastern Front, German authorities found an ever-growing requirement for self-propelled Pak and Flak weapons. By that time the Germans had a large number of own-made tank chassis and captured vehicles available, which could easily be converted to the role of SPG. Besides, the gradual increase in Allied air supremacy by 1943 demanded the introduction of specialised self-propelled Flak weapon-carriers with increased firepower and thicker armour as a means of protecting ground units from fighter and bomber attacks. The German situation stimulated a great deal of development in self-propelled anti-aircraft systems, notably the Flakpanzer IV series using the chassis of the *Panzerkampfwagen* IV. Flakpanzer saw active service but they could not do a great deal to mitigate the terrible effects of the Allied air threat in the last year of the war.

Flakpanzer PzKpfw I Ausf. A

The most interesting conversion based on the modified PzKpfw I Ausf A was *Flakpanzer* I (Sd.Kfz.101) armed with a 20mm Flak 38 L/112.5 gun. It was most likely based on the modified *Munitionsschlepper* I Ausf A (Sd.Kfz.111), a light ammunition carrier. The gun was mounted on the floor in place of the original turret. The chassis was overloaded and engines were used up leading to poor performance. Approximately 24 were produced in early 1941 by Alkett in Berlin and all equipped three batteries (each equipped with eight vehicles) of Flak Abteilung

◆ Flakpanzer PzKfw I Ausf. A
with 2cm Flak 38.

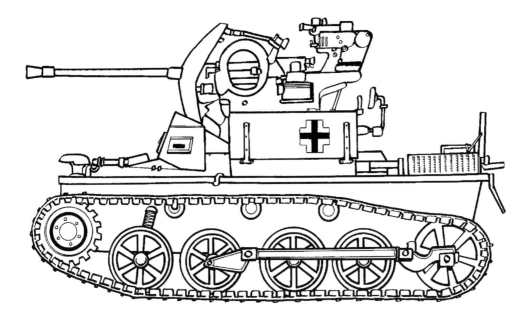

614. In addition, each battery had eight *Munitionsschlepper* I Ausf A (Sd.Kfz.111) ammunition carriers. The last of these interesting conversions was lost at Stalingrad in January 1943. Along with the Flakpanzer I, there was also the PzKpfw I modified and mounted with 15mm MG 151/15 *Dreilling* (triple) heavy machine guns.

◆ Profile Flakpanzer I SdKfz 101(with 2cm Flak 38.

Flakpanzer 38 (t)

The second self-propelled anti-aircraft gun fully mounted on track was the Flakpanzer 38 (t) Ausf. L (SdKfz 140) sometimes named *Gepard*. Appearing in late 1942, it was composed of a light 2cm Flak 38 gun mounted on the chassis of a Czech-made CDK/Praha TNHP 38, re-designated by the Germans as Panzerkampfwagen 38 (t). The SdKfz 140 was an improvisation consisting of the ex-Czech 38 (t) tank chassis modified so that the gun could be mounted on two cross beams at the rear of the chassis, to form a firing compartment at the rear protected by an octagonal 10mm thick armoured shield; the upper part of each of the eight plates was hinged at the bottom, and had to be folded outwards when going into action giving full 360 degree traverse but poor protection to the crew.

The SdKfz 140 weighed 9.8 tons and had a crew of four: the driver, commander and two gunners operating the light 2cm Flak 38 gun. Issued to the Flak platoons of tank battalions, it was an interim solution before more efficient Flakpanzers were available. Some 162 were built and production was stopped in 1944. Some of them equipped the 12th Waffen SS Division Hitlerjugend, which took part in the fighting during the Battle of Normandy in June and July 1944.

The chassis of the CDK/Praha TNHP 38 was also used for the design of the *Jagdpanzer* 38(t) (Sd.Kfz. 138/2), later known as *Hetzer* ('baiter'), a popular and successful German light tank destroyer. A version included the *Bergepanzer Hetzer* 38(t), a light recovery vehicle, a number of which could have become Flakpanzers fitted with a 2cm Flak 38. The war ended before these proposed converted models were put into production.

◆ Flakpanzer 38 (t) Ausf. L
SdKfz 140 *Gepard*.

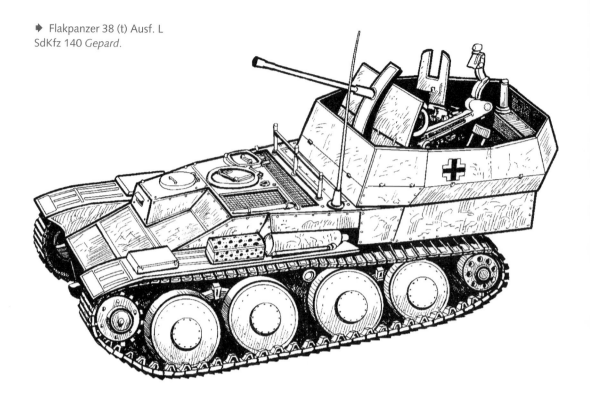

Panzerkampfwagen PzKpfw IV

As the Flakpanzer 38 (t) did not prove completely satisfactory, this combination was followed by other models using guns with stronger firepower placed on the chassis of the *Panzerkampfwagen* PzKpfw IV with several variants.

Put in production in late 1943, the Panzerflak IV F SdKfz 161 *Möbelwagen* ('furniture van') was composed of the chassis of a Panzerkampfwagen PzKpfw IV upon which a four-barrelled 2cm gun Vierling 38 (with a devastating rate of fire of 800 rounds per minute) was centrally mounted in a box-shaped firing emplacement. The nickname 'furniture van' came from the hinged, slab-sided 10mm thick armoured shields that dropped down when the weapon came into action. The *Möbelwagen* had a crew of five and carried 3200 rounds. There were also other versions armed with one 3.7cm Flak 43 or one 8.8mm anti-aircraft gun. A total of 211 of these vehicles were built.

There was a variant, introduced in December 1943, the Panzerflak IV 3 *Wirbelwind* (whirlwind). This had the same features as the *Möbelwagen* but the fighting emplacement was greatly improved. Instead of folding armoured plates, which took precious time to put down before operating the weapon, the vehicle had an open-top octagonal fully revolving turret designed to give better protection to the gun and crew. Some 140 *Wirbelwinds* were built. A variant, the Flakpanzer IV *Ostwind* (east wind) was produced from March 1944 on; it was similar to the *Wirbelwind* but armed with a 3.7cm Flak 43 gun, placed in a turret, whose armour thickness was increased to 25mm. Only around 40 IV *Ostwinds* were built.

◀ Flakpanzer IV.

◀ Flakpanzer IV
Wirbelwind/Ostwind.

⬆ T-34 Flakvierling. There were also a few Flakpanzer using captured enemy tanks showing how the German field workshops were adept and ingenious at producing extemporised fighting vehicles, such as the Fahrgestell Bren (e), which consisted of a captured British Universal Bren Carrier converted to take a 2cm Flak 38 gun protected by a shield. Another example was the depicted Russian T-34 converted to a Flakpanzer. The turret was removed and replaced by a 2cm Flakvierling in a revolving armoured turret. A few seem to have been used to protect the headquarters of Panzerjäger Abteilung 653 in Galicia, Poland, in early 1944.

FLAKPANZER PROJECTS

Up until the end of the Second World War various other elaborate Flakpanzer types were designed. None ever entered mass production but they paved the way for the modern anti-aircraft weapons mounted on tanks developed in the 1950s.

The Flakpanzer *Kügelblitz* (ball lightning) had the chassis of a PzKpfw IV and a rotating enclosed turret with a rounded 'skullcap' housing, armed with a twin 3cm Flak 103/38 guns designed by the Rheinmetall Company. A modern feature of this weapon was the belt feed for the ammunition giving a cadence of 425 rounds per minute with a range of 5700m. With a height of only 2.3m, the *Kügelblitz* had a low silhouette. Only six prototypes were built, and this pre-series, built by Deutsche Eisenwerke AG, Werk Stahlindustrie in Duisburg, was delivered by the end of 1944 to the newly formed *Panzerflak-Ersatz und Ausbildung Abteilung* (tank anti-aircraft replacement and training regiment) at the training camp of Ohrdruf in the province of Thuringen.

◆ Flakpanzer *Kugelblitz*.

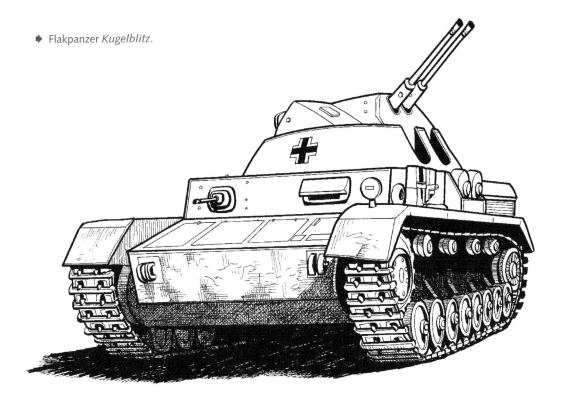

Each company had three platoons, and each platoon was equipped with four *Wirbelwind*, four *Ostwind*, four *Möbelwagen* and four *Kugelblitz*. It seems that this unit was used against the Red Army on the Oder front in early 1945, but there is no further information concerning their fate. The German military archive in Koblenz has a photograph which shows two abandoned destroyed *Kugelblitz* on a roadside somewhere in East Germany, but it is generally believed that the *Kugelblitz* never saw action. It represents, however, another of those very late wartime German experimental vehicles, and the forerunner of post-war anti-aircraft designs produced on both sides of the Iron Curtain.

Another project, known as Flakpanzer 341 *Colian*, consisted of the chassis of a PzKpfw V Panther Ausf. D with a completely enclosed turret armed with a twin 3.7cm Flakzwilling 43 mounted side-by-side. Designed by Rheinmetall-Borsig and Krupp in December 1943, this heavy 40-ton Flakpanzer was to have a crew of four and an ammunition supply of 104 rounds. The twin guns were to have a rate of fire of 500 rounds per minute, and an elevation of −5 to +80 degrees. The turret only weighed approximately 9060kg. The *Colian* was never produced, as its firepower was rather weak (although it was also envisaged to mount a twin 5.5cm Flak guns) compared to the cost involved. There was another project using the hull of a Panther Ausf. D, known as *Flakpanzer Panther mit MG-151/20 Flakvierling*. This had a mechanised, fully traversable closed turret armed with four echeloned MG 151 Mauser Flak guns with an effective ceiling of 900m and a rate of fire of 750 rounds per minute. This project was never produced and abandoned in late 1943. Other Flakpanzer projects using the chassis of a Panther tank included a Panther with a 5.5cm twin mount in an open turret (Gerät 58), and a Panther with a twin 3.7cm mount in a closed turret (Flakpanzer 3.7cm *Flakzwilling* 44). These designs remained on the drawing board as it was soon clear that all Panther production capacity was needed for combat tanks and no chassis were available for Flakpanzers.

Another project, designed by Rheinmetall-Borsig, involved the lengthened chassis of a *Luchs* (light reconnaissance tank) which would have carried an open-top revolving turret mounting one 3.7cm Flak gun.

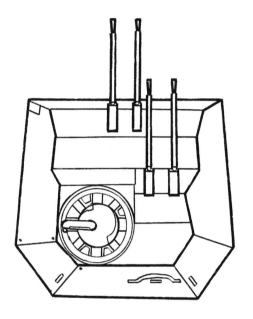

◀ Plan of the turret of a Flakpanzer Panther with 2cm Vierling MG-151/20.

◀ Flakpanzer Panther with 2cm Vierling MG-151/20 (Flak-quad).

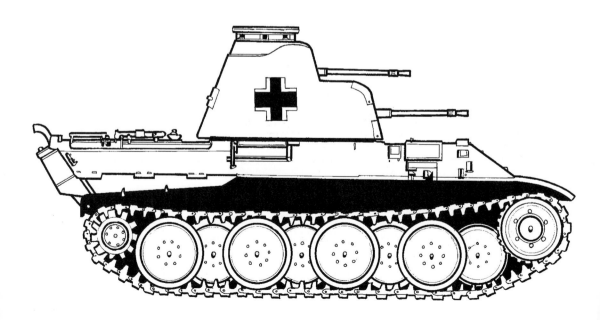

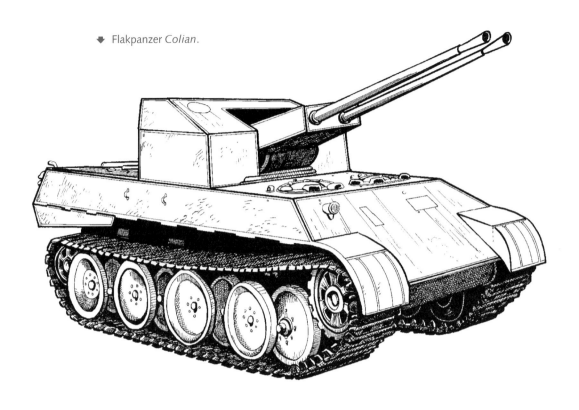

⬇ Flakpanzer *Colian*.

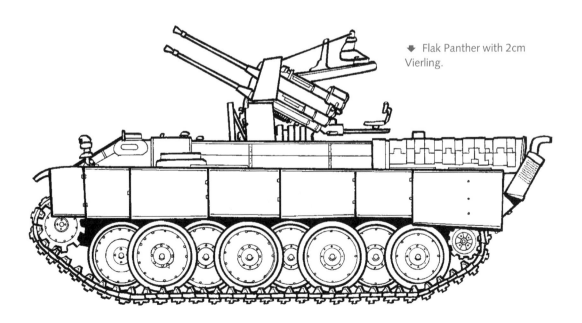

⬇ Flak Panther with 2cm Vierling.

FLAK BUNKERS

The German military engineering authorities had gained good experience of bunker construction, starting in the First World War, and continuing in the period 1935–1938 with the establishment of the Oder-Warthe-Bogen fortification at the eastern border with Poland. Another important fortification project was the Westwall (Siegfried Line) built between 1938 and 1940 facing the Maginot Line at the western border with France, where standardised bunkers were used. The German use of bunkers culminated in the construction of the Atlantic Wall in the period 1941–1944, stretching from Norway to the Franco-Spanish border in order to repulse any Allied landings in Western Europe.

The Germans distinguished several levels of fortification ranging from simple field works to enormous and sophisticated concrete structures.

FIELD FORTIFICATIONS

If a Flak troop (or any other infantry unit) was deployed in a certain position for a few days or longer, the crews generally constructed temporary fieldworks for the protection of both the gun and personnel. The longer the unit stayed in one

➡ Anti-aircraft machine-gun pit. The pit was a simple excavation about 1.50m deep and about 2m in diameter accommodating two men, a firer and a loader.

position the stronger it was constructed. The Germans employed two main levels of field fortification: *Feldmässig* (field fortification, F) and *Verstärkter Feldmässiger* (reinforced field fortification, VF).

Feldmässig (field fortification, F)

Field fortifications were used when a position was to be occupied for a short time. How the Flak gun was deployed depended heavily on the materials available, which could be affected by the nature of the surrounding country but also by shortages of or distances to available materials. The gun was deployed on an open road or in a field without any construction around it, and if the situation required it, the weapon could stay on its carriage. Occasionally the gun was taken off its carriage and a beam of earth, sand, snow, stones, sandbags or logs was erected around the gun position, always taking every possible advantage of cover, camouflage and concealment in the shape of the surrounding ground features.

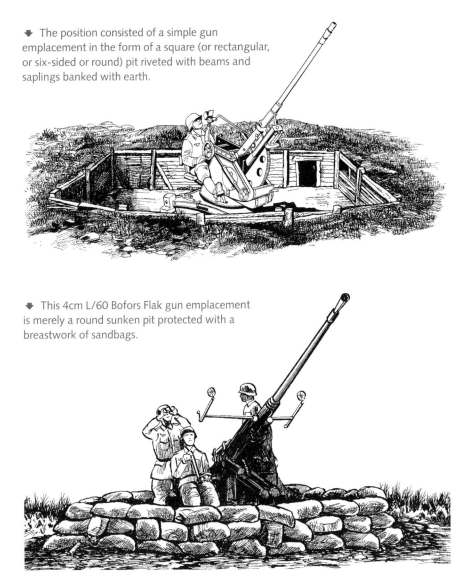

◆ The position consisted of a simple gun emplacement in the form of a square (or rectangular, or six-sided or round) pit riveted with beams and saplings banked with earth.

◆ This 4cm L/60 Bofors Flak gun emplacement is merely a round sunken pit protected with a breastwork of sandbags.

Verstärkter Feldmässiger (reinforced field fortification, VF)

Reinforced field fortifications were used in the case of semi-permanent occupation of a position. A parapet of wood, timber, light concrete or bricks was erected around the gun's position. Temporary works were also built in order to shelter the gun, ammunition and material as well as the crew both against attack and the

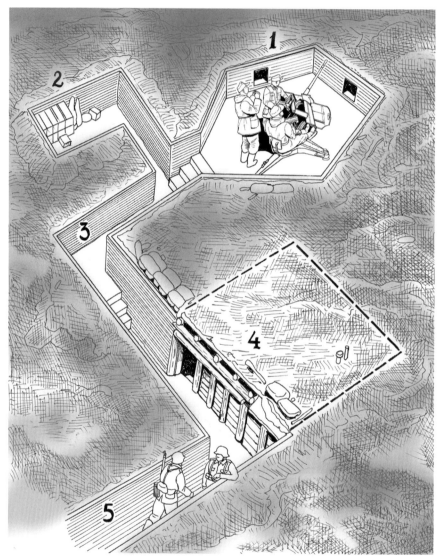

⬆ VF position for a 2cm Flak 38 gun. The position included a camouflaged combat emplacement for the gun (1); a niche (2) that could be dug underground containing boxes of round magazines, spare barrels, cleaning gear, spare parts and tools; and a trench (3) leading to a subterranean crew shelter (4), this being made of concrete, masonry or log walls filled with rock or packed earth, with a thick roof made of several layers of logs, clay, earth and rocks. Another trench (5) connected the emplacement with the rest of the position. The *déblai* (excavated earth) was removed and the sides and the roof of the shelter (possibly also that of the ammunition niche) were covered over with sods of turf to ensure the position blended into the surrounding terrain.

elements. Elaborate designs for the construction of field fortifications, obstacles, ammunition stores and crew shelters were available, based on First World War principles. The VF category included stone and concrete defence works divided into the following subcategories:

Subcategory D	roofs and walls 30cm thick, able to resist rifles and shell splinters
Subcategory C	roofs and walls 60cm thick able to resist machine gun and light artillery fire
Subcategory B-1 *alt* (old)	roofs and wall 1m thick able to resist up to 10.5cm gun fire
subcategory B-2 *neu* (new)	roofs and walls 1.50m thick able to resist up to 15.5cm gun fire

However, enemy pressure, as well as a lack of resources and time did not always allow the construction of ideal Flak and field positions. As a rule VF Flak positions were always deep, kept as small as possible, camouflaged, and built flush with the ground in order to present a low profile, both for concealment and to offer less of a target. As can be easily imagined, VF reinforced field fortifications displayed no real uniformity but rather a great deal of initiative and improvisation.

◀ Each German infantryman – and also each Luftwaffe Flak gunner – was issued a *Schanzzeug* (entrenching tool) with a short wooden handle and a fixed square blade. The small spade was carried in a leather cover often attached to the waist service belt.

Tobruk

Amongst the VF open combat emplacements, the so-called *Ringstand* occupied a very particular place. The *Ringstand* was better known as *Tobruk* by the Allies because it resembled a similar type of position, a small roofless bunker built by the Italians near Tobruk in Libya during the North African campaign. It is not known if Italian military engineers shared their designs with their German counterparts, so the origin of the popular name *Tobruk* remains a mystery. The *Ringstand* could also find its origin in a small armoured observation post, called *Schnecke* ('snail' because of its form), built in the *Festen* (fortresses) around Metz in eastern France at the end of the nineteenth century and beginning of the twentieth century. It should be noted that the British developed a rather similar defensive post. Known as the TTRT turret, this had the appearance of a cylindrical pit, and was intended to be manned by one soldier serving a light machine gun placed in a small fully revolving turret allowing a 360-degree arc of fire.

The German *Ringstand* was probably designed in April 1941 by a commission of the German *Festungpionere* (engineer corps) as a cheap substitute for the expensive

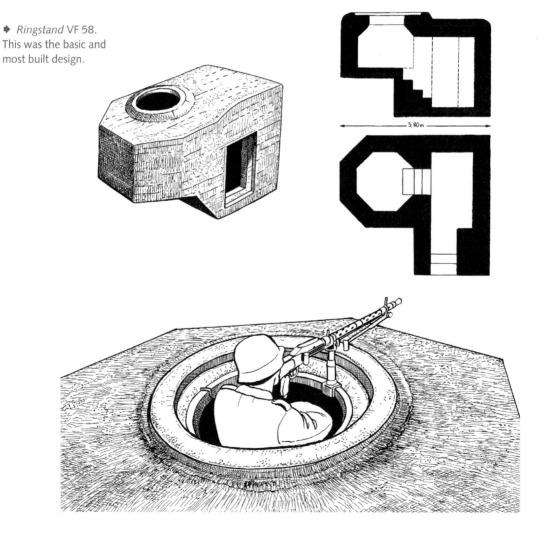

◆ *Ringstand* VF 58. This was the basic and most built design.

3,80 m

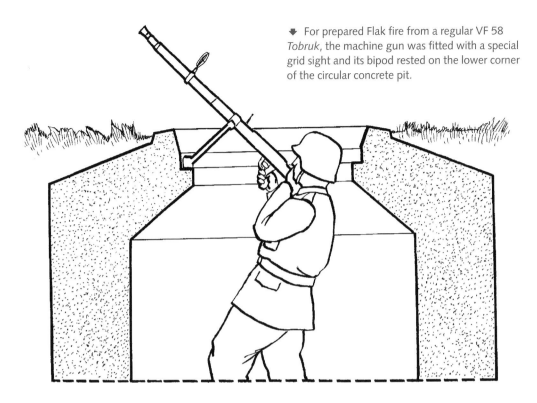

⬇ For prepared Flak fire from a regular VF 58 *Tobruk*, the machine gun was fitted with a special grid sight and its bipod rested on the lower corner of the circular concrete pit.

machine-gun armoured turrets at a time when priority was given to armoured vehicles. The simple *Tobruk* was approved by Hitler in early 1942 and was soon widely used by the German Army (particularly in the Atlantic Wall). It was a small independent one- or two-man combat bunker. It was also often found integrated into an army bunker as an observation and close-range defence element (in that case named *Offener Beobachter*, 'open observatory').

As a separate unit the *Tobruk* was built in 40cm *Verstärkt festmaßig* (VF, reinforced field fortification) thickness. It was basically a concrete foxhole, composed of a small 1.60m high open pit in which a soldier could stand upright with only his head and shoulders exposed. The upper opening was 80cm in diameter, and either circular, hexagonal or octagonal in shape. The edge of the upper opening was fitted with a circular rail having a double function: it enabled to fix a lid for camouflage purposes and for preventing infiltration of rain, dust or sand; the rail also supported a *Ringstandlafette* (a special rotating mounting) for a machine gun. Often a small room (of various dimensions) was added to serve as an ammunition recess and shelter. It was accessible by means of a narrow curved corridor or staircase.

Tobruks existed in numerous variants indicated by letter R (*Ringstand*) or Vf (reinforced field fortification) or occasionally L (Luftwaffe) followed by one, two or sometimes three figures. The most frequent was coded *Ringstand* VF 58 observatory/combat emplacement armed with one machine gun. Variants included models armed with a 5cm *Granatwerfer* (mortar), flame-thrower, light 5cm KwK anti-tank gun, and a small rotating tank-turret (often from captured French tanks like the Renault R 35, Renaultft 17, char B-1 bis, Somua). Special variants were issued for light Flak guns (coded R 65a, R70, and R 80). They had a wider pit, broad enough to house a light Flak gun, and a lower parapet to allow a full traverse. The model L10 (*Stand für Flakrichtgeräte* issued in March 1943) was a slightly enlarged *Tobruk* designed and adapted to take a Flak aiming device.

The *Ringstand/Tobruk*, although made of light VF construction was able to take the high pressure of an explosion due to its circular form. It was reported that a 250kg Allied aeroplane bomb detonating about 5m from a *Tobruk* caused only several thin and barely noticeable cracks, and the position remained totally intact. In case of a direct hit, however, the same bomb had a disastrous effect: the occupants would all be pulverised and the bunker would be completely wrecked.

*Tobruk*s were an important tactical feature on the battlefield. Sited in mutually supporting groups, they provided all-round defence against attacks from the front, flank or rear. The *Tobruk* was maximally standardised, it was cheap, rapidly built, easy to camouflage, adaptable and multifunctional. Widely used in all theatres of operation (for the Atlantic Wall a rough estimate can be made for more than 10,000), many of them still exist today along European shores.

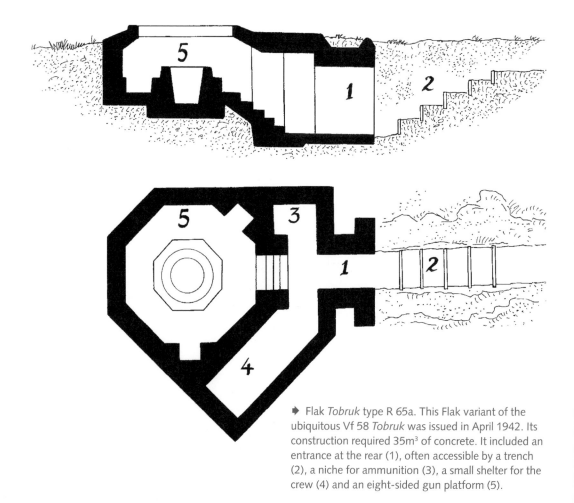

→ Flak *Tobruk* type R 65a. This Flak variant of the ubiquitous Vf 58 *Tobruk* was issued in April 1942. Its construction required 35m³ of concrete. It included an entrance at the rear (1), often accessible by a trench (2), a niche for ammunition (3), a small shelter for the crew (4) and an eight-sided gun platform (5).

PERMANENT FORTIFICATIONS

Ständiger Ausbau

The elaborate *Ständig Ausbau* (permanent construction, *St* in short) included all concrete works able to resist heavy bombardment. This was divided into four sub-categories:

Baustärkte E   5m thick. Very expensive, this was reserved for exceptional bunkers e.g. U-Boote shelters and important headquarters.

Baustärkte A (StA) 3.5m thick, making it capable of resisting anything up to 1800kg aerial bombs and 52cm artillery rounds.

Baustärkte A-1   the non-frequent intermediary 2.5m concrete thickness.

Baustärkte B (StB) the standardised 2m concrete thickness, designed to resist up to 500kg aerial bombs and 22cm artillery fire. Most German bunkers were constructed in StB. In the case of a permanent occupation of a position, Flak guns were placed in a fully fortified position either in a *Bettung* (concrete gun platform) or in a bunker.

Luftwaffe Flak Bunkers

Bunkers designed, built and used by the Luftwaffe during the Second World War originated from experience gained in 1938 by the creation of the *Luftverteidigungszone West* (LVZ-W, zone of air defence west). This zone was formed shortly before the war, in 1938, as a part of the Westwall (Siegfried Line). As stated above, the LVZ-W was a massive deployment of light and heavy anti-aircraft guns in a belt 30km deep stretching from the Black Forest to the Saar and later extended, first to Aachen, then to the Heligoland Bight and finally to Schleswig-Holstein. After 1939 the Luftwaffe modified its designs for its own purpose owing to German Air Force General Karl Kitzinger who had served as an army engineer. However the LVZ-W was largely incomplete and even mythical by 1939. It strength, greatly exaggerated in the media, was used by the German propaganda machine to deceive the public both at home and abroad.

As the air war above Germany proceeded, a wide radar chain (called the Kammhuber Line) was established along Germany's northwest border towards Aachen extending from Lübeck to Liège in Belgium, with forward posts in western France, Denmark, Belgium and the Netherlands. The line included radar stations, searchlights, Flak guns and interceptor aircraft. In addition, Flak guns were established around the most likely targets: main cities, ports and industrial installations. In order to shelter weapons and equipment, the Luftwaffe designed and developed bunkers, which were on the whole rather similar to the Heer's since the *Festungpioniere* (Army Engineer Corps) were generally recognised as the highest authority.

In view of the limited scope of the Luftwaffe's functions (protection of Flak artillery and radar equipment), the number of *Regelbauten* (standard bunkers) was rather limited. Air Force bunkers were prefixed by a letter L (meaning Luftwaffe to designate their origin) and a figure from 400 to 494. A first batch of designs included all Flak bunkers from L401 to L470 (types between L401 and L435 had variants and options suffixed *A* or *a*) for Flak artillery. These were generally

✦ A heavy Luftwaffe Flak battery generally consisted of four 8.8cm or 10.5cm guns arranged in a quadrilateral with a main fire control centre some 100m away. An auxiliary command centre was often positioned centrally between the four guns. The battery was protected against low level attacks by a light flak gun. (1) The core of a Luftwaffe battery included a fire control-leading bunker (this could be types L412A, L421A, L424, L425, L424A, L425A, L428 or L429). (2) Radio and communication bunker (L490, L483 or L484). (3) Radar post bunker (L405, L404A or L426). (4) Heavy Flak gun bunker (L401, L401A, L418, L422, L422A or L436). (5) Ammunition bunker (L407, L407A or L413). (6) Light Flak guns bunker (L402, L409, L409a, L409A, L410, L410A, L419 or L435A or L470). (7) Power plant bunker (L406, L406A or L427) and service buildings. (8) Searchlight shelter (L411, L411A, L420, L420A or L430). (9) Water bunker (L414 or L415). (10) Enclosed perimeter with barbed wire and minefield. (11) Entrance to the complex guarded by checkpoint, road obstacles, armed *Tobruk* or artillery casemates L415A or 416A. Depending on the location, the battery was camouflaged so it could blend in as much as possible with the surrounding terrain. The armed bunkers could be covered with camouflage netting/material, but this was not to hinder the operation of the guns. If paint was used the colours also reflected the surrounding terrain.

composed of an open platform with a parapet housing the gun called a *Bettung* (see below). Under the platform there was a bunker. One or two entrances led to a gas lock. This was a small intermediate room between the bunker and the external environment, completely airtight owing to two armoured doors. The gas lock isolated the interior of the bunker from contamination should the enemy attack using poison gas. This small chamber gave access to a corridor leading to a crew chamber and an ammunition store.

A second batch (types L479 to L494) regrouped all bunkers connected to detection, communication and fighter command stations. Roof and wall thickness was standardised according to army and navy *Regelbau* (standardisation of construction).

Most of the Luftwaffe bunkers were of standardised permanent type *Ständig B* (StB with walls and roof 2m thick). The same standardisation was applied to equipment, ventilation systems, communication devices, furnishers, armoured doors and shutters, *Tobruk* pits and close range defence elements.

Marineflak Bunkers

The Kriegsmarine anti-aircraft artillery was called *Marineflakabteilung* (in short MFLA or MaFla). It was intended to protect naval installations, warships and long-range navy coastal artillery. The MaFla was therefore deployed near important harbours, building yards, U-Boat bases and main coastal artillery batteries. Navy anti-aircraft batteries could be permanent ground installations similar to the Luftwaffe Flak batteries. For their permanent ground Flak batteries, the navy engineering services designed shelters for plants and searchlights,

The *leichte Flakstand* FL242 (light Flak gun emplacement) was issued in March 1942. It included an entrance with gas lock, an ammunition-store and a crew chamber with an emergency exit. This feature, called a *Notausgang*, was a narrow horizontal gallery 60cm wide and 80cm high in the thick troop chamber wall. It emerged outside in a vertical rectangular, square or semi-circular pit in which rungs allowed a man to climb up. The emergency exit played an important role in morale as the crew did not feel trapped. Access to the gun emplacement on the roof was done by means of an external staircase. Length was 11m, width was 10.45m and height was 6.40m. Construction required 640m³ of concrete; 93 FL242 bunkers were built. Top: platform. Bottom: ground plan of FL242 with (1) entrance (2) stairs to the platform (3) gas lock (4) troop quarters (5) emergency exit (6) ammunition store.

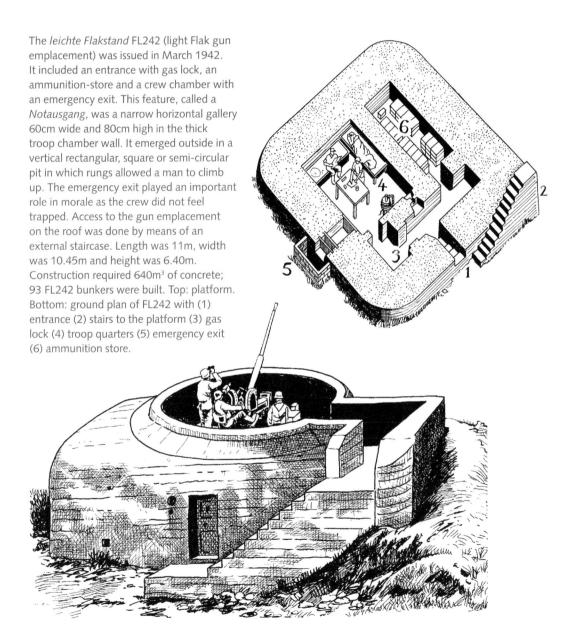

ammunition stores, radar stations, command posts, fire leading stations and
armed emplacements. From 1939–1940 the Kriegsmarine anti-aircraft artillery
was coded 'Fla' with designs indicated by Fla 1 to Fla 108 (e.g. Fla 14 was an
open emplacement for heavy guns). These early bunkers had a VF thickness of
30–80cm. As the war proceeded, the bunkers were redesigned according to the
standard Army Regelbau's regulations. The *Marineflakabteilung* bunkers were then
identified by the prefix FL (short for 'Flak') and three numbers between 200 and
354. Radar, measuring instruments, range finders, communication devices and
guns were similar to Luftwaffe Flak, but each Wehrmacht branch designed its own
anti-aircraft bunkers.

ARTILLERY BUNKERS

Given the vertical nature of anti-aircraft fire, a Flak gun could not be placed in a
casemate (this being a closed concrete firing chamber with a roof and walls) but
had to be installed in an open platform fitted with a parapet, known in German
as a *Bettung*. The gun had to have a free and unobstructed field of fire, therefore
without buildings and high vegetation around it. If the Flak position was placed
in an occupied area at risk of enemy ground action (including partisan/resistance
fighter attacks) a defensive perimeter was also constructed. This often consisted of
an extensive trench system called a *Stutzpunkt* (literally 'support point') hemmed
with barbed wire, obstacles and landmines, and defended by concrete casemates
armed with anti-tank guns, mortars and machine guns. The position was never

⬆ L2 emplacement for 2cm or 3.7cm Flak gun. Issued in January 1943, the standardised
light *Bettung* L2 had a total length of 8m and its construction required 61m³ of concrete.
The gun is shown here protected by a tarpaulin. The cross section (top) shows the covered
ammunition niche (1), the combat platform for the gun (2) and the rear opening to let the
gun in and out (3).

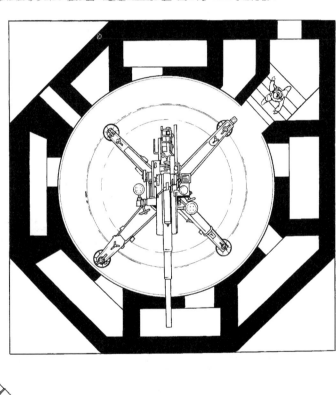

Bettung L4 for 8.8cm Flak gun. The standardised open emplacement L4 was 10m in length and its construction required 92m^3 of concrete. The work was issued in January 1943. Ammunition niches were placed in the thick parapet and additional rounds could be stored apart in another bunker.

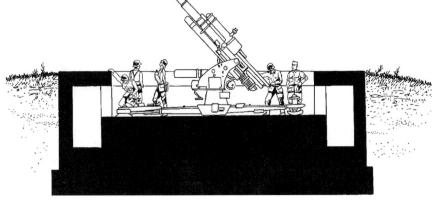

left unattended, but guarded day and night by sentries and patrols. During daylight hours there were armed watch-guards with binoculars on duty in the positions.

When the gun was not in use it was protected against the elements with tarpaulins, muzzle covers etc. When the gun was in action these were stored in a wooden crate, or the tarpaulins were simply thrown on the parapet. Gun crewmen's helmets, gun cleaning equipment like oil, grease and cleaning rags, metal container for the rangefinder and a field telephone were placed on wooden racks. There could also be a rifle stand for the crew's personal weapons. In the event of an attack, the sentry would first sound the alarm; then would rip off the tarpaulin and muzzle cover and unlock the gun. By that time, the rest of the gun crew should have arrived. In battle, all personnel had to wear their steel helmets. The Alarm (Flak alarm) for specific areas in the predicted flight path of enemy intruders was often raised in advance by telephone or radio from command and control headquarters linked to radar stations.

There was always a gun blast/muzzle flash safety area around larger guns. This was 30m from the centre of the gun for calibres of 8.8cm and above, as anything unprotected outside the parapet up to a range of 30m could sustain serious damage if the gun fired below 5 degrees. The crew shelters for the larger guns were

◆ This 10.5cm *Schiffskanone* L/60 in *Einheitslafette* (naval gun on standardised mount) was protected by a naval armoured turret emplaced into a circular concrete pit. It could be used against aircraft, ships and ground targets.

therefore always placed some distance from the weapon. The opposite applied for light automatic guns; the crew shelter was always placed only a few metres away to reduce reaction time. If it was placed outside the parapet, it was often shielded with an earth bank reaching up to or just above the entrance. There was always an opening in one of the sides of the platform (the width of which depended of the size of the gun's carriage), making it possible to emplace or remove the gun. The opening was often closed with removable plates and arranged in a zigzag or chicane pattern, so the *Bettung* could still be entered but at the same time protected from firing down the length of the position.

There was often a protective deflection bar made of wood or iron placed on the top of the parapet. The purpose of this was to prevent the gun crew from hitting other positions or friendly installations nearby in the heat of battle. As an aid to the gunners and commander the numbers 1–12 (in clock fashion) were often painted on the inside of the parapet. Number 12 was set at north to help locate the target (3 o'clock being east, 6 being south and 9 being west). There were also

◆ Flak *Bettung* (concrete gun platform).

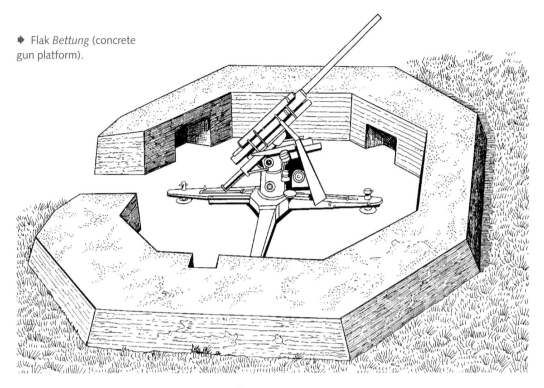

♦ Flakbunker type L 401A. The *S-Flak-Geschützstand* (heavy Flak emplacement) was issued in January 1942. It was designed to house an 8.8cm or a 10.5cm anti-aircraft gun. Its construction required 840m³ of concrete. The bunker included a combat terrace accessible via an external stair; two entrances with gas lock defended by a caponier; a room for the crew; and an ammunition store.

◆ Flakbunker type L 402. The
L-Flak-Geschützstand (light Flak
emplacement) was issued in
February 1942. It was designed to
house a 2cm light gun or a 2cm
Flak-quad. Its length was 10.1m,
its width was 9.6m, its height was
6.3m and its construction required
450m³ of concrete. Right: the
bunker with entrance (1); crew
quarters (2); and ammunition
store (3). Below: terrace with 2cm
Flak-quad.

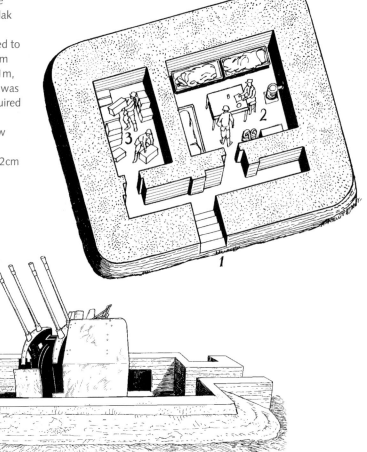

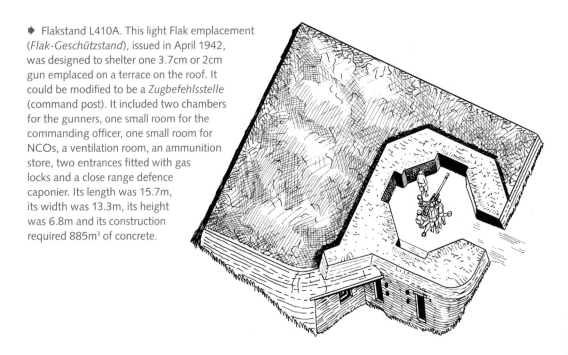

◆ Flakstand L410A. This light Flak emplacement
(*Flak-Geschützstand*), issued in April 1942,
was designed to shelter one 3.7cm or 2cm
gun emplaced on a terrace on the roof. It
could be modified to be a *Zugbefehlsstelle*
(command post). It included two chambers
for the gunners, one small room for the
commanding officer, one small room for
NCOs, a ventilation room, an ammunition
store, two entrances fitted with gas
locks and a close range defence
caponier. Its length was 15.7m,
its width was 13.3m, its height
was 6.8m and its construction
required 885m³ of concrete.

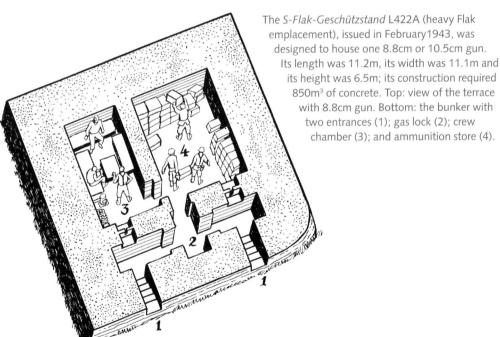

The *S-Flak-Geschützstand* L422A (heavy Flak emplacement), issued in February1943, was designed to house one 8.8cm or 10.5cm gun. Its length was 11.2m, its width was 11.1m and its height was 6.5m; its construction required 850m³ of concrete. Top: view of the terrace with 8.8cm gun. Bottom: the bunker with two entrances (1); gas lock (2); crew chamber (3); and ammunition store (4).

painted profiles of prominent landmarks on the sides of the pit with the exact range to those landmarks noted beside them. This helped both the gunner and the commander to calculate the exact range to the target. Boards on the walls with aircraft silhouettes or technical data about the gun's ballistics were also common.

The ammunition for the gun was often stored in recesses or niches build into the parapets, or in closets placed in the corners of the position. For single round guns, the recesses had shelves. For automatic guns, they contained either preloaded clips, or magazines or new ammunition boxes. Hinged doors or a removable wooden board covered the front of the recesses to protect the ammunition against the elements. On or above these doors, written in chalk or paint, were the type of fuzes that the ammunition within had – e.g. Zt.Z (*Zeitzünder*) or A.Z. (*Aufschlagszünder*) – time fuzes and percussion fuzes (time fuzed means that it detonates after a specific amount of flight time, percussion fuzed that it has to hit something to detonate). The reason was to prevent any shells falling back down to earth and harming friendly forces or civilians. Often the projectiles had both types of fuzes.

The ammunition, clips and magazines were always kept in pristine condition. Quite often it was unpacked, cleaned with oiled rags and then repacked/reloaded.

FL243/FL 249 heavy Flak gun emplacement (*schwere Flakstellung*). The bunker FL243, issued in March 1942, was especially designed by Kriegsmarine engineers to house a 10.5cm gun placed inside a *Drehhaube* (a rotating armoured turret). Its length was 19.6m, width was 18.8m, height was 6.1m and its construction required 645m³ of concrete. The bunker basement included a crew chamber, a gas lock and several ammunitions stores placed in the breastwork of the emplacements. The fully revolving armoured turret, placed on the roof, gave excellent protection to the crew, the 10.5cm SKC/32 gun and ammunition. It was fitted with a ventilator, an emergency exit and an electric engine for moving the turret, allowing a full 360 degrees traverse. The *schwere Flakstellung* bunker FL249 was the same as the FL243 *Flakstellung* only in mirror image. Top: the armoured turret; bottom: ground plan with: (1) emplacement of turret (2) caponier (close defence room) (3) crew chamber (4) entrance with gas lock.

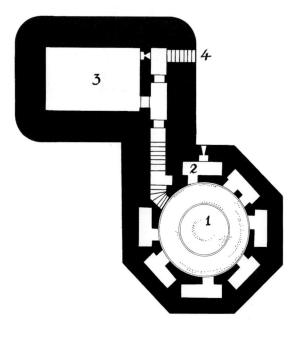

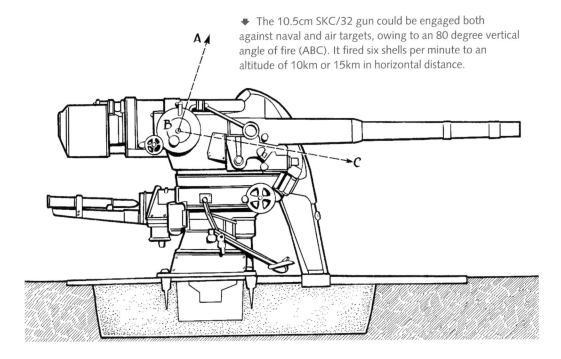

The 10.5cm SKC/32 gun could be engaged both against naval and air targets, owing to an 80 degree vertical angle of fire (ABC). It fired six shells per minute to an altitude of 10km or 15km in horizontal distance.

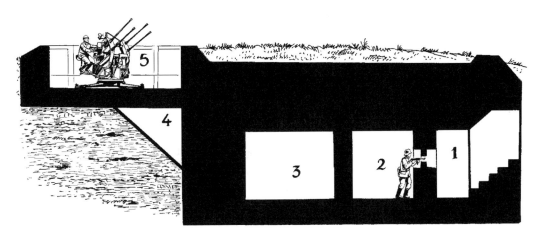

The *leichte Flakstand* type FL247 (light Flak gun emplacement), issued in March 1942, included an entrance with a gas lock (1), a troop chamber (2), a room for the commanding officer and an ammunition store (3). An internal staircase (4) furnished with a gas lock gave access to the external gun platform (5). Overall length was 18.20m, width was 9.5m, and total height was 5.3m. Construction required 600m³ of concrete.

New ammunition for the automatic guns did not arrive ready to use in clips or magazines; a certain number of clips or magazines belonged to the gun and they were refilled after use. Spent cartridges were removed as soon as possible by the crews. Often they was just shovelled up or thrown out of the position as soon as there was a lull in the fighting; afterwards they were collected for reuse since German industry was always short of raw materials.

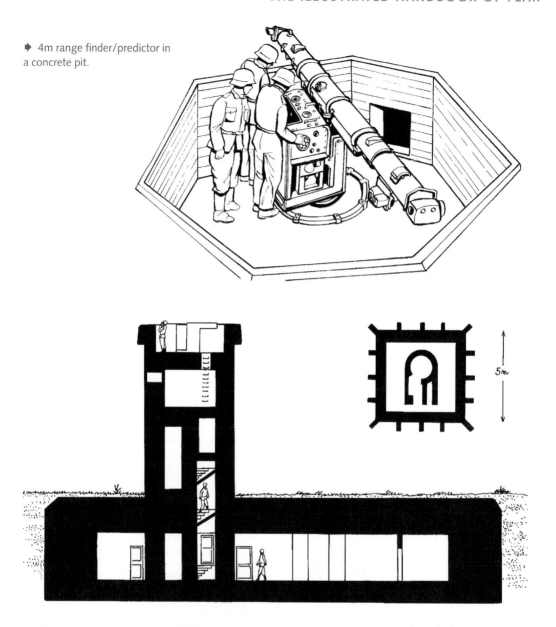

◆ 4m range finder/predictor in a concrete pit.

♠ Cross-section *Flagruko* type FL250. A command post of the Navy Flak, called *Flakgruppenkommandostand* or *Flagruko* in short, coordinated the defence in a region or in a sector. Equipped with sophisticated calculation and communication instruments, they connected radar stations to Flak batteries. The heart of the *Flagruko* was a room where information such as strength, speed, height and direction of enemy aircraft were projected on large vertical glass maps in order to determine what targets were going to be attacked. When supposition became certainty, the alarm was raised in the menaced sectors where Flak batteries were scrambled and issued fighting orders. The *Flagruko* FL250, issued in March 1942, included a square concrete tower with a top platform fitted with detection and observation equipment. The tower was 5m by 5m wide and had a height varying from 10–20m. The bunker had a length of 25m, a width of 23.80m and its construction (tower included) required 2500m³ of concrete. The subterranean bunker included an entrance with a gas lock defended by a caponier, a ventilation room, a water store, an engine room with fuel store, several chambers for the crew, a large command/computing room, and a telephone and radio exchange room. Two FL250s were built in France (notably at Saint-Marc near Saint-Nazaire), three in Denmark, four in the Netherlands (notably at Den Helder, Hoek van Holland, Walcheren island in Zeeland), and several others in Germany.

FLAK FIRE CONTROL BUNKERS

Flak fire control stations (called *Flakleitstände*) were the brains of anti-aircraft batteries. They were characterised by their top arranged as an open round or polygonal emplacement in which rangefinders were placed, and small open *Ausgucke* (recesses or pits) fitted with observation and communication instruments. The terraces and recesses were placed on top of an underground bunker housing various areas including calculation and working rooms, a ventilation room and

↑ *Flagruko FL250.*

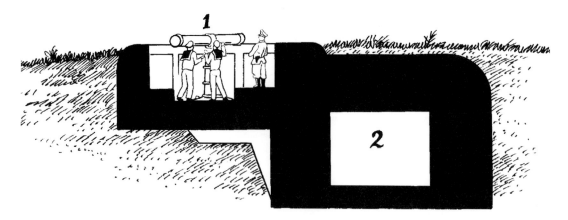

⬆ The fire control post for heavy Marine Flak battery type Flakleitstand FL351, issued in January 1944, included a platform (1) with a round pit in which a range finder was placed, as well as small recesses for observation and communication. The subterranean bunker only comprised a single entrance with gas lock leading to a work room (2) where data and information were gathered, analysed and transmitted to Flak batteries. Overall length was 11.5m and width was 10.5m. Similar designs were the FL304 and FL306. Other bunkers with the same function but larger and more elaborate (including more rooms such as a ventilation room, crew, NCOs and officers' quarters, engine room, fuel store and water supply) were types FL 244, FL 255, FL311, and FL314.

The heavy *Flakleitstand* type L403A (fire leading post for heavy anti-aircraft guns) was issued in April 1943. Its length was 19.35m, its width was 15.1m, its height was 6.60m and its construction required 1150m³ of concrete. Top: the terrace. Bottom: (1) terrace (2) troop chamber (3) work room.

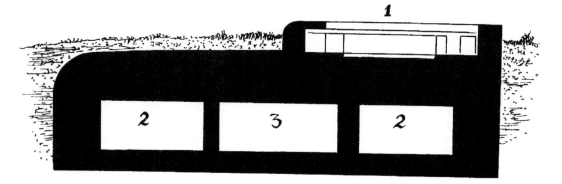

⬆ Terrace of the *Flakleitstand* type L424A. The fire leading station L424A for heavy Flak artillery was issued in January 1944. Its length was 11.8m, its width was 10m, its height was 6.7m and its construction required 650m³ of concrete. The bunker included two entrances, a gas lock, a ventilation room, a radio and telephone room and a calculation and command room connected to the observers on the terrace outside.

personnel chamber. The highly specialised crews received information from observatories and radar posts, calculated the angle of fire, the distance to the target and issued orders by telephone or by wireless radio to batteries gunners (e.g. the ammunition type to employ and moment to fire). After firing, the crew observed the results and indicated corrections. Kriegsmarine and Luftwaffe Flak fire leading stations were not standardised and there were many local improvisations and special constructions.

AMMUNITION BUNKERS

For obvious security reasons, ammunition stores (*Munitionsunterstände*) were always placed at a safe distance from living quarters and active armed emplacements. Roads, tracks or paths were set up to enable communication. A (camouflaged) concrete platform was often built in front of the ammunition store so that supply trucks could park. However, scattering units presented disadvantages; indeed if the ground was upset, if roads and tracks were destroyed or impracticable, the guns in the active armed emplacements could no longer be supplied.

The ammunition stores were generally simple, not being equipped with a gas lock or caponier; they sometimes included a *Tobruk* housing a guard. In some case they could be used to shelter equipment, material or supplies, even wounded soldiers in an emergency. Often the internal layout of the bunker was designed in order that the doors leading to the stores were placed laterally inside the corridor, in other words the entrances to the ammunition stores opened into a gallery that led to the main exit/entrance on either sides. So if the main entrance

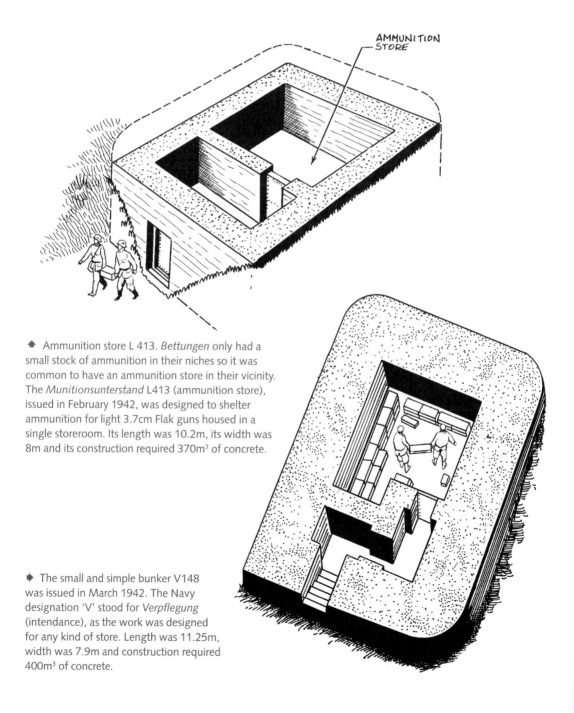

♠ Ammunition store L 413. *Bettungen* only had a small stock of ammunition in their niches so it was common to have an ammunition store in their vicinity. The *Munitionsunterstand* L413 (ammunition store), issued in February 1942, was designed to shelter ammunition for light 3.7cm Flak guns housed in a single storeroom. Its length was 10.2m, its width was 8m and its construction required 370m³ of concrete.

♦ The small and simple bunker V148 was issued in March 1942. The Navy designation 'V' stood for *Verpflegung* (intendance), as the work was designed for any kind of store. Length was 11.25m, width was 7.9m and construction required 400m³ of concrete.

was directly shot at, the projectiles could not reach the ammunition stores. Small ammunition was packed in boxes and cases, and heavy shells were stored on shelves. Ammunition was also stored in non-standardised concrete bunkers or stone storehouses concealed underground or covered with earth.

SEARCHLIGHT BUNKERS

Searchlights were fragile and expensive pieces of equipment. In order to protect them a number of concrete *Scheinwerferunterstände* (searchlight shelters) were designed and built by both the navy and air force. These generally included a platform with a parapet on top, an underground garage with sliding doors, and often a chamber for the crew with a gas lock and emergency exit.

Issued in March 1942, the Luftwaffe bunker type L411 was designed to shelter a 60cm searchlight. The roof (top) was arranged as a terrace where the searchlight was put in operation. The ground plan (bottom) shows the internal layout of the bunker with (1) entrance (2) garage for searchlight (3) crew quarters (4) fuel and supply store. The length was 11.8m, its width was 11.4m, its height was 6.3m and its construction required 600m³ of concrete.

The Kriegsmarine bunker type Fl 277 (also referred to as M277 or S277) was issued in January 1943. Intended to emplace a 150cm searchlight, its construction required 920m³ of concrete. Seventeen FL277s were built in the Atlantic Wall, sixteen in Denmark and one in France. Top: general view of bunker Fl 277, here shown without camouflage. Bottom: ground plan with garage (1) closed with concrete or armoured sliding doors; engine room/workshop/fuel reserve (2); emergency exit (3); crew chamber (4) with gas lock; and small close-combat post (5) defending the entrances. The bunker's length was 13m, width was 12.8m.

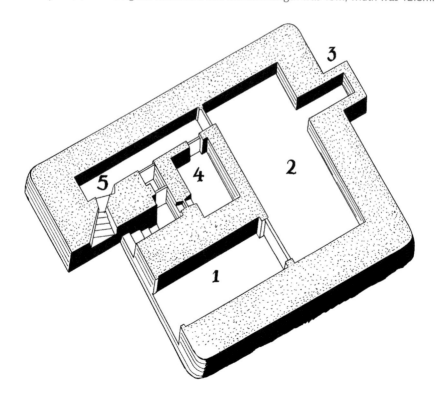

RADAR BUNKERS

The size of a radar bunker depended on the type of radar used. Generally it consisted of an underground bunker with various chambers for men and equipment, a ventilation system and stores. The radar aerial was fixed upon one or more strong poles (or on a concrete tower) resting on the roof of the bunker. It should be noted that both the Kriegsmarine and the Luftwaffe developed their own bunkers. For the same Mammut radar, the navy designed bunker type V143, and the Luftwaffe types L485/1 and L485/2.

An important German air-detection radar installation, part of the strategic Atlantic Wall defences, can still be seen at Douvres-la-Délivrance, north of Caen in Normandy. Completed in the autumn of 1943, the northern part of the station included a large Siemens *Wasserman* long-range radar and associated structures. The larger southern zone had two intermediate-range *Freya* and two short-range *Würzburg-Riese* radars, as well as command and infirmary bunkers,

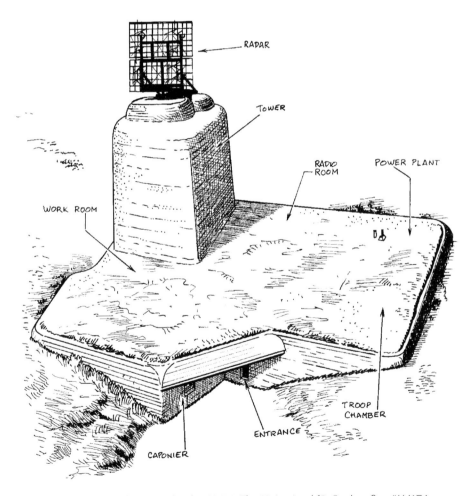

♠ Radar *Freya* installed on navy bunker V174. The *Unterstand für Funkmeßgerät* V174, issued in March 1942, was composed of a 7.8m high tower on top of which a naval FuMO *Seetakt* radar was installed. The tower was part of a bunker with a length of 14.7m and a width of 10.2m; its construction required 850m³ of concrete. Nine V174s were constructed in the Atlantic Wall, all in Denmark.

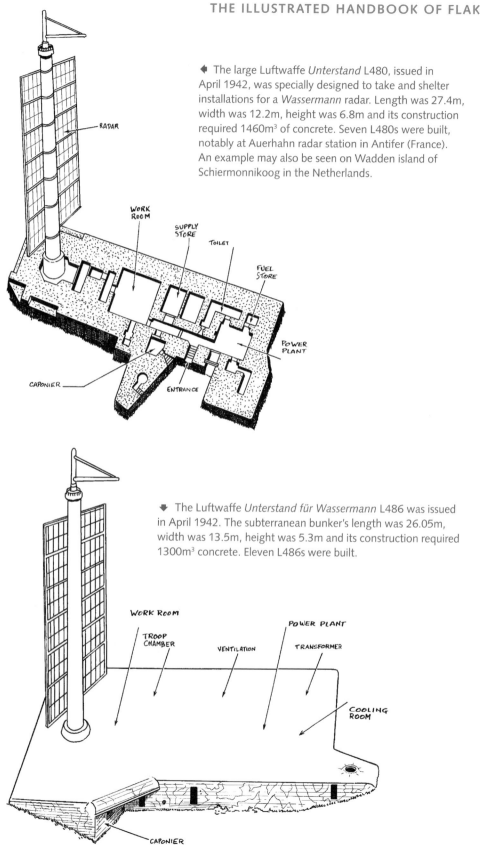

◀ The large Luftwaffe *Unterstand* L480, issued in April 1942, was specially designed to take and shelter installations for a *Wassermann* radar. Length was 27.4m, width was 12.2m, height was 6.8m and its construction required 1460m³ of concrete. Seven L480s were built, notably at Auerhahn radar station in Antifer (France). An example may also be seen on Wadden island of Schiermonnikoog in the Netherlands.

RADAR

WORK ROOM

SUPPLY STORE

TOILET

FUEL STORE

POWER PLANT

CAPONIER

ENTRANCE

▼ The Luftwaffe *Unterstand für Wassermann* L486 was issued in April 1942. The subterranean bunker's length was 26.05m, width was 13.5m, height was 5.3m and its construction required 1300m³ concrete. Eleven L486s were built.

WORK ROOM

TROOP CHAMBER

VENTILATION

POWER PLANT

TRANSFORMER

COOLING ROOM

CAPONIER

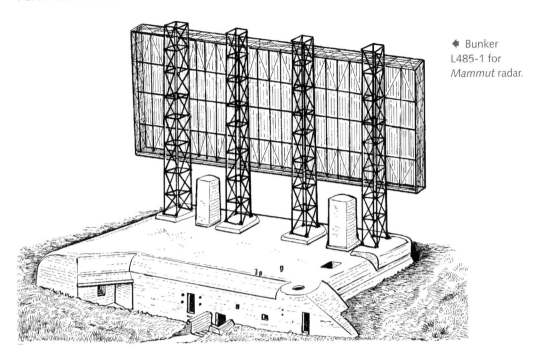

◀ Bunker L485-1 for *Mammut* radar.

◆ The large *Mammut* radar bunker L485/1 had a length of
25.2m, its width was 23.9m and its height was 6.5m.
An example of this bunker still exists at the former
StP 13 and StP 13a on the Pointe du Raz
(Brittany, France), as well as at Kijkduin and
Den Helder (the Netherlands).

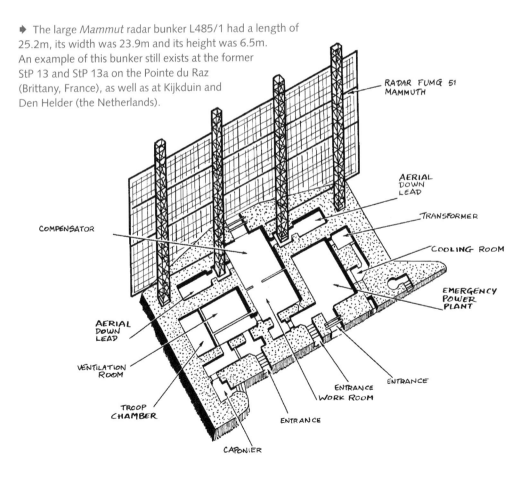

RADAR FUMG 51 MAMMUTH

AERIAL DOWN LEAD

COMPENSATOR

TRANSFORMER

COOLING ROOM

EMERGENCY POWER PLANT

AERIAL DOWN LEAD

VENTILATION ROOM

TROOP CHAMBER

ENTRANCE WORK ROOM

ENTRANCE

ENTRANCE

CAPONIER

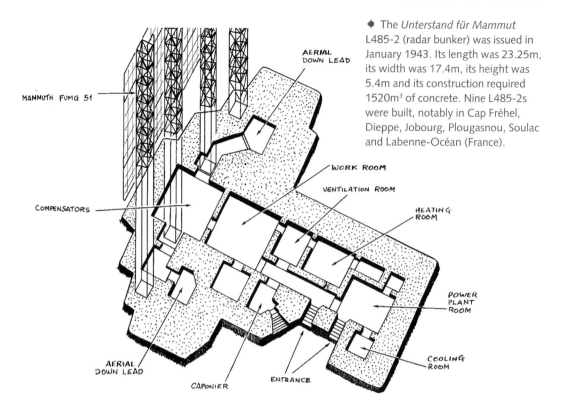

MAMMUTH FUMG 51

AERIAL
DOWN LEAD

COMPENSATORS

WORK ROOM

VENTILATION ROOM

HEATING
ROOM

POWER
PLANT
ROOM

COOLING
ROOM

AERIAL
DOWN LEAD

CAPONIER

ENTRANCE

◆ The *Unterstand für Mammut* L485-2 (radar bunker) was issued in January 1943. Its length was 23.25m, its width was 17.4m, its height was 5.4m and its construction required 1520m³ of concrete. Nine L485-2s were built, notably in Cap Fréhel, Dieppe, Jobourg, Plougasnou, Soulac and Labenne-Océan (France).

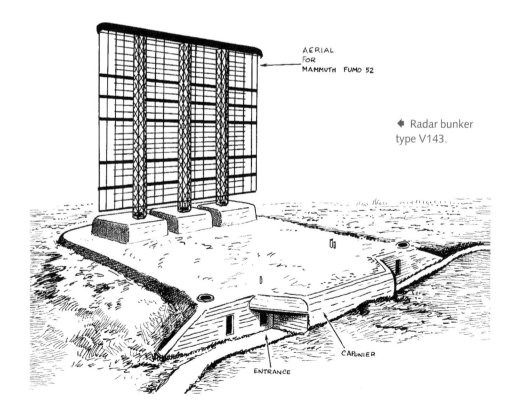

AERIAL
FOR
MAMMUTH FUMO 52

◆ Radar bunker type V143.

CAPONIER

ENTRANCE

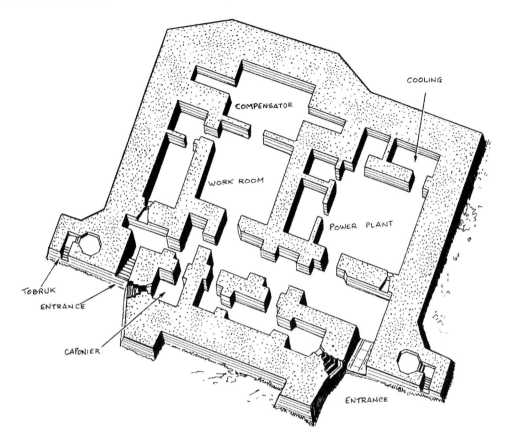

COOLING

COMPENSATOR

WORK ROOM

POWER PLANT

TOBRUK

ENTRANCE

CAPONIER

ENTRANCE

⬥ The large *Unterstand* V143, issued in March 1942, was especially designed to house a *Mammut* radar with a maximum range of 400km. The large aerial (27m long and 10.5m high) was placed on the roof by means of three concrete blocks. The bunker length was 20.5m and width was 18.2m. Six V143s were built. Units can still be seen today at the former Wn Sickingen near Framzelles (northern France), north of Fécamp (Normandy) and at Omonville-la-Rogue at the western extremity of the Cotentin peninsula (Normandy).

garages and artillery emplacements. The radar station covered 3 hectares, and was heavily fortified with bunkers, machine guns and minefields. Some 230 Luftwaffe personnel were based there, including electricians, engineers and 36 air controllers.

MISCELLANEOUS BUNKERS

A static Luftwaffe or MaFla battery always included several bunkers enabling the operation of the weapons and the Spartan life of the garrison. When a group of bunkers could not be linked to the normal civilian electricity network, power plants were installed to produce energy, to load accumulators and electric batteries which were used to supply wireless radios, electrical signal devices, emergency lamps, corridor lights, galleries, machine-guns turrets and observation cupolas.

⬆ A German radar station (shown here on a coast somewhere on the Atlantic Wall) could be equipped with either a long-range *Mammut* radar placed on a L485 bunker (1), or a *Wassermann* radar placed on a L480 bunker (2), or a short-range *Würzburg* radar (3) housed in a garage type L405 (4). The station generally included a command post (5), which could be a L408 type, a power plant (6) type L406, a water supply bunker (7) type L415, and various service and logistics buildings (8). The station was defended against air attacks by various light and heavy Flak guns placed in bunkers (9) such as types L409 and L410. The whole position was arranged as a *Stützpunkt* with a barbed wire fence and minefields (10), and defended by trenches and various army bunkers and *Tobruks* armed with anti-tank guns, mortars and machine guns facing both the sea and the land.

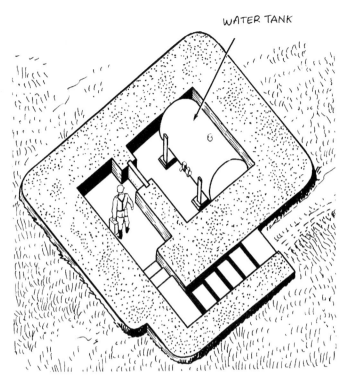

WATER TANK

Water supply bunker type L415. Water was indispensable not only for the men but also to cool engines and machines. The Luftwaffe engineering corps designed two small *Wasservorratsunterstände* (water supply bunkers): type L414 for a well and type L415 for a cistern. The construction of the bunker depicted required approximately 200m³ of concrete.

The operating of radar, radio equipment and searchlights required a lot of energy. This was provided either by the civilian network, or by a generating set composed of a diesel engine and a dynamo, which transformed mechanical energy into electricity. Several bunkers were designed for the purpose of protecting such vital power plants. The depicted Luftwaffe *Machinestand* L406 was issued in March 1943. Its length was 12.6m, its width was 10.1m and its construction required 630m³ of concrete. The fuel store was placed externally for safety reasons.

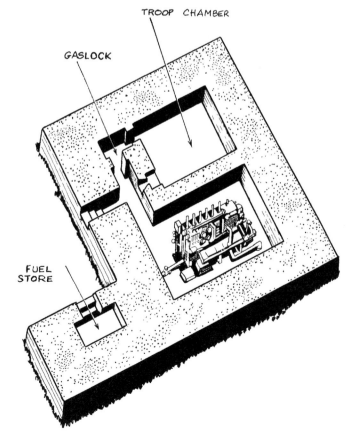

TROOP CHAMBER

GASLOCK

FUEL STORE

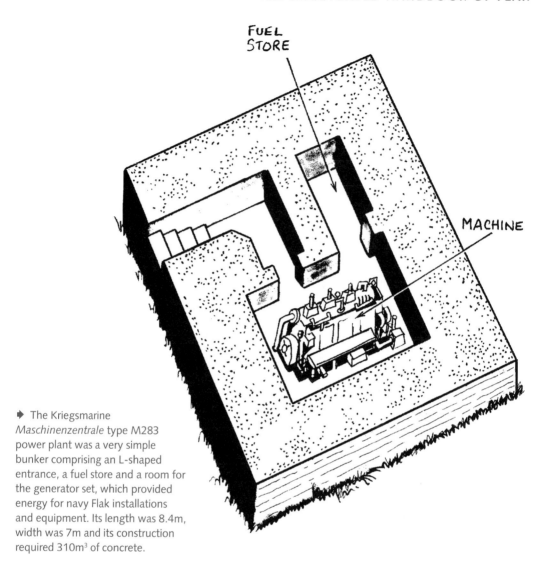

FUEL
STORE

MACHINE

◆ The Kriegsmarine
Maschinenzentrale type M283
power plant was a very simple
bunker comprising an L-shaped
entrance, a fuel store and a room for
the generator set, which provided
energy for navy Flak installations
and equipment. Its length was 8.4m,
width was 7m and its construction
required 310m³ of concrete.

Water supply was a major problem, being vital for both the men and for cooling
plants and weapons. Special logistics bunkers were designed e.g. water stores,
and also underground first aid posts, dressing stations, infirmaries and hospitals.
Local improvisations for searchlight shelters, water supply and kitchen bunkers
were numerous. They were often built in Vf (field fortification) with no regular
standardised *Regelbau* number. Although not designed for a combat function, some
of these logistical works were furnished with fighting elements including caponier
and close range entrance defence crenels in corridors.

FLAK TOWERS

A *Flakturm* (Flak tower) was a huge concrete anti-aircraft tower, fitted with a terrace armed with Flak guns and anti-aircraft equipment. In August 1940, Hitler gave the authorisation to build these enormous Flak positions, which had no equivalent anywhere at the time. In Berlin, Hamburg and Vienna they were constructed in pairs composed of one *Gefechtsturm* (G-Turm, combat tower armed with guns) and one *Leitturm* (L-Turm, fire control tower often also armed with light guns) including radar stations and Luftwaffe command posts which coordinated and conducted anti-aircraft fire.

◀ Radar/Flak
L-tower in Vienna.

➧ G-Flakturm Ausgarten in Vienna.
The tower was in construction
Bauart 3.

The Flak towers, the design of which Hitler took a personal interest in and even made some sketches for, were designed by Minister Albert Speer, and constructed by the *Organisation Todt* (a conglomerate of building companies created by the engineer Fritz Todt). The construction of Flak towers had top priority and the German national rail schedule was altered in order to facilitate the shipment of the necessary materials, namely concrete, steel and lumber to the construction sites. The overall shape, size and style of Flak towers varied to some extend with time and space but there were three main *Bauarten* (styles).

Bauart 1   Square G-towers with a length of 70.5m and a height of 39m, usually armed with four twin 12.8cm guns placed in gun pits located at the four corners, and a number of 3.7cm and 2cm quad guns. The L-towers were 50m in length, 23m in width and 39m in height, usually armed with four 2cm quad guns.

Bauart 2   Square G-towers, 57m in width and 42m in height, usually armed with four twin 12.8cm guns placed in massive circular gun pits located on the roof and sixteen 2cm quad guns. The L-towers were 50×23×44m, and usually armed with ten 2cm quad guns.

Bauart 3   Large circular G-tower, 43m in diameter and 54m in height, usually armed with four 12.8cm twin guns and eight 2cm quad Flak guns.

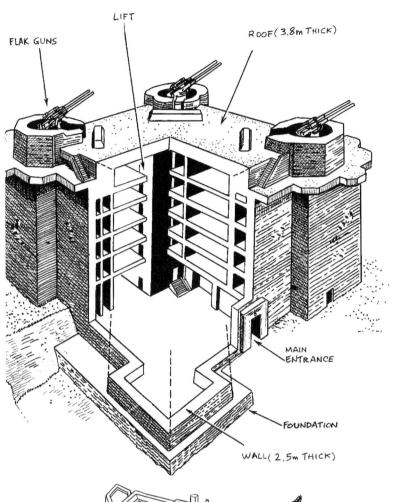

FLAK GUNS

LIFT

ROOF (3.8m THICK)

MAIN
ENTRANCE

FOUNDATION

WALL (2.5m THICK)

◀ Cross-section
G-Flakturm
Heiligengeistfeld
in Hamburg. It
was 47m high and
each side was 70m
long. It displayed
the Bauart 1 with
a terrace arranged
for four angle
concrete pits each
armed with one
highly effective
12.8cm Zwilling
(twin) Flak-guns.
The inside of
the building was
arranged as a
shelter for 18,000
civilians.

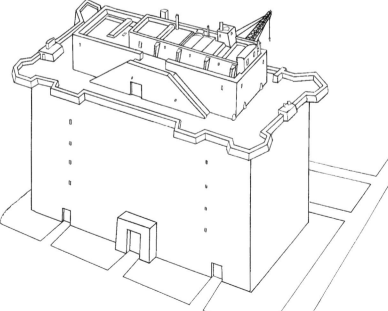

◀ L-Turm
Heiligengeistfeld
Hamburg. This
fire-control tower
was a variant of
Bauart 1.

On the whole Allied aircraft crews tried to avoid the Flak towers. They were able to sustain a formidable rate of fire (about 8000 rounds per minute) from their multi-level guns, with a range of up to 14km in a full 360-degree field of fire.

All Flak towers, whatever shape they had – local variants existed with slightly different sizes – had common features. They were generally a little higher than the average urban constructions around them so that guns and searchlights had a wide arc of fire, and their concrete walls and ceilings were up to 3.5m thick. The different floors were arranged as ammunition stores, shelters for rescue teams, doctors and medical personnel, police squads, firemen and bomb clearance units. There was a lot of space left for civilians and hospital purposes.

The towers were thus both active armed emplacements and passive defence objects and an extension of the air raid shelter programme (see Chapter 6). For example, the air defence of Berlin included six large towers – built in 1941/1942 – that rose above the city in the neighbourhoods of Humboldthain and Friedrichshain, and from the grounds of the Berlin Tiergarten (zoological park). The twin towers situated in the zoo included the normal pair of one L-Turm coupled to one G-Turm. The L-tower was a radar and communication control centre bristling with antennae and light guns. The heavily armed combat G-tower was very large covering almost the area of a city block. It was designed as a huge five-story warehouse, 40m (132ft) high, with concrete walls 2.4m (8ft) thick. The gun battery placed on top of the roof included eight heavy twin 12.8cm Flak guns placed in four open concrete pits,

⬇ G-Flakturm Wilhelmsburgstrasse (Hamburg). This combat tower was a variant of the Bauart 2 with large turret on each corner making it look like a massive medieval fortress.

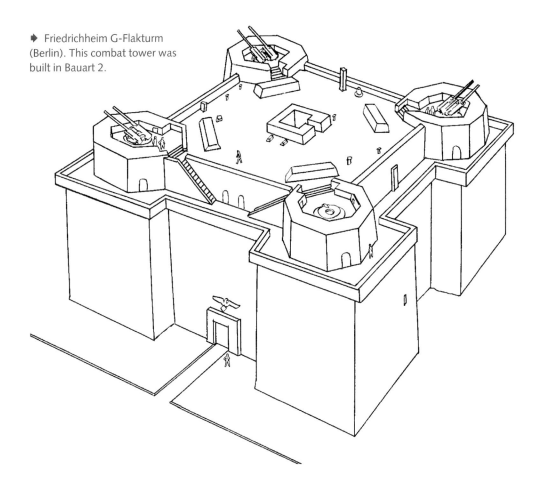

◆ Friedrichheim G-Flakturm (Berlin). This combat tower was built in Bauart 2.

plus several 2cm and 3.7cm Flak guns positioned in a lower terrace. The top floor of the tower housed the 100-man artillery garrison with ammunition brought to the upper terrace by means of a goods elevator. Beneath that was a 95-bed Luftwaffe hospital with X-ray room and two fully equipped operating theatres staffed by 6 doctors, 20 nurses and 30 medical orderlies. The next floor down was used to store for treasures from Berlin museums, including numerous priceless Egyptian, Greek and Roman antiquities, Gobelin tapestries and a vast quantity of paintings and coin collections. The two lower floors were arranged as *Luftschutzraum* (public air shelters) for 8000 people (or 15,000 in cramped conditions). The G-tower was entirely self-contained with a water supply, kitchen, food store, emergency services and a power plant. The Berlin Zoo towers were one of the last points of defence during the battle for Berlin in April 1945.

At Vienna in Austria, the anti-aircraft defences included six high Flak-Türme designed by architect Friedrich Tamms (1904–1980) and built in the period 1942–1945 by Franz Fuhrmann of the Viennese building authority, the companies Philipp Holzmann and Gottlieb Tesch and the Organisation Todt. Since the availability of local manpower continuously diminished due to enlistment, prisoners of war, foreign and forced labourers were increasingly employed in the construction. Cement was delivered for the main part from Mannersdorf am Leithagebirge and to a lesser extent from Rodaun. The gravel came from the quarries of Padlesak in Felixdorf and Gustav Haager at Heidfeld by the Preßburger

➡ G-Flakturm Wilhelmsburg,
Hamburg (Bauart 2).

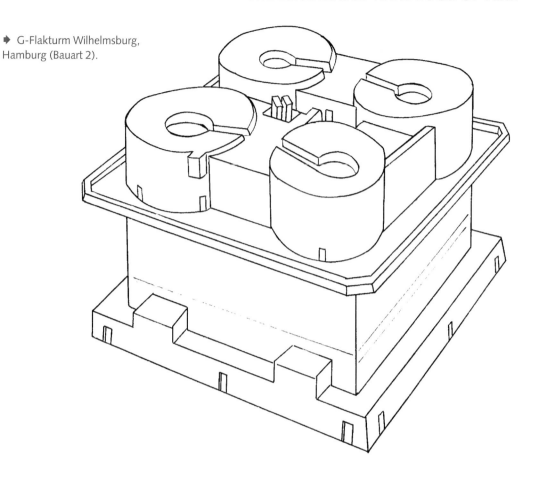

track. Sand was delivered by inland boats on the Danube Canal, for which the United Construction Supply Factory (Vereinigte Baustoffwerke AG) built sand silos in the area of the Weißengerberlände. A connecting track of the tram system through the Drorygasse had existed in that area since 1918. Although it had been dismantled in 1925, it was reconstructed in 1941 and extended by two tracks in the following year after the construction of another silo. For the déblai material from the excavations of the foundations, a disposal site was laid out at the Kratochwjlestraße, which likewise received a tram connection. The Vienna G-towers were armed with twin 12.8cm Flak guns with a range of about 20km. They served not only as an artillery emplacement but also as provisional hospitals, housed radio stations and strategic technical services, and provided a large facility to shelter the population.

It was envisaged that after the war was won the Flak towers would be clad in marble as Nazi memorials to German soldiers killed in action. As things turned out the Flak towers were meant to be demolished, but in most cases that was not feasible and as a result many of them stand today.

AIR RAID PROTECTION SERVICES

THE AIR OFFENSIVE ON GERMANY

Aircraft technology had made such huge advances during the 1930s that the possibility of sudden aerial attack had to be taken into consideration. It was no longer sufficient to protect soldiers deployed on the frontline, but also rear-area units, bases and headquarters. It was also necessary to safeguard industry and the civilian population far in the interior of the country. During the Second World War – as in no previous modern war (with the exception of the Spanish Civil War) – civilians outside the battle areas were involved in the conflict not only through privations, restrictions, the rationing of food and clothing, but also through deadly direct attack by air raids.

British air attacks on Germany began in late 1939 but at first caused little damage. They continued in 1940 as retaliation for German air raids on civilian targets during the Battle of Britain. Heavy British and American air raids started in earnest during the spring of 1942. As range, frequency and size of the raids increased, so too did the casualties and damage inflicted. The German people knew the horrors of war at first hand, the warning sirens, the sound of aircraft engines overhead, the falling and explosions of bombs, the night sky lit by Flak bursts, the flames of burning buildings; and next day saw the smoking ruins in their streets. The Allies believed they could smash the German war machine by large-scale bombardment. Bombers of the RAF (by night) and USAAF (by day) carried out large-scale destruction raids on key targets with two main aims: first to reduce and destroy industrial war production, and secondly to lower civilian morale.

By June 1943 '1000-bombers raids' started with devastating effect, and an appalling new phase of the air war above Germany began. On 24/25 July, 1943 repeated Allied attacks on Hamburg provoked a firestorm killing 42,000 people, injuring 100,000 and destroying 225,000 homes and 3600 industrial and business buildings. In one raid in October 1943, 2.5km^2 of Hanover were destroyed; in all 15,000 tons of bombs were dropped on the city. The small port of Emden in East Frisia (where a submarine factory had been built in 1938) was attacked in December 1941 causing 30 casualties, in June 1942 (31 dead), in October 1943 (27), in August 1944 (46) and in September 1944 (46). By the end of the war, Emden was one of the most utterly destroyed cities in Germany, with about 90 per cent of its buildings in ruin.

Berlin became the focus of Allied air attacks between November 1943 and April 1944. The capital of the Reich was repeatedly smashed by 50,000 tons of explosive, making 400,000 Berliners homeless; in all 37 per cent of homes were destroyed. In Cologne 60 per cent of homes were destroyed; 53 per cent in Hamburg; 66 per cent in

Dortmund; and 33 per cent in Munich. By 1945, 20 of Germany's major cities were laid waste and classed as being virtually wiped out, and nineteen others, including Berlin, were severely damaged. One of the final major air attacks of the war in the West was a succession of controversial and some argue pointless bombardments on Dresden on 13 and 14 February 1945, which killed as many as 25,000 civilians.

By June 1945 RAF Bomber Command reported that 657,674 tons of bombs had been dropped on Germany. The total tonnage dropped by the British and the Americans has been estimated to 2,697,473 tons, of which 50 per cent was dropped on cities, and the rest on military, transport and industrial areas. Estimates show that about 300,000 German civilians died and 780,000 were injured.

Yet the Allied air raids did not achieve their goals, and the effectiveness of the Allied air offensive has been endlessly disputed in the post-war period. Until mid-1944, German war production was still rising and it was only in the winter of 1944/45 that industrial production, armament output, communications and transportation totally collapsed. As for the German people, many had low morale and lost trust in Hitler's regime, but many others, in spite of heavy casualties and privations, were not dispirited and showed extraordinary resilience. Almost to the end, air raids were an integral part of daily life in most German cities, and made people more determined to hold out.

From the start of the Second World War, the German authorities had considered air raid precautions, but the RAF's initial inability to carry out serious raids led to a public sense of anticlimax. The smashing Blitzkrieg victories of the period 1939–1940 assured the public at large that the country was safe from air attack and that the war would soon be won. The continuation of the war, the first German military setbacks, and the first serious Allied air attacks forced the German authorities to lower their triumphant tone, to take a number of measures, and to reconsider and develop air raid precaution services. Two principal levels of defence were organised. First, fighter defence, and anti-aircraft artillery and searchlight were controlled by Luftwaffe commanders in their various regions, called *Luftgaue*. Secondly, ground defence of cities and their population was effectively a Nazi party affair with several organisations, rescue, police and fire brigade forces.

GENERAL MEASURES

Blackout

For German civilians, the first clouds of war appeared with the introduction of instructions and measures with regard to the possibility of attacks from the air. A blackout in time of war or the threat of war referred (and still does today) to the practice of collectively minimising external light, including upward-directed or reflected light. During the Second World War it was principally intended to prevent crews of enemy aircraft from being able to navigate to their targets by sight. Open fires were forbidden, street lighting was turned off, and lights in homes and large public buildings were minimised by tarring windows, hanging lightproof curtains and screens to obscure all openings, or by replacing white bulbs with blue-tinted ones. Motorists were required to cover all but a small slot on their vehicle's headlights, and the same restriction was applied to public transportation vehicles including trains, buses and trams.

The blackout had several drawbacks. Although the shortage of fuel considerably reduced the density of traffic, vehicle accidents increased. Darkness also encouraged crimes such as murder, rape, robbery, burglary, and street prostitution. This not-withstanding, the police strictly enforced the blackout, and offenders were punished.

Gas Masks

The use of poison gas during the First World War gave rise to widespread fears during the inter-war period. The gases used were generally classed into four groups, based on their properties. Lachrymators (White Cross, according to the German system of classification) were tear gases whose main purpose was simply to encumber the enemy by forcing him to don his gas mask and exhaust its protective capacity. Sternutators, or sneezing, coughing, and vomiting gases (Blue Cross) were initially designed to incapacitate the enemy, but later used to force him to remove his mask to vomit or sneeze and make himself vulnerable to lethal gas. Vesicants, or blister gases (Yellow Cross) were heavy, persistent aerosols which nullified the ground for either side, and which would raise huge blisters on the skin, and cause permanent scarring. The actions of vesicants on the mucous membranes of the throat and other internal membranes could be fatal, and could cause blindness. This class included the various mustard gases, as well as Lewisite. Probably the most famous victim of this class of substances was a certain Gefreiter (Corporal) Adolf Hitler, whose temporary blinding in 1918 left him with a lifelong hatred of combat poison gas, which is probably one of the reasons why Germany never used it in the Second World War, in combat. Lung irritants, or suffocating gases (Green Cross), a sort of catch-all classification, included chlorine as well as phosgene, the latter being a particularly dreaded substance filling the lungs of the victim with fluid that could result in sudden death some 48 hours after the attack. Phosgene was additionally classified as a lethal gas, because of its potential effect, but there was only one gas that could be immediately lethal, and that was hydrocyanic acid (HCN), or hydrogen cyanide gas. Death could occur within seconds or minutes of the inhalation of high concentrations of this substance.

⬆ M38 gas mask.

➡ Gasmask canister and gas sheet pouch. Combat gases were not used in the Second World War and the gas mask box ended up being a convenient container for various items used by frontline troops.

Most people in the 1930s expected gas warfare to be a feature of any future conflict. The belief that major cities would sustain horrific casualties once the enemy could attack from the air with explosive, incendiary and gas bombs led to pre-war planning. The German civil defence literature reflected the anxiety of the time, describing in great detail how bomb shelters were to be made secure from both bomb blasts and poison gas, and how to use gas masks. It is also significant that all German bunkers intended to shelter personnel were fitted with a gas lock. When the Second World War broke out the fear of enemy gas attack was real, and the German population and soldiers on duty were issued with gas masks. Before and during the Second World War, the Germans used three models, namely the *Gasmaske* 24, 30, and 38, as well as special respirators designed for use by young children. Basically they were made of rubberised cloth and leather or entirely of rubber, and included a face piece with eye pieces, and a changeable oval-shaped filter screwed onto the snout. The gas mask was carried in a *Tragbüchse für Gasmaske* (case for gas mask), a cylindrical, robust, rather cumbersome and heavy fluted steel canister with a lid. Inside the lid was a hinged compartment for spare eyepiece lenses.

Another item was available against combat gases on the field, the *Gasplane* (gas sheet), a treated protective fabric, thick paper or rubberised sheet (2m x 1.2m) intended to protect the wearer from sprayed blister agents. The gas sheet was carried in a rubberised fabric pouch with a flap, generally attached to the gas mask canister's sling and worn over the chest. The gasmask case (24.5cm in length and 12.5cm in diameter) hung on a shoulder sling across the small of the back or was slung around the neck when riding a bicycle or motorbike. In practice the canister and pouch were carried in whatever way the wearer found least encumbering.

While combat gases were not used by the German Army during the Second World War, the Germans did stockpile large quantities of chemical weapons. Gases were not employed possibly through fear of retaliation, but more likely because of the mobility of the combat. Morality was not an issue; the Nazis used gases such as Zyklon B (a cyanide-based insecticide) in the gas chambers of extermination camps during the Holocaust.

Civilian Evacuation

Another measure taken by the Nazi regime directly related to and caused by Allied air raids was the evacuation of civilians and the *Kinderlandverschickung* (KLV, literally the 'sending of children to the land'). Begun in September 1940, the KLV was the evacuation to the countryside of children from cities at risk of bombing. Initially the evacuation scheme was voluntary, and applied only to children of school age from Berlin and Hamburg who lived in suburbs and parts of the cities without sufficient air raid shelters. By October 1940, some 62,000 children under the age of 14 had been evacuated from Berlin, and 42,000 from Hamburg to the provinces of Bavaria, Silesia and Thuringia.

The scheme became more extensive and eventually compulsory as the war dragged on and the Allies stepped up their bombing campaign. In April 1942, there were already 850,000 evacuated civilians. By June 1943 a wholesale evacuation from the Ruhr Gebiet (Germany's most industrial region) was carried out with 1 million women, children and elderly evacuated. This was followed by the evacuation of another million women, children, elderly and invalids from Berlin in August 1943. The evacuation was a large program carried out by the *Nationalsozialistishe Volkswohlfahrt* (Nazi Welfare Organisation, NSV), supervised by the Nazi Party. It was the party Gauleiter (Senior Nazi Party administrative leader) of each *Gau* (district) who, as State Defence Commissioner, gave the order to evacuate, determined areas of reception, and arranged for transport and billets.

Local authorities cooperated with the NSDAP and the Hitler Youth, notably girls of the BdM (the female branch of the Hitler Youth) and women of the NSV and NSF were involved in the care of KLV children.

Evacuated women, children and the elderly were housed in vacant apartments and properties, spare rooms, youth hostels, farms, monasteries and holiday camps, all of which were registered, requisitioned and occupied according to a system of priority. Special KLV camps, approximately 5000 of them, were also arranged mainly in the rural regions of Germany, but also in the Warthegau area of Poland, Upper Silesia and Slovakia. The camps varied in size and capacity; the largest of them could accommodate over 1200 children. Each camp was run by Nazi approved teachers and a Hitler Youth leader. These camps began replacing many bigger city junior and grammar schools, most of which had been closed due to the bombings. In the period 1940–1945, over 2.8 million German children were sent to the KLV camps.

➧ Girl of the BdM-KLV.

As can be imagined, the forced evacuation of civilians had psychological repercussions. It also created gigantic logistic and organisational problems. Some evacuees could be accommodated by relations or friends, but the majority could not. Although acts of genuine generosity and solidarity were numerous, the large-scale evacuation was on the whole unpopular with all those involved. Those whose properties were requisitioned for billets resented the unwelcome guests as hungry intruders. The evacuees themselves were often sent to uncomfortable or badly organised billets and were depressed, disoriented and homesick. There was often ill feeling between the locals and evacuees, rich and poor, urban and rural people. The combination of shortages, difficulties of all sorts, and frustrations was worsened by a sense of unfairness, as in many cases the burden of providing billets was avoided by the wealthy and those with Party connections.

The destruction of homes by Allied bombing and the evacuation scheme had a traumatic impact on social life as families were split up and juvenile crime rose. By 1945, Germany was a chaotic nation. Many of the evacuation camps themselves had to be evacuated again before the advance of the Russian Red Army. Other KLV camps were overrun with thousands of children, many of whom were orphaned. More than 16 million civilians were refugees from the German eastern provinces, fleeing in haste rather than waiting for the vengeful Soviet troops. There were 4,500,000 displaced persons in Germany (foreign, forced and slave labourers), plus 2 million prisoners of war of different nationalities. Public transport, especially the railway, was wrecked, as were most public utilities.

Hitler was shaken by the heavy Allied air raids, although less by the casualties amongst the German population than by the destruction of valuable industrial sites producing weapons and ammunition. When it came to visiting bombed towns to boost morale, Hitler was totally uninterested. Shattered German cities and disheartened refugees did not sit comfortably with the Führer's dream of a Thousand Year Reich. In his mind a great people must perish heroically, so the ordinary men, women and children of Germany had to die for failing to win his war; they could expect no sympathy from their Führer. Hitler once declared: 'If the German people are incapable of winning the war, then they can rot!' He remained true to his megalomaniac programme '*Weltmacht oder Niedergang*' ('world power or ruins'), and considered that if Germany lost the war it meant that the 'Aryan nation' had not stood the test of strength, and in that case the German people deserved no better than to be totally destroyed.

Air Raid Shelters

Air raid shelters were built specifically to serve as protection against enemy air raids. The Nazi authorities recognised that such protection would be vital in any future war, and the planning of a programme of construction was begun after Hitler came to power in January 1933. The first modest steps were taken in 1934, but few shelters were actually constructed. Indeed in the pre-war period and even after the Second World War had started, these projects were a low priority. This was partly due to a national atmosphere in which the building of air raid shelters for civilian use was regarded as defeatist; Hitler declared that the war would be short and victorious, and that Britain would come to terms. However he authorised an emergency programme in 1940, but it was not until 1941 – when it became clear that the war would last longer than expected and when the British Royal Air Force launched increasingly daring air raids on Germany – that Hitler gave the order to activate the programme.

Before the civil defence effort could begin in earnest and before adequate shelters were available in large numbers, pre-existing edifices such as underground stations, tunnels, mine galleries and railway arches were used to safeguard people during air raids. Trenches were also dug in private gardens or public parks. Cellars and basements were also used. They were the most common type of ad hoc shelter, since they could be easily modified to accommodate the residents of a building, the workers of a factory, the children of a school or the personnel and shoppers in a department store. The authorities encouraged such arrangements and published pamphlets on the reinforcement of ceilings, preparation of survival kits, storage of food and water and the digging of

◆ *Luftschutz* (air protection) bunker at Osnabrück. This circular concrete bunker had two entrances.

◀ *Luftschutzraum* at Trier
(Rhineland-Palatinate).

emergency exits and escape passages. However, these shelters could bring their own dangers, as heavy machinery and materials, water storage facilities above the shelter, and insufficient support structures, such as pillars and beams beneath the shelter ceiling, all threatened to cause the collapse of basements. When burning buildings and apartment blocks above them collapsed, the occupants often became trapped in basement shelters, which were often overcrowded after arrivals from other buildings rendered unsafe through earlier attacks. Occupants could perish from collapsing debris or carbon monoxide poisoning.

The inadequacies of the subway stations, cellars and basements became apparent when a firestorm began during an incendiary attack on Hamburg in July 1943. A 'firestorm' or a 'fire typhoon' occurred when individual fires caused by incendiary bombing combined into a major conflagration. The heat generated by the blaze created a giant column of rapidly rising hot air, which sucked cool air into the centre of an inferno causing high winds that fanned and intensified the existing flames. The heat generated by the fire typhoon was so intense that metal melted, and those caught in shelters were carbonised; in some cases only a stump or grey ash remained. There were an estimated 43,000 casualties, and thousands people died a horrible death inside the private and public shelters.

A better form of protection was offered by collective concrete bunkers, a peculiarly German type of construction designed to relieve the pressure German authorities were facing to accommodate additional numbers of the population in high-density housing areas, as well as passers-by on the streets during air raids. In contrast to any other shelters these buildings were considered completely bombproof. They also had the advantage of being built upwards, much cheaper than being built downwards by excavation.

Air raid bunkers, always placed in the middle of a city, were regularly controlled and inspected by the authorities, and came in several shapes and sizes. According to their capacity, they were sub-classed into categories including *Luftschutzhäuser* (air raid protection houses), *Luftschutzunterstände* (air raid protection bunkers) and *Luftschutztürme* (air raid protection towers). The *Luftschutzraüme* (air raid protection buildings) were the largest and the most effective. They consisted

◆ Air raid bunker for 1500 people.

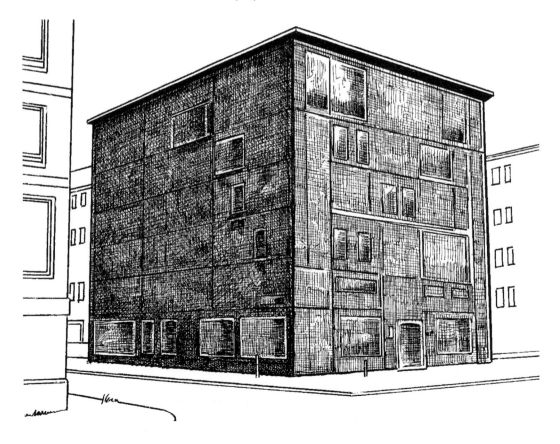

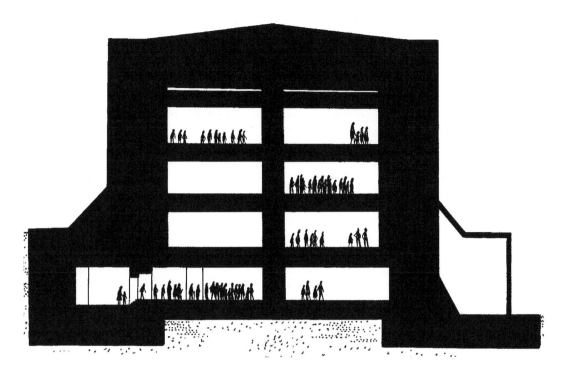

♠ Cross-section *Luftschuztraum* (2000 persons).

usually of large concrete blocks built above ground with walls between 1m and 3m thick, with huge lintels above doorways and openings. The thickness of the roofs, based on military research and tests, had the following thickness standards: 1.40m could resist 230kg (500lbs) bombs; 2m 460kg (1000lbs) bombs and 2.50m 920kg (2000lbs) bombs.

Concrete shelters were primarily designed to protect people, but were also meant to protect administrative centres, important archives and works of art. Their structures took many forms, usually a square block or a straight tower with a square plan, but also lower and longer rectangular shapes, as well as round towers, huge medieval-like concrete keeps, pyramidal constructions and shell-shaped (ant hill) in order to deflect bombs. Whatever their shape and capacity, all *Luftschützraüme* offered Spartan accommodation. They included a reception hall and staircases (and lifts in the largest ones) leading to many rooms in the storeys. They had an infirmary, water (provided by a well or the urban water system), lavatories (male and female) and emergency lamps fed by batteries. Electricity came from the national power grid and transformer stations, although large shelters often had their own emergency power plant. All corridors and rooms were lit and clearly marked to facilitate circulatio, and fire extinguishing apparatus was available in large numbers.

All shelters had a telephone connection, and those for over 300 persons often included radio receiving and transmitting equipment. Attention was also paid to the danger of poisonous gases. Decontamination procedures included a sequence of undressing, washing and medical attention. In large structures, each function had a separate room. Shelters included gas detectors, decontamination devices, containers

⬇ *Luftschutzturm* Johannisbollwerk
(Hamburg).

for contaminated clothing, changing rooms, heavy armoured gas-tight doors with
a peephole and sealed with either rubber or felt, gas locks, washing facilities and
medicine cabinets. A ventilation system was always available. The air was drawn from
pipes through dust filters; the air flow could be interdicted by a stopcock, then the
air flow passed through more filters, including a gas filter. Finally, the air was passed
through the extraction mechanism, powered by hand or electricity, and finally the
fresh air was delivered into the rooms. It was calculated that the ventilation system
would provide $30m^3$ of fresh air per person per hour. Chimneys, ventilation shafts,
intake stacks and exhaust pipes for the evacuation of used air (and possibly poison
gas contaminants) were also designed to be totally gas tight.

For blackout purposes, particular attention was paid to darkening in the event of
or during an air raid, but shelters generally had no or very few openings (all sealed

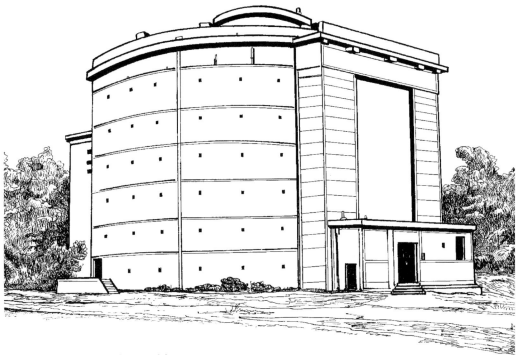

⬆ Air raid tower at Breslau Frankfurterstrasse.

by armoured shutters) except for a main front entrance and several emergency exits. Shelters were closed monoliths with a constant interior temperature of 7 –10°C. Regulations recommended that they be heated to 17°C with the use of stoves or heated air.

The construction of these huge concrete buildings was generally carried out by the *Organisation Todt* (a conglomerate of building companies placed under Nazi supervision), and coordinated and managed by the *Reichsluftschutzbund* (Reich Air Defence League). A distance of 500m was officially considered the farthest that a person should need to travel to reach a shelter during an aerial attack, but this could not always be observed everywhere. Some shelters were decorated in a 'Nazi style' and were also used as propaganda objects. Their monumental construction had the additional objective of reassuring the public. At the start of the war the few shelters that were completed were often designed to blend in with their surroundings, with bombproof roofs covered with tiles, trompe-l'oeil windows and doors, and concrete walls revetted with bricks. Later in the war, some were camouflaged, but they were of little interest to Allied airmen.

At the beginning of Allied air raids on Germany, public concrete shelters were not numerous and were reserved for Nazi Party members and relatives of soldiers who had died at the front. The main cities of Germany were secretly classed into three categories depending on their value for the war economy, which determined the availability of concrete shelters. With the intensification of the Allied bombardments, their number, disposition and capacity were increased and standardised for 500, 1000, 2000 or 4000 persons. A few of them had a yet larger capacity, up to 12,000 and even 18,000 persons. In fact large multi-storey shelters were much more economical; the 500-person shelters required a volume of 3m^3 of concrete per person, whilst the 4000-person shelter required only 1.8m^3. At the end

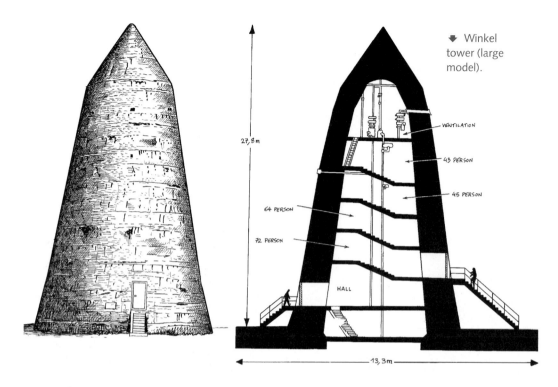

↓ Winkel tower (large model).

This shell-shaped bunker was known as the *Winkelturm* (after the designer and architect Leo Winkel) and codenamed RL3-40/5. Patented in 1934, some hundred examples in five different models were built in the period 1936–1941. The diameter of the Winkel tower was 8.4–10m, the height was 20–30m with a minimum wall thickness of reinforced concrete of 0.8–1.5m. This and the rocket-like shape offered good bomb-deflecting capability. The largest towers could shelter more than 500 people, the smaller ones 164. Winkel towers were adopted by the German National Railroad Company because they could be placed in the limited space available in congested rail yards. Equipped with air conditioning and a water supply, they held the largest number of occupants and required less space than most of the other types. They were intended mainly as protection for factory workers and railroad personnel, and they appeared most often in areas of heavy industry and rail centres, principally in the Ruhr Gebiet. Some of them are still standing today, such as those in Bremen, Darmstadt, Duisburg, Düsseldorf, Berlin, and Solingen (at the corner of Gasstrasse and Luneschlosstrasse). Nineteen Winkel air raid shelters were built at Zossen-Wünsdorf, the wartime headquarters of the Wehrmacht, located south of Berlin.

of the war – by overcrowding – the air raid shelters could accommodate up to 75 per cent of the population in all principal German cities. When cellars, basements and underground metro stations had shown the limits of their usefulness, *Luftschützraüme* became the last safe places.

Massive as the public shelters and the previously described armed Flak towers were, their value diminished when the weaponry of aerial bombing changed in 1943. As the scale and the frequency of Allied bombing increased and effectiveness grew, more of the German urban population flocked to the public bunkers. These became overcrowded by five to six times their design capacity. Records showed bunkers intended for 18,000 people were used in practice by up to 60,000 persons. Needless to say overcrowding made the service provision inadequate; sanitary arrangements were overstretched, ventilation became ineffective, there were insufficient bunks and scenes of panic amongst occupiers were not uncommon.

🔺 *Luftschutz* shelter at Münster Lazarettenstrasse.

🔻 Air raid shelter at Aachen.

After the war it was decided to get rid of the air raid shelters, which were seen as ugly relics of Hitler's regime, and horrible reminders of the carnage of the Allied bombing campaign. Many light concrete and brick shelters were destroyed, but a number of the large concrete *Luftschutzraüme* may still be seen today, as the dangers and cost of demolishing such structures sited in the middle of densely populated residential areas were too high. During the Cold War, some concrete air raid bunkers and other Nazi shelters were used by the German Federal government, Allied occupation troops and NATO as store places, headquarters, offices, archives and shelters. Others have been converted for civilian purposes such as storage, parking lots and museums. At Emden one of the 31 concrete air raids shelters built during the Second World War now houses an historical museum in Holzsägerstrasse 6.

It should be noted that Hitler and the main Nazi leaders were not only interested in sheltering the Germans from air raids, but also particularly concerned about their own safety. Wherever Hitler went he first issued orders for building bunkers for his

personal protection. The meeting with the French Marshal Philippe Pétain in October 1940 – at a time when Allied air activity was extremely limited – took place in the small village of Montoire because there was a convenient tunnel in the vicinity where the Führer's train could shelter in case of an airstrike. There were underground concrete bunkers and command Führer's Headquarter (FHQu) systems in Rastenburg, Berlin, Rodert, Bruly, Obersalzberg, Munich, Salzburg, Bad Nauheim, in Silesia and Thuringia. These complexes were guarded, fenced, and included accommodation for escort troops and staff, and were linked by a communication system. Nearby there was an airfield and whenever possible access to the railway.

Hitler's exaggerated fear inspired his entourage. Göring had extensive underground installations for his personal protection in his home at Karinhall near Berlin and in Castle Feldenstein near Nuremberg, which he hardly visited. The road from Karinhall to Berlin, 40 miles long and leading through lonely woods, was provided with concrete shelters at regular intervals for fear of an Allied air attack. The Gauleiters (Nazi region administrative governors) were ordered by Hitler to have additional air shelters built outside the cities for their personal protection.

◆ Policeman of the *Ordnungspolizei*. This policeman of the Gendarmerie (rural police) wears the widely issued *Mantel* (greatcoat) and the typical shako (kepi or cap). When worn on parade, a horsehair plume was inserted behind the cockade down to the left side of the kepi.

POLICE AND FIRE BRIGADES

Ordnungpolizei

Nazi Germany was a *Totalstaat*, a dictatorial state, and Nazi rule extended to all departments of public life, culture, education and the most intimate details of private and family life. In a state where all civil and human rights were totally abrogated, where all duties and responsibilities converged on the Führer, where citizenship was limited to 'Aryans', where Jews were eliminated from political, economic, cultural and social life from the German *Volksgemeinschaft* (folk community), the police apparatus was a large and complex organisation including many police and intelligence services. In 1939 these were centralised into a body controlled by Heinrich Himmler's SS, and known as the *Reichssicherheitshauptamt* (RSHA, Main Office for Security of the Reich) headed by Himmler's deputy, Reinhard Heydrich. The RSHA symbolised the close connection between the SS (a party organisation) and the police (a state organisation); in fact the SS and police were inextricably linked. The RSHA included several major organisations, notably the armed Waffen SS, the *Sicherheitspolizei* (Sipo or security police) repressing and spying on the population including the infamous Gestapo (Secret State Police), the *SS Sicherheitsdienst* (Security Service of the SS), the *Wirtschafts-und Verwaltungshauptamt* (SS economic and administrative office which controlled the economic enterprise of the SS and administrated the concentration and extermination camps) and several others.

An important sub-branch was the *Ordnungspolizei* (Orpo, literally the order police), the regular domestic uniformed police. Himmler spared no effort in ensuring that the SS directly or indirectly controlled every important policing function in Nazi Germany. In April 1934 he was appointed Chief of the German Police in the Ministry of Interior, and – by gradually combining all existing German police forces – the lines between the national police and the SS began to blur. The Orpo came under the control of the SS in 1936. It was headed by SS Oberstgruppenführer (General) Kurt Dalüge (1897–1946), who reported directly to Reichsführer-SS Heinrich Himmler, and who did his best to nazify and militarise the Orpo. Kurt Dalüge was appointed Deputy Protector of Bohemia and Moravia in 1942, and replaced by SS Obergruppenführer Alfred Wünnenberg as Orpo Chief.

The Orpo was composed of seven *Ämter* (main departments) as follows:

Amt I	*Kommando*	High Command including various inspectorates
Amt II	*Verwaltungs-und Recht*	Administration and Justice
Amt III	*Wirtschaftsverwaltung*	Budget and Economy
Amt IV	*Technische Nothilfe*	TeNo Technical Emergency Service
Amt V	*Feuerwehr*	Fire Brigades
Amt VI	*Kolonialpolizei*	Colonial Police founded in 1941 intended to control Germany's future overseas possessions when the war was won
Amt VII	*Technische SS und Polizei Akademie*	SS and Police Technical Academy

The Orpo – totalling some 250,000 policemen in 1939 – had several branches including *Schutzpolizei des Reiches* (Shupo regular uniformed security police), *Gemeinde Polizei* (urban municipal police) and *Gendarmerie* (rural police) each with sub-branches. The police corps brought together the city and municipal uniformed forces that had been organised on a state-by-state basis and covered the towns and cities, whereas the *Gendarmerie* (in Württemberg known as the *Landjäger*) covered small towns and rural areas. It also included various technical, administrative and auxiliary services such as rescue squads and police units on rivers, as well as air defence and air raid precaution units.

Fire protection police and fire brigades were part of the Orpo from 1938. The Orpo was charged to ensure interior order, and therefore it was militarily structured and organised with uniforms and ranks similar to those of the Wehrmacht. The ranks of the German police were as follows:

Generaloberst der Polizei	no exact equivalent, approximately General
General der Polizei	General
Generalleutnant der Polizei Lieutenant General	Major General
Generalmajor der Polizei	Major General
Oberst	Brigadier General
Reichskriminaldirektor	Colonel
Oberstleutnant	Lieutenant Colonel
Major	Major
Hauptmann der Gendarmerie	Captain
Oberleutnant	First Lieutenant
Leutnant	Second Lieutenant
Meister	Sergeant Major
Hauptwachtmeister	Sergeant Major
Kompaniehauptwachtmeister	Master Sergeant
Revieroberwachtmeister or *Zugwachtmeister*	Technical Sergeant
Oberwachtmeister	Staff Sergeant
Wachtmeister	Sergeant
Rottwachtmeister	Corporal
Unterwachtmeister	Private First Class
Anwärter	Private

Owing to their green uniforms, members of the Orpo were also referred to as *Grüne Polizei* (green police).

At regional level the Orpo was controlled by inspectors called *Inspekteur der Ordungspolizei* (IdO) in each *Land* (province). In the annexed territories and later in the occupied European countries a senior officer was in charge, the *Befehlshaber der Ordnungspolizei* (BdO). Indeed, the Orpo spread to occupied countries during the war and was militarised, becoming more of a military force than an organisation of public servants. Some 100 battalions were raised from the Orpo (each about 550 men) and served in the ranks of the Wehrmacht as anti-partisan units. Some members of the Orpo were drafted in 1940 to form the 4th Waffen SS Panzergrenadierdivision 'Polizei 1'. Some Orpo policemen – particularly those who were under disciplinary punishment – volunteered to constitute *Einsatzgruppen* (murder squads) in Poland and Russia in 1939–42. Other volunteers formed SS-Polizei regiments in 1943. At the beginning of 1945 a number of Orpo policemen were drafted into the *Volkssturm* and to form the 35th Waffen SS Grenadierdivision 'Polizei nr.2'.

The Allies regarded the Orpo as a dangerous service, and after the German capitulation in May 1945 it was purged of its Nazi members. It was, of course, rapidly reactivated, and many of its personnel continued business as usual, performing valuable general police services for the Allied occupation forces. In the post-war period the *Ordnungpolizei* became the *Volkspolizei* (Vopo) in the communist eastern Germany (DDR) and – under the name *Schutzpolizei* (Schupo) – in the western Federal Republic of Germany (BRD).

Fire Defence

Prior to 1938 fire brigades operated independently in villages, towns and cities. Formations were usually part of the municipal services administrated by the local authorities under the leadership of the mayor. The national *Feuerschutzpolizei* (Fire Protection Police, FSP) was founded in 1938 as an amalgamation of several fire fighting services. In view of the necessity for air raid protection, fire brigades were incorporated into the overall police system. About 90 of the larger German cities were ordered to transfer their existing fire fighting personnel to the newly created Fire Protection Police. As stated above, the *Feuerschutzpolizei* was a branch of the *Ordnungspolizei* and as such came under SS authority. The 'police' aspect of the FSP is explained by the fact that the corps was not only responsible for fighting fires, but also had police powers; in case of emergency (when no regular policemen were available) members could be called upon to carry out police duties, such as maintaining order and making arrests.

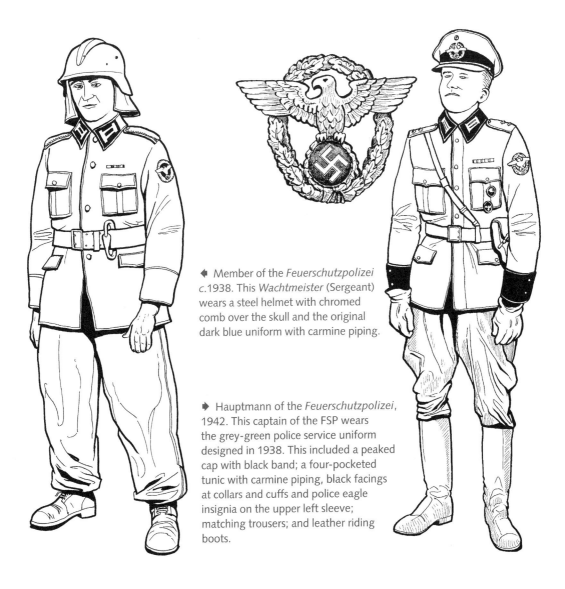

◀ Member of the *Feuerschutzpolizei* c.1938. This *Wachtmeister* (Sergeant) wears a steel helmet with chromed comb over the skull and the original dark blue uniform with carmine piping.

▶ Hauptmann of the *Feuerschutzpolizei*, 1942. This captain of the FSP wears the grey-green police service uniform designed in 1938. This included a peaked cap with black band; a four-pocketed tunic with carmine piping, black facings at collars and cuffs and police eagle insignia on the upper left sleeve; matching trousers; and leather riding boots.

The Fire Protection Police included several regiments. Feuerschutzpolizei Regiment 1 was based in Saxony and, after the outbreak of the Second World War, some of its units were engaged in occupied countries such as the Netherlands, France, namely at Le Havre, Saint-Nazaire, Brest and Lorient, as well as in Romania at the Ploesti oilfield. Feuerschutzpolizei Regiment 2 was based in Hannover; Feuerschutzpolizei Regiment 3 was based in East Prussia and also saw service in Poland; Feuerschutzpolizei Regiment 4 was based in occupied Ukraine; Feuerschutzpolizei Regiment 5 was based in Czechoslovakia; and Feuerschutzpolizei Regiment 6 was based in the occupied Netherlands.

The smallest administrative area was the *Wachtbezirk* consisting of several *Schutzpolizei Reviere* (Protection Police Wards). Operational areas for actual fire fighting were determined independently, however, and zones were drawn in conformity with tactical considerations. The usual operational unit engaged in the first instance was known as a *Zug* (squad, plural *Züge*). In exceptional cases a larger unit, the *Gruppe*, was called out. The commanding officer leading the local units of the *Feuerschutzpolizei* was called *Kommandeur* or *Leiter*. He directed

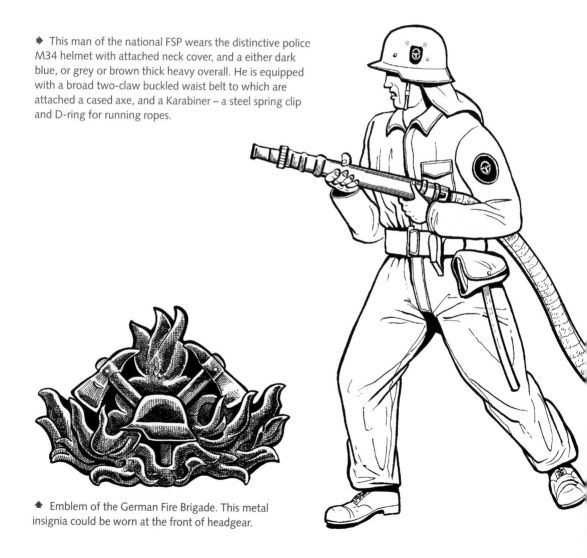

◆ This man of the national FSP wears the distinctive police M34 helmet with attached neck cover, and a either dark blue, or grey or brown thick heavy overall. He is equipped with a broad two-claw buckled waist belt to which are attached a cased axe, and a Karabiner – a steel spring clip and D-ring for running ropes.

◆ Emblem of the German Fire Brigade. This metal insignia could be worn at the front of headgear.

◆ This fireman of the *Feuerschutzpolizei* wears the distinctive early police M34 helmet with cup-type vents and a thick leather neck protection cover attached to the rear of the liner by means of five leather lugs. A unique feature of the police helmet was that it had a profile featuring a sharply angled brim in the ear guard section rather than the regular slight curve of the Wehrmacht M1935 helmet.

◆ Police/fireman crested helmet. There was a variant especially designed for firemen. It was actually the same as the M34 with the addition of an aluminium crest on top.

◆ This fireman badge was black with the Gothic letter F (for '*Feuer*', fire) in white, and often worn on the lower left sleeve.

fire fighting and fire prevention, allotted the respective zones of operation to the subordinate units, and supervised the organisation and operation of the *Feuerschutzpolizei* under his command. For administrative purposes he was responsible to the *Oberbürgermeister* or *Bürgermeister* (burgomaster, always a NSDAP member) because the costs involved in maintaining the FSP were borne by the local community.

The size of the Fire Protection Police was fixed in accordance with the population of the city. However, in those cities with more than 870,000 inhabitants or with harbour installations, important industrial areas or zones presenting particular fire hazards, the establishment of the *Feuerschutzpolizei* formations

◆ The *Feuerwehr Ehrenzeichen* (Fire Brigade Medal) was instituted in December 1936. Designed by the artist Herbert Knötel, it was available in first and second class, and awarded for merit and for long service in the fire brigade.

was determined on an individual basis. In towns with more than 150,000 inhabitants, auxiliary fire-fighting units called *Freiwillige Feuerwehren* (volunteer fire brigades organised into tactical units called *Gruppen*) were established on a voluntary basis to supplement the *Feuerschutzpolizei*. In small towns and villages fire protection was also organised on a voluntary basis, and when the *Freiwillige Feuerwehren* were inadequate, an obligatory fire service, the *Pflichtfeuerwehr* (Compulsory Fire Brigade) was established, manned by all available able-bodied males aged 17 to 65. These firemen, like their FSP colleagues, were considered *Hilfspolizei* (Auxiliary Police), and their leaders were appointed and directed by the local chief of police.

Other auxiliary part-time firemen were *Werkfeuerwehren* formed by the management of individual factories, and manned by employees of the company. The Hitler Youth also contributed volunteers, known as *Hitler Jugend Feuerwehrscharen* (Hitler Youth Fire Companies), composed of *Scharen* (companies of 45–50 boys), trained and equipped by the local fire chief. Each *Schar* usually comprised three *Kamerafschaften* (fire-fighting squads) placed at the disposal of the local fire and police officers. It is estimated that when the Allied air offensive on Germany reached its peak in 1943/44, the FSP (including regiments, voluntary, compulsory units and auxiliary formations) totalled about 2 million members. As the war dragged on and Germany crumbled, still more men were drafted in the Wehrmacht for front line duty, and increasingly women, as well as foreign auxiliaries (draftees and volunteers from Poland, the Ukraine and other occupied nations) had to fill the ranks of the FSP as auxiliaries, but they were, of course, deprived of police powers.

Officers of the FSP usually wore *Ordnungpolizei* green uniforms with pink-carmine piping and police insignia. Firemen's service dress included a dark blue uniform and various overalls with the FSP carmine-red police eagle on an oval green-grey patch and a district designation on the upper left sleeve. In operation they wore the distinctive police helmet with a leather flap attached at the rear to protect the neck from embers and water. On the right side of the helmet there was a swastika decal, and on the left side the police decal – a wrath of oak leaves with an eagle holding a swastika in the middle.

CIVIL DEFENCE

In general terms, the German civil defence system was composed of regulations and measures to prepare civilians for an enemy attack, primarily from the air. It used the principles of emergency operations, prevention, preparation, response, emergency evacuation and recovery. Programmes of this sort were initially discussed in the interbellum between 1918 and 1939, when air power represented a yet unknown but real threat. Before things went that far, General Douhet's possible thesis that 'the bomber will always get through' represented a real danger, and most industrial nations had taken measures for civil defence dedicated to the protection of civilians from air strikes. In Germany active measures (*Luftverteidigung*, 'air defence') included the development of fighter/interceptor aeroplanes and anti-aircraft artillery. Passive measures (*Luftschutz*, 'air protection') included services dealing with air raid precautions: protection of the population; sounding air alarms; first aid; rescuing and treating victims; prevention of panic; fire-fighting; bomb disposal; smoke screens; decoy sites; and camouflage of potential targets. As the air war on Nazi Germany escalated, the *Luftschutz* department and other services related to air raid precautions became vital, and they saw an increase in the scope of their activities, personnel numbers, funds and equipment.

Emergency Technical Rescue (Technische Nothilfe, TeNo)

The *Technische Nothilfe* was a corps of specialised troops for rescue and repair, created in Berlin as early as September 1919 by the Weimar Republic. Headed by lieutenant and engineer Otto Lummitzsch, its original purpose was to make sure that vital services such as electricity, gas and communications would continue to function in the event of popular strikes. At the same time other technical units were created in other German towns for the same purposes, and in November 1919 all TeNo units were placed under the tutelage of the Ministry of the Interior. Directives were issued in February 1920 and the corps, headed by a *Vorstand* (Administration Council) and a *Haupstelle* (Central Office), was organised into 13 *Landbezirke* (regional directives) including 333 *Ortsgruppen* (local groups).

In the late 1920s the TeNo's tasks were extended and its personnel – composed of volunteer engineers, craftsmen, technicians and general workers – were used as a specialist reserve group for emergency response, dealing with damage done by natural disasters such as floods, railway accidents and air raid preparation. In 1929 the TeNo became a registered association called *Technische Nothilfe eingetragener Verein*, still presided over by Otto Lummitzsch and deputies from the Ministry of the Interior in the Administration Board. The potential value of the TeNo was fully recognised by the Nazis, thus the service was continued after January 1933, although naturally after a reorganisation along Nazi lines. A swastika was added to the association's emblem and Chairman Lummitzsch was called Reichsführer der TeNo.

In March 1934, Lummitzsch, who was married to a half-jewess, was dismissed and replaced by SA-Gruppenführer Hans Weinrich who maintained Erich Hampe (Lummitzsch's deputy) as Stellvertreter (deputy). From 1937, the TeNo became a technical auxiliary corps of the police and was absorbed into the *Ordnungpolizei* (Amt IV) and was therefore attached to the SS when all German police forces were placed under the leadership of Reichsführer SS Heinrich Himmler.

The TeNo was headed by police and SS officers: Hans Weinrich, now promoted SS-Gruppenführer und Generalleutnant der Polizei from June 1937 to June 1943, and then by SS-Gruppenführer und Generalleutnant der Polizei Dipl. Ing. Willy Schmelcher from 15 October 1943 to May 1945. However the TeNo kept a relative autonomy from the police and SS in its function. It was not part of the Air Protection

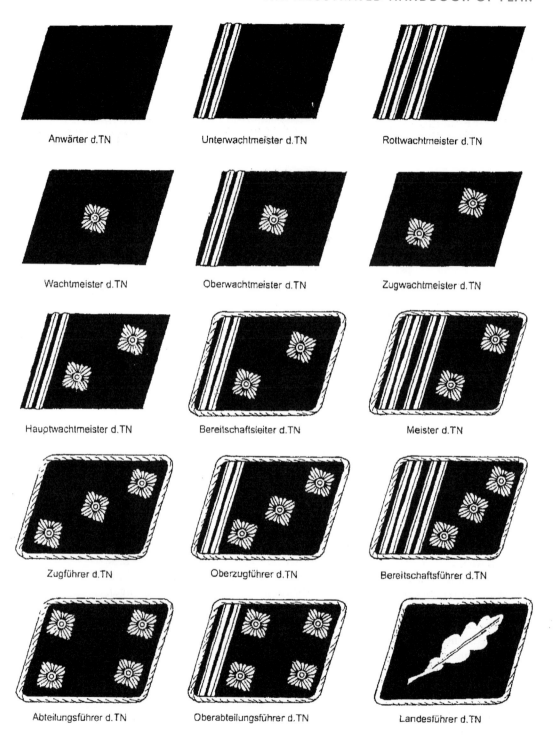

Anwärter d.TN

Unterwachtmeister d.TN

Rottwachtmeister d.TN

Wachtmeister d.TN

Oberwachtmeister d.TN

Zugwachtmeister d.TN

Hauptwachtmeister d.TN

Bereitschaftsleiter d.TN

Meister d.TN

Zugführer d.TN

Oberzugführer d.TN

Bereitschaftsführer d.TN

Abteilungsführer d.TN

Oberabteilungsführer d.TN

Landesführer d.TN

◆ Collar patches of the *Technische Nothilfe* (TeNo, Technical Emergency Corps). Shown here are the left collar patches indicating rank, which were quite similar to those of the SA, SS, Waffen SS and NSKK.

Technische Nothilfe

↑ The cuff title of the TeNo was worn on the lower left arm.

◄ Emblem of the TeNo.

Police, but its services cooperated closely with the civil defence, notably with the *Sicherheits und Hilfsdient* (SHD, Assistance and Security Service), fire brigades and the German Red Cross. In March 1939, a decree made the corps an auxiliary police service and its personnel were allowed to carry light weapons (pistols and carbines).

The TeNo had four branches, each identified by its own *Waffenfarbe* (colour of service): *Technischedienst* – TD technical service (blue); *Luftschutzdienst* – LD air raid protection (red); *Bereitschaftsdienst* – BD, emergency service (yellow/orange); and *Allgemeiner Dienst* – AD, general service (green). It had its own newspaper called *Die Räder, Zeitschrift der Technischen Nothilfe* (the Wheels Magazine of the TeNo). With the intensification of Allied air raids on Germany, the tasks of the *Technische Nothilfe* were greatly increased; the services played a major part in the air war and in many cases its members became heroes of the Reich. The TeNo was active in Germany as well as in the occupied territories; in Holland and Norway local versions were formed.

The basic TeNo unit was the *Zug* (company), and five companies formed an *Abteilung* (battalion). TeNo battalions were motorised and distributed throughout cities, industrial centres and major traffic hubs, and emphasis was placed on maintaining public services and responding to public dangers, both during and after air attacks. The TeNo provided the proficient manpower and expertise for industrial and building projects, they dealt with breakdowns in public services including gas leaks in damaged buildings, controlling exposure to chemical warfare agents, the maintenance of the public water system, repairing electrical power outrages, air raid clearance, and other problems resulting from bombing raids. They fought fires, tunnelled under piles of rubble in search of victims and survivors, cleared waterways, repaired lock-gates, helped defuse unexploded bombs, demolished houses to create fire breaks, repaired generating plants, pumping stations and communication systems, and even helped evacuate casualties.

Most of the men of the TeNo possessed great technical skills, from engineers to technicians and skilled and semi-skilled specialists in construction work, public utilities operations, communications, metal salvage and other related fields. They were equipped with specialised vehicles (identified by a wide white band) and tools including tractors, trucks, mobile cranes, electric saws, heavy power pneumatic drills, pumps, winches, air-compressed pile drivers, earth and debris moving equipment, generators and compressors. TeNo men worked with and supported other air raid services including the fire brigades, German Red Cross, the RLB and the *Nationalsozialistische Volkswohlfahrte* (NSV, Nazi People's Welfare Organisation) (see below).

The TeNo was originally a state force created to cope with public emergencies, but increasingly it began to work with the police and the army in a supporting role.

◆ TeNo Private.

◆ TeNo rank was indicated by the collar patch. This *Wachtmeister* (Sergeant) wears the Tyr-rune badge indicating specialisation on his left arm, and – being in service of the Army – a yellow brassard with the words *'Deutsche Wehrmacht'*.

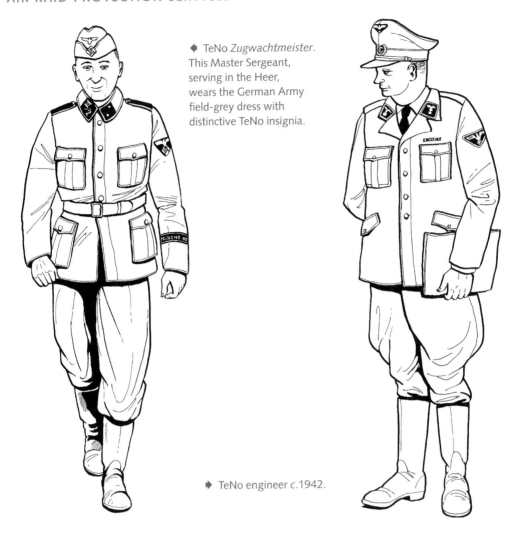

◀ TeNo *Zugwachtmeister*.
This Master Sergeant,
serving in the Heer,
wears the German Army
field-grey dress with
distinctive TeNo insignia.

◆ TeNo engineer *c*.1942.

TeNo men gradually assumed police tasks such as detecting looters and searching and guarding crashed Allied planes. They were employed in construction and repair work but also in many other technical tasks in connection with the armed forces. Parts of TeNo units were incorporated into the German Army as *Technische Truppen* (technical troops) and *TeNo Kommandos* for engineering purposes such as construction and repair work on military installations, buildings and fortifications. In this role members were charged with re-establishing or repairing damaged utilities in areas where water and power services were crucially needed, including facilities related to shipping, inland transportation and airfields.

Before the war the members of the TeNo were originally German men over military age, and the general requirements for membership were as for the SS and police. To fill its ranks during the Second World War, the organisation was forced to relax its entrance policy, recruiting pro-Nazi foreign volunteers –most physically able German men were already serving in the armed forces – including Dutchmen, Flemings, Walloons and Frenchmen. For menial tasks (e.g. clearing debris), the TeNo also employed forced labour provided by prisoners of wars and concentration camp inmates. By 1943, the TeNo had over 100,000 members.

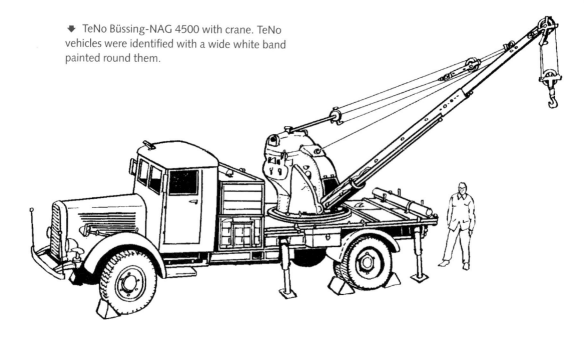

TeNo Büssing-NAG 4500 with crane. TeNo vehicles were identified with a wide white band painted round them.

The TeNo and other German air raid services were completely overwhelmed by the end of the war. By that time many TeNo personnel were armed to protect key positions, employed to guard destroyed buildings, ruined factories and bombsites against theft and pillage. Some were drafted into the army to form demolition squads with retreating front-line fighting units. In late 1944 and early 1945, Germany was exhausted and needed still more combatants. As a result of a large comb-out, the youngest and fittest TeNo men were drafted into German fighting formations such as the Waffen SS and the *Volkssturm*.

Like all German uniformed organisations the TeNo had their own ranks and distinctive insignia, rather similar of those of the SA, NSKK and SS. The ranks of the TeNo included the following:

Anwärter der TeNo	Private
Unterwachtmeister der TeNo	Private 1st Class
Rottwachtmeister der TeNo	Corporal
Wachtmeister der TeNo	Sergeant
Oberwachtmeister der TeNo	Staff Sergeant
Zugwachtmeister der TeNo	Master Sergeant
Hauptwachtmeister der TeNo	no equivalent, perhaps Warrant Officer or Senior NCO
Bereitschaftsleiter der TeNo	no equivalent, perhaps Warrant Officer or Senior NCO
Meister der TeNo	no equivalent, perhaps Warrant Officer or Senior NCO
Zugführer der TeNo	Second Lieutenant
Oberzugführer der TeNo	First Lieutenant
Bereitschaftsführer der TeNo	Captain
Abteilungsführer der TeNo	Major
Oberabteilungsführer der TeNo	Lieutenant Colonel
Landesführer der TeNo	Colonel

The *Reichsführer der Teno* was the leader of the Corps, assisted by a deputy bearing the title of *Stellvertreter Reichsführer der TeNo*. TeNo ranks were indicated by a left collar patch on a man's tunic.

Members of the TeNo wore various uniforms varying from green police dress to fatigue suits when on duty and when working in difficult and dirty areas. The fatigue suit, made of strong white herringbone twill material, included a shapeless jacket and trousers. When assisting the Wehrmacht in the field, they were issued field-grey Heer uniforms. In November 1940, Hermann Göring made a deal with Himmler allowing the creation of two TeNo battalions (TeNo-Einsatzgruppe Luftwaffe West) totalling 2000 men subordinate to the Luftwaffe who wore the greyish-blue air force uniform but retained their black rank badges and specific insignia. A number of TeNo personnel served in North Africa alongside the Luftwaffe on airfield construction and repair; they wore the typical DAK (Africa Corps) tropical uniforms.

TeNo men wore a distinctive sleeve eagle with a swastika and a cogwheel enclosing a sledgehammer making a T combined with the letter N. A cuff-title with the indication *Technische Nothilfe* in Gothic letters was often worn on the left sleeve. When incorporated into the German Army, TeNo personnel wore a yellow or white brassard carrying the words '*Deutsche Wehrmacht*' on the left upper arm. Armbands were often worn by German non-military and paramilitary units, or foreign workers serving as auxiliaries. Armbands and cuff titles were worn not so much as political trappings, but to allow for the easy identification of men dressed in anonymous overalls while working or clearing rubble on bomb sites. Officially the armband established the wearer as a genuine member of the Wehrmacht entitled to the same rights as those afforded to regular German armed forces personnel.

TeNo officers wore a buckle with the TeNo symbol surrounded by a laurel wreath. Reflecting their tough role, rank and file men had a broad-bladed parade hewing

▲ TeNo Honour Badge. Instituted in April 1935 the *Ehrenzeichen der Technischen Nothilfe* was awarded to members who joined between 1919 and 1923. The year of entry was marked on a scroll.

▲ The *Rettungsmedaille* (life saving medal) was instituted in 1833 as a Prussian award. It was reinstated in June 1933 with the addition of a swastika on the Prussian imperial eagle. The medal was awarded to any person who rescued someone from great peril at the risk of his own life. The medal was worn on the breast and the ribbon only could be worn in the second buttonhole of the tunic.

knife, introduced in November 1939, while officers had an elegant double-edged dagger bearing the eagle as a guard. Personnel who had successfully passed through the TeNo Reich Training School were allowed to display the silver and black arrow-shaped Tyr-rune badge on the left upper sleeve of their coat or jacket. There were no specifically TeNo awards, but brave men could qualify for medals such as the *Luftschutz Ehrenzeichen* (Civil Defence Decoration) or the *Rettungsmedaille* (Saving Medal).

In 1945 the Allies dissolved the TeNo, but the corps was re-established in 1950 in West Germany. Known as the *Technisches Hilfswerk* (THW, Technical Relief) it still exists today, with civil defence responsibilities; it also participates in worldwide disaster relief efforts.

◆ *Luftschutz Ehrenzeichen*. Instituted in January 1938 and designed by the artist Egon Jantke, the Civil Defence Medal (also known as Air Raid Protection Honour Award) was awarded in 1st and 2nd Class for service in the civil defence.

National Air Protection League (Reichsluftschutzbund, RLB)

The *Reichsluftschutzbund* was created in April 1933. This predated the revelation that the newly established Nazi regime was developing a secret air force in defiance of the 1919 Versailles Treaty. Already a *Reichsluftfahrtministerium* (National Ministry for Air Travel, RLM) had been created and placed under the leadership of Hermann Göring, and the RLM's *Luftschutzamt* (Air Defence Department) took effective control over defence and protection services. The purpose of the RLB was to instil widespread support and encourage volunteer labour for a large air defence organisation, and owing to Minister Josef Göbbels's propaganda

◆ Emblem of the *Reichsluftschutzbund* (RLB) National Air Protection League. The emblem consisted of the traditional German *Gardenstern* (an eight-pointed star), the monogram RLB and a swastika.

◆ Breast badge of the RLB. The badge was worn in white embroidered cloth form on the uniforms, on the breast or on the upper left sleeve. In decal silver-grey form it decorated the front of helmets.

hundreds of thousands of German citizens volunteered to serve in its ranks. By June 1935 the voluntary status of the RLB was abandoned, and membership was practically mandatory for every able-bodied adult. By 1938 it was estimated that the League had 12.6 million members.

The RLB was organised into 15 *Landesgruppen* (regions), each divided into *Untergruppen* (sub-regions), *Ortsgruppen* (districts) and finally into precincts at village or city neighbourhood level. The role of the RLB was to train all households and provide educational services related to air raid precautions. This included providing wardens and firewatchers who were trained to respond to air attacks. Before the war members supervised all civil defence training throughout Germany. They instructed the public at large by giving practical demonstrations, forwarding official instructions, arranging educational lectures and presenting film shows. For the purpose of public information the RLB had two periodical publications, *Der Reichsluftschutz* (the National Air Protection) and *Deutsche Flugillustrierte* (German Air Illustrated), and the fortnightly illustrated *Die Sirene* (the Siren).

After the outbreak of the Second World War and the start of the air offensive against Germany, theory was put in practice. General responsibilities of the RLB members included helping in bomb disposal, fire fighting and establishing camouflage of potential targets, for example by building ground decoys and setting up smoke screens and camouflage netting. Prior to the creation of the *Luftschutzpolizei* (LSP, Air Protection Police) in 1942, the RLB was divided into two main sub-branches with distinctive responsibilities.

Firstly the *Selbschutz* (Self-Protection Service) encompassed all the responsibilities related to protecting families and citizens in residential areas. It was, as it were, the first line of domestic defence against air attack. The *Selbschutz*, under the supervision of house wardens placed under the leadership of the local police chief, was composed of volunteers and part-timers who managed home shelters and fire prevention, reported incidents and accidents, performed first aid, and mounted rescues and fire fighting when necessary until more specialised services could intervene. Members had to supply their own service dress and equipment. They also had to make do with ad hoc vehicles including requisitioned cars towing water pumps and commercial trucks converted into ambulances.

Secondly the *Erweiterter Selbschutz* (Extended Self-Protection Service) was responsible for overseeing individual buildings, business premises, hotels,

↑ RLB flag.

↑ RLB belt buckle.

↑ RLB belt buckle (variant).

◆ Introduced in 1936, the RLB dagger was awarded to select individuals between the ranks of *Führer* (Lieutenant) and *Präsident* (President). The dagger had a total length of 39cm, a flat pommel, a grip and scabbard wrapped in blue-black morocco leather and extended eagle's wings on the cross guard.

◆ Fireman of the RLB.

public institutions and facilities and places of entertainment (cinema, theatres) that did not possess their own air raid protection teams. In these cases, members of the *RLB-Erweiter Selbschutz* were normally employees, civil servants, factory workers, or other labourers who worked in these buildings or institutions. They operated in the same way as the *Selbschutz*, but with more resources including first aid and simple rescue equipment, and their semi-professional leaders were trained by the police and the fire brigade, and received payment from the League.

The amateurish approach of both RLB Self-Protection Service and Extended Self-Protection Service was made to work by the steadfastness and selfless behaviour of the volunteers. Their role was a passive one, reacting to air attacks and their results. They did not take military measures against raids in any way, and did not possess police powers. RLB members were authorised to control civilians during and after air raids, assist and provide medical and evacuation duty, organise repair services for buildings, utilities and transportation, care for wounded animals and livestock, assist with fire-fighting, and provide rescue and ambulance services to victims. The RLB was also required to cooperate with other services. In case of emergency they served to augment the effectiveness of existing services provided by the *Feuerwehrpolizei* (Police Fire Brigade), *Sicherheits und Hilfsdienst* (Security and Assistance Service) and *Luftschutpolizei* (Air Protection Police).

The RLB was not affiliated to the Nazi Party, although many of its prominent leaders were NSDAP members. It was a civilian organisation with both full-time regular cadre personnel and a large number of unpaid part-time volunteers, but in fact it was a semi-official Nazi-sponsored organisation. In March 1934 members of the RLB were authorised by law to wear uniforms based on the Nazi Party model, including a peaked cap, tunic, overcoat, swastika armband, riding breeches and leather boots. In typical Nazi fashion the League's members had ranks, emblems, daggers, flags, badges and medals, but they were not armed.

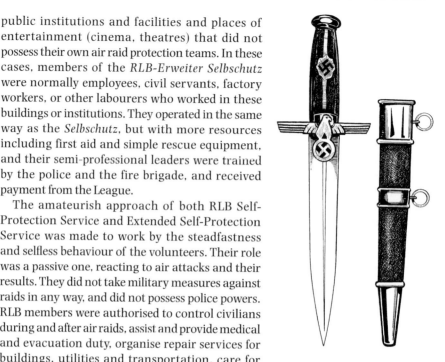

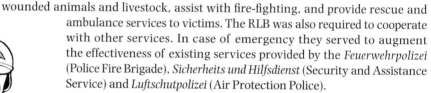

◆ *Luftschutz* armband. The armband was green with the words 'Luftschutz-NSDAP' in white or black lettering.

The ranks of the RLB were as follows:

RLB Präsident	President of the League
Vize Präsident	Vice-President
Gruppenführer	Major General
Hauptführer	Captain
Oberführer	First Lieutenant
Führer	Second Lieutenant
Obertruppmeister	Master Sergeant
Truppmeister	Staff Sergeant
Obertruppwart	Sergeant
Truppwart	Corporal
Obertruppman	Private 1st Class
Truppmann	Private

The facing colour used by the RLB was lilac, appearing on the collar patch, shoulder strap underlay and as piping to tunics and trousers. A variety of armbands were worn, often displaying the RLB eight-pointed starburst *Gardenstern* emblem. As in all other organisations, wartime pressure on manpower resulted in the recruitment of women and youths to release male members for front line military duty. By 1943, the RLB counted about 22 million members.

Security and Assistance Service (Sicherheits und Hilfdienst, SHD)

The Security and Assistance Service was formed in 1935 as a mobile civil defence organisation for the most vulnerable cities and towns in Germany. It differed from other civil air raid protection services in that it was national rather than regional and local. Units of the SHD were mobile and responsible for heavy rescue work, unlike the members of the *Reichsluftschutzbund* (Reich Air Defence League) discussed above.

Prior to 1939, the SHD consisted of volunteers and skilled professionals. Following the outbreak of the Second World War, members of the *Sicherheits und Hilfdienst* were conscripted as reservists stationed in their home cities, but were required to rotate duty and were temporarily *kazerniert* (housed in barracks) as needed; they were allowed to sleep at home on alternate nights. Serving in the SHD was a reserved occupation, and therefore members were exempt from military service, and were not allowed to take part in any other occupation while a member.

The SHD was organised into five main groups consisting of: decontamination squads; fire-fighting troops; repair work teams; veterinary service groups; and medical units. In 1940, a number of *Sicherheits und Hilfdienst Abteilungen* (battalions) were formed to serve as a mobile reserve for those cities most heavily hit by Allied air raids. The battalions were self-supporting, motorised in order to be able of quick transfer, and well equipped with cutting tools, hydraulic jacks, wrecking tools and pile drivers. Each area of Germany was required to form a battalion to be sent where needed. As the Reich Air Ministry/ Luftwaffe had control of the national air raid protection services, SHD personnel wore Luftwaffe blue-grey uniforms and fatigues with the letters SHD on the collar patches, and armbands with the name of the service often in yellow Gothic script.

⬇ Fireman of the Security and Assistance Service (*Sicherheits und Hilfdienst*, SHD). This SHD man wears the greyish blue Luftwaffe uniform with SHD collar patch, armband and *Luftschutz* helmet.

The ranks of the SHD were as follows:

SHD Mann	Private
Truppführer	Corporal
Gruppenführer	Staff Sergeant
Hauptgruppenführer	Master Sergeant
Stabsgruppenführer	Warrant Officer
Zugführer	Second Lieutenant
Oberzugführer	First Lieutenant
Bereitschaftführer	Captain
Abteilungsführer	Major
Abteilungsleiter	Lieutenant Colonel

In spring 1942, after a series of devastating air attacks on Lubeck and Rostock in North Germany, the *Sicherheits und Hilfdienst* units proved unable to cope. As a result the entire system of German civil air defence and rescue was reorganised. This was done on 1 June 1942 by creating a brand new organisation, the *Luftschutzpolizei*.

Air Protection Police (Luftschutzpolizei)

The *Luftschutzpolizei* came under the control of the *Ordnungspolizei* (Orpo, German Order Police), although Göring's Luftwaffe was still responsible operationally. The corps, formed to replace the mobile battalions of the SHD, was thus placed under the command of Reichsführer SS Heinrich Himmler in his capacity of Chief of the German Police. Members were exempt from military conscription. When

◆ This member of the *Luftschutzpolizei* wears a greyish-blue Luftwaffe uniform (note that he has retained the *Sicherheits und Hilfdienst* collar patch) with a green armband bearing the words 'Luftschutz-NSDAP' in Gothic letters.

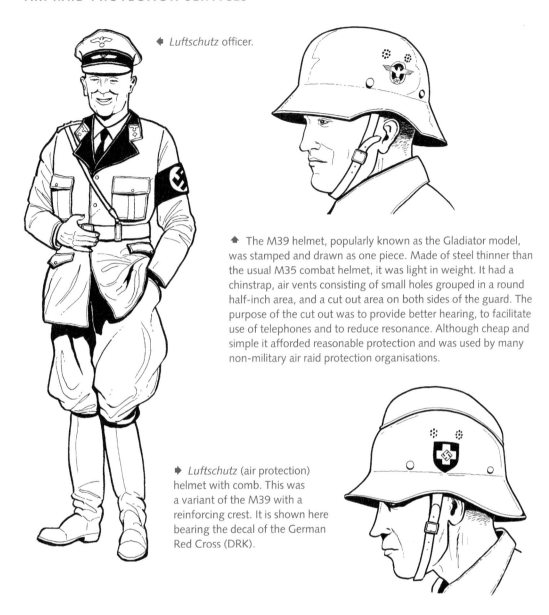

◆ *Luftschutz* officer.

♣ The M39 helmet, popularly known as the Gladiator model, was stamped and drawn as one piece. Made of steel thinner than the usual M35 combat helmet, it was light in weight. It had a chinstrap, air vents consisting of small holes grouped in a round half-inch area, and a cut out area on both sides of the guard. The purpose of the cut out was to provide better hearing, to facilitate use of telephones and to reduce resonance. Although cheap and simple it afforded reasonable protection and was used by many non-military air raid protection organisations.

♣ *Luftschutz* (air protection) helmet with comb. This was a variant of the M39 with a reinforcing crest. It is shown here bearing the decal of the German Red Cross (DRK).

the *Luftschutzpolizei* was formed the existing mobile *Sicherheits und Hilfdienst Abteilungen* were transferred directly into the Lufwaffe where they became *Luftschutz-Abteilungen*, or motorised air protection battalions. Fifty-five such units were known to have been formed, numbered as Luftschutz-Abteilung 11 through 60, and Luftschutz-Abteilungen VI, XI, XII, XIII and XVII. These 55 Luftschutz-Abteilungen were controlled by eight *Luftschutz-Regimentsstäben* (regimental headquarters). They continued to deal exclusively with fire fighting, rescue work and debris clearing operations when they were transferred to the Luftwaffe. The Air Defence Policemen wore a Luftwaffe field-grey uniform with slate-grey piping, though the cap had a black band, and distinctive police insignia were retained. They generally wore light steel helmets painted dark blue bearing the Luftschutz winged decal insignia.

Air Raid Warning Service (Luftschutz Warndienst, LSW)

The *Luftschutz Warndienst* was an important civilian organisation absorbed by the Luftwaffe in 1942. The LSW was responsible for the timely warning of incoming enemy air raids and attacks on German cities, towns and installations. It functioned at all times, day and night, by taking reports from its members, from the *Flugmeldedienst* (Warning Service) and from the various related police organisations, after which the information was processed and the air raid sirens were sounded prior to an attack. The service was also responsible for the sounding of the all-clear siren once a raid was over. When the frequency of Allied raids increased, refinements and a more elaborate system were introduced giving 12-minute and 6-minute warnings. Information on the movements of Allied bombers was improved by 1942 (notably by the introduction of radar) and the progress of attack formations and raids were broadcast.

⬆ Badge of the Air Raid Warning Service (*Luftschutz Warndienst*, LSW). It was embroidered in silver-grey on dark-green and was worn on the left sleeve.

➡ This LSW woman wears the blue/grey Luftwaffe female auxiliary uniform including a single-breasted jacket, matching skirt and field cap. She wears the LSW eagle on the breast and on the cap, and a green LSW cloth badge on the upper left sleeve. Her rank (*Haupthelferin*, platoon leader) is indicated by two white sleeve rings and three pips on the lower left sleeve.

⬆ Collar patch of the LSW.

⬆ *Helferin* of the LSW, 1944. This female auxiliary wears a Luftwaffe uniform with trousers for outdoor activity. The wearing of trousers by women was a dilemma for the conservative Nazi authorities, who were always worried about the change in gender roles forced by wartime necessity. She wears the LSW eagle on the breast and on the cap, and a green LSW cloth badge on the upper left sleeve.

The LSW and the other air raid protection services and organisations counted many women in their ranks. Members wore Luftwaffe blue-grey uniforms and a variety of fatigue and overalls for heavy duty service. The letter LSW appeared on the dark green patches worn by the personnel.

Nazi Drivers' Corps Emergency Service (Katastrophendienst)

From 1943 onwards, even the Nazi Party had to involve some of its formations and associations with the air services, which became increasingly strained. Some units of the *Nationalsozialistisches Kraftfahrkorps* (NSKK, National Socialist Drivers' Corps) were engaged to support the various existing rescue teams on the home front. The NSKK was created in 1931, largely to increase the mobility of the SA and provide transport for Nazi Party members. After the purge of the SA in 1934, the corps became a *Gliederung* (major branch) of the NSDAP and turned to the

◀ Member of the National Socialist Drivers' Corps (*Nationalsozialistisches Kraftfahrkorps*, NSKK).

◀ NSKK *Obersturmmann*.

training of drivers for the eventual use of the armed forces. With a membership on a voluntary basis, the NSKK had its own regional organisation divided into *Motorobergruppen* and further into *Motorgruppen*.

At the outbreak of war the NSKK fulfilled three important functions. It organised pre-military training in the motorised branch of the Hitler Youth; it provided an auxiliary transportation service in the communications zone in support of the Armed Forces; and it trained tank crews for the German Army. For the transport function NSKK units were organised into separate *Brigaden* (brigades). As the Allies intensified bombardments on German towns and cities, a special branch was hastily created, known as the *Katastrophendienst* (Nazi Drivers' Corps Emergency Service), which performed various roles including transport, evacuation and ambulance driving, but also police, protection, heavy rescue, fire fighting and debris-clearance duties.

Factory Air Protection Service (Werkluftschutzdienst)

As the air offensive against Germany proceeded, the RLB could not cope with the frequency and scale of attacks, and a new service was created, known as the *Werkluftschutzdienst*. Each important industrial site had such a service organised and trained by the State Group for Industry under the Minister of Economics. At local level the Factory Air Protection Service was headed by a leader appointed

◆ This policeman of the *Werkschutzpolizei* wears a standard grey uniform with a cuff title bearing the word '*Werkschutz*' and a chevron indicating his rank.

◆ *Werkschutz* officer.

by the police department. The work leader commanded several squads of firewatchers, fire fighters, decontamination men, first aid helpers and – where a manufacturer used animals – veterinarians. The squads were drawn from staff and employees, and in case of emergency, the work leader might call upon all factory personnel to assist his teams. Here again many German women, and pro-Nazi foreign volunteers served in all capacities. The *Werkluftschutzdienst* was also responsible for providing instructions, preventative precautions and the running of air raid shelters for the personnel. When damage or fires were beyond the capabilities of the factory squads, fire brigades and other medical and rescue services were called in to give assistance. The Factory Air Protection Service was also required to cooperate with other services. In case of emergency it was at the disposal of the local authorities to be engaged as an auxiliary municipal rescue and fire-fighting unit.

The *Werkluftschutzdienst* also included squads of *Werkschutzpolizei* (Factory Air Protection Police) who were persons privately employed by factory owners to act as overseers, guards and watchmen. It must be remembered that the German industry employed not only German workers but also many foreign volunteers and still more forced foreign labourers. Members of the Factory Air Protection Police were to see that prisoners were kept disciplined, obedient and subdued. Another important task was the prevention of sabotage and theft.

Guardsmen of the *Werkschutzpolizei* were subject to regulations issued by the Air Ministry, not by the police authorities. They wore various darkish grey Luftwaffe items, or dark blue surplus paramilitary uniforms or Lufthansa uniform including headdress, tunics, jackets and overcoats. When available arm badges, Orpo insignias and sometimes collar patches displayed the company's logo or emblem.

POST-RAID SERVICES

Along with air defence and protection organisations, which carried out heavy rescue work, there were a number of non-military services such as the Nazi Welfare Organisation (NSV), the Nazi Women Association (NSF) and the German Red Cross (DRK), which took care of air raid victims, the homeless, evacuees and refugees. They played an important role in nursing the wounded, providing assistance, overseeing evacuations, supplying and controlling billets, managing public and field kitchens, and providing replacement clothes and other essentials, while the Missing Persons Bureau (VNZ) would collect information on casualties and take over the identification and burial of the dead. Also after a raid, anything retrievable was salvaged from ruins, damaged factories and demolished homes. Anything recovered and still usable was removed and stored in warehouses by the *Selbschutz* (Self Protection Service) or by the local Nazi party authorities. Goods were either reclaimed by the owners or offered to other bombed-out victims when they were re-housed.

Nazi People's Welfare Organisation (Nationalsozialistische Volkswohlfahrte, NSV)

The NSV, like Robert Ley's DAF (German Labour Front), was the 'social' arm of the Nazi state. The organisation was founded in September 1931 by a Nazi municipal councillor (later SS Gruppenführer), Erich Hilgenfeldt, in the district of Wilmersdorf in Berlin. Originally the NSV's function was modest and limited: it was designed as an emergency aid group providing relief for NSDAP members during the depression of 1929–1932. Soon its activities encompassed the whole of Berlin, and owing to the support of Josef Göbbels and the patronage of Hitler, the organisation devoted itself to the welfare of party members and their families, especially mothers and juveniles.

After the Nazis came to power the NSV grew in influence and stature, as in 1933 Erich Hilgenfeldt received Hitler's mandate for all matters of charity and the people's welfare at national level. Hilgenfeldt soon usurped the place of both private and public welfare agencies, effectively subordinating organisations like the German Red Cross. The NSV became one of the largest Nazi party organisations, with some 16 million members in 1942. A large proportion of these were women, as the drain of manpower to the armed forces allowed women to take over posts which ten years before would have been considered 'men only' jobs. The structure of the NSV was militarised and based on the organisation of the Nazi Party.

The NSV had nursing auxiliaries, known as *NS-Schwestern* – female Nazi Party members contributing their time to the organisation – and included several sub-agencies, such as the WHW (Winter Relief), the Tuberculosis Relief, the Dental Relief and the Mother and Child Relief. The Nazi welfare organisation constituted a large empire within Germany, disposing of millions of Reichmarks raised by 'voluntary' due-paying members, state funds, collections and donations. Actually 'voluntary' contributions were docked from salaries and wages, and failure to give spontaneously and generously was reported to the authorities and police. Like Robert Ley's German Labour Front, the NSV enjoyed a relatively high reputation; there were, however, rumours of large scale corruption, with the saying 'There goes the Winter Relief!' marking the passage of a luxurious Nazi Party car.

During the war, the NSV's task was to care for, feed, house and comfort all German civilians who were injured or hungry, and those who had lost everything in Allied mass air raids. Outwardly a charitable organisation, the NSV also had an unsavoury side: the implementation of Hitler's racial policy through the preferential treatment of those of pure German blood. The clothing and money collected under the aegis of the NSV's Winter Relief were not made universally available to the needy. From the start Jews, Gypsies, the 'asocial', 'hereditary ill' and other 'enemies of the regime' were disqualified from receiving aid. Racial objectives were pursued by the NSV, notably in its Mother and Child Relief. Only the 'biologically valuable parts of the German nation' received support. Women who were 'hereditarily ill and inferior' or had an 'asocial disposition' were barred from post-natal care. Women, babies and young children were categorised according to whether they were 'worthy of help', 'hereditarily healthy' or of 'lesser value'.

From 1935, the NSV became involved in adoptions, and by 1937 a new sub-agency was created, the NSV Reich Adoption Service, dealing with only 'healthy and racially pure' children. During the war, the NSV's attempts to appropriate the field of adoption led to conflicts with the *Lebensborn* agency ('Well of Life', a eugenic organisation directed by the SS). Questions of respective competence were settled in a spirit of compromise. In the occupied Netherlands for example, the NSV was responsible for the care of children born to German soldiers by Dutch mothers. In occupied Norway, the *Lebensborn* agency secured a monopoly of germanising mothers and children in their care. Both the NSV and the *Lebensborn* were involved in the kidnapping of 'Aryan' children in occupied Europe. Orphans of 'German blood' were taken from their homes or from their foster parents, or were simply abducted from kindergartens, schools, and even off the streets. They were placed in NSV homes, given new names and educated in a military and 'racially sound' fashion.

◆ Since the late 1930s, all Hitler Youth members actively participated in local air raid drills, evacuating buildings and providing first aid treatment to the wounded and fighting fires as auxiliaries to the professional fire departments. When war broke out the Hitler Jugend was quickly mobilised to provide auxiliary support in their neighbourhoods. From January 1943, members of the HJ aged 15 and above were called up to serve as *Helfer* (auxiliaries) in the various branches of the *Luftschutz*. Many also served in the Luftwaffe Flak operating anti-aircraft guns and searchlights. The idea, of course, was to allow the Luftwaffe to release Flak men the Germans desperately needed for frontline combat duty, and replace them with Hitler Youth recruits. On the left a girl member of the *Bund Deutsche Mädel* (BdM, the female branch of the Hitler Youth) wears the BdM winter uniform including a *Kletterweste* (brown four-pocket suedette tunic), dark blue Melton cloth skirt and white stockings. The boy on the right wears the distinctive dark blue HJ uniform composed of a soft peaked cap, two-pocket pullover service blouse and matching baggy trousers. On the left upper sleeve he wears the red-white-red HJ armband with swastika and the *Gebietsdreieck* (triangular badge) indicating district.

Nazi Women's Association (NS-Frauenschaft, NSF)

Nazism was very much a male movement in tone and character; it emphasised physical struggle, toughness and military-style camaraderie, leaving little place for 'feminine' values. From the start a woman's position in society was inferior and the NSDAP barred females from membership. According to the anti-feminist ideology, women could not think logically or reason objectively, since they were 'ruled only by emotion'. The Luftwaffe was the only German arm employing large numbers of women in uniform (there were approximately 100,000 *Helferinnen* in 1944) serving as auxiliaries in air warning, telephone and teletype departments. On the whole women were repressed and had little official influence.

◀ HJ fire brigade volunteer.

◀ The emblem of
the DFW displayed
a triangle with the
words *'Deutsches
Frauenwerk'*, a
circular swastika
and the Algiz (rune)
symbol of life.

◀ Emblem of the
*Nationalsozialistische-
Frauenschaft* (Nazi
Women's League).
It bore the initials of
the German words
for Faith, Hope and
Charity.

A series of legislative measures sought to encourage marriage and raise the birth rate. The creation of new roles within party and public organisations – such as the *Nationalsozialistische-Frauenschaft* – made possible the active involvement of many women in the Third Reich. The NSF was a *Gliederung* (limb) of the NSDAP. Created in October 1931 the *Nationalsozialistische-Frauenschaft* was reorganised after the Nazi seizure of power in 1933. It was the overall body coordinating all existing women's groups and associations, such as the Women's League of the Red Cross, the Women's League in the *Deutsche Arbeitsfront* (the German Labour Front), and the Women's Labour Service.

In the period 1933–1937, women were expelled from work, their rights of inheritance were curtailed, they were refused higher education and barred from access to senior professional posts. The removal of women from many sectors of employment caused resentment. However in the period 1938–1945, the Nazi regime launched a wide scale re-armament policy programme and during the war the majority of males were drafted in the armed forces. This created a large labour shortage and Nazi officials found themselves in the contradictory position of having to encourage, even demand, women to work. For this purpose, a branch of the *NS-Frauenschaft* was created, known as the *Deutsches Frauenwerk* (German Women Labour, DFW). Although officially the NSF still presented being a housewife and a mother as the exemplary criterion of womanhood, the DFW dealt with urban housewives' organisations, and prepared them to replace men in workshops, factories and shops. Increasingly, women opted for better-paying jobs in heavy industry and weapons plants in the larger towns, leaving behind jobs as servants and on farms. Open to all German 'Aryan' women, the DFW, however, was a non-compulsory organisation.

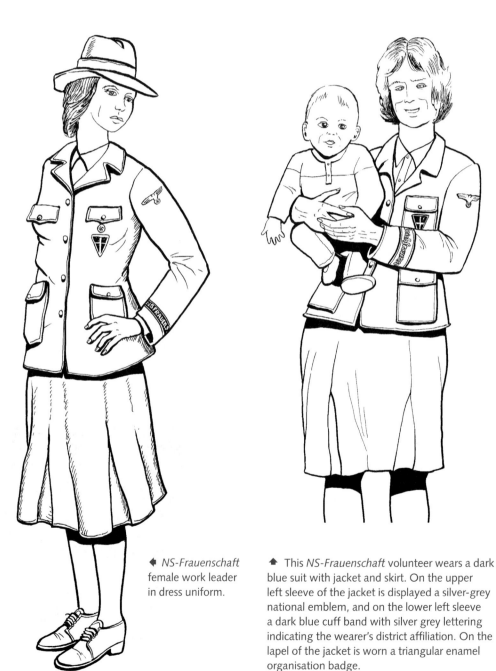

◀ *NS-Frauenschaft* female work leader in dress uniform.

▲ This *NS-Frauenschaft* volunteer wears a dark blue suit with jacket and skirt. On the upper left sleeve of the jacket is displayed a silver-grey national emblem, and on the lower left sleeve a dark blue cuff band with silver grey lettering indicating the wearer's district affiliation. On the lapel of the jacket is worn a triangular enamel organisation badge.

The purpose of the NSF was to keep German women firmly under the control of the exclusively male NSDAP. The NSF was placed under the leadership of Gertrud Bäumer and then under Gertrud Scholtz-Klink. A blonde, blue-eyed, slender woman, Gertrud Scholtz-Klink was married to a postal clerk and bore him six children. Active in various Nazi organisations, she was promoted to *Reichfrauenführerin* (leader) of the NSF and other women's organisations in 1934. Despite the imposing and sonorous title she possessed, her leadership was more token than actual, and her views on a woman's role closely mirrored those of the state. She was the prototype of the militant Nazi woman, expected to tread softly, avoid difficult issues and seek to teach all German women how to organise their households according to the policies of the party and consistently praising the 'sacred character' of National Socialism.

Although it tolerated a small but vocal faction, the NSF firmly encouraged women to pay deference to male supremacy, to embrace their secondary role, to emphasise the joys of child-bearing, to raise their children as patriots, to support the ideas and beliefs of Nazism, and to see that all commands of the party were unconditionally carried out in daily life. NSF members gave aid and comfort to fatigued mothers, instructed adolescent girls, dealt with cases involving children, offered enlightenment on such subjects as cooking leftovers, making clothes with good German cloth, and raising babies.

Not all of the NSF's activities were benevolent. The leadership of the organisation, mirroring Hitler's view, regarded any kind of feminism or women's liberation as anathema. Some of its members became guards in concentration and work camps for 'deviants' and Jewish women. During the last year of the Second World War, women of the *NS-Frauenschaft* provided rear-echelon support to the *Volkssturm* (Home Guard). By 1935 about 11 million out of the country's 35 million females belonged to the NS-Frauenschaft.

The official NSF uniform consisted of a dark blue-black suit including a jacket, a skirt and a fedora hat. On the upper left sleeve of the jacket was sown a silver grey national emblem (with the inevitable eagle and swastika). The wearer's district affiliation was indicated by a silver grey cuffband often worn on the lower left sleeve. An enamel organisation badge was usually worn on the lapel of the jacket.

⬇ The German Red Cross emblem consisted of a black eagle with wings down, bearing a white swastika and holding a red Greek cross in its claws.

The German Red Cross (Deutsches Rotes Kreuz, DRZ)

The International Movement of the Red Cross was founded at the instigation of the Swiss industrialist and philanthropist Henri Dunant (1828–1910) after the terrible Battle of Solferino, Italy, on 24 June 1859. Dunant, then travelling in Italy on business, witnessed the aftermath of the battle where more than 38,000 casualties from all sides were callously neglected and left to die, and some prisoners were subjected to ill treatment or shot out of hand. Dunant wrote a book (*Un Souvenir de Solferino* published in 1862), created a committee (including Gustave Moynier, General Henri Dufour, Louis Appia and Theodore Maunoir), and travelled all over Europe to spread and promote his ideals, which were on the whole well received. Owing to Dunant's generous efforts (which led ultimately to his financial ruin in 1867, but also to the first Peace Nobel Price in 1901), the concept of a permanent, neutral, international humanitarian organisation gained momentum. The

◆ The *Medaille für Deutsche Volkspflege* (German Social Welfare Medal) was instituted by Hitler in May 1939, and awarded to those who distinguished themselves in social and nursing work. The award had three classes according to achievement. The medal had a diameter of 38mm with the obverse displaying the DRK emblem and the words '*Medaille für Deutsche Volkspflege*' on the reverse. The ribbon was red with white edges, and after 1942, crossed swords could be added as extra distinction.

◆ The DRK *Schwesternkreuz* (German Red Cross Nurses' Cross) was instituted in July 1937. It was awarded in four classes, in silver or in gold for long service in the DRK.

International Movement of the Red Cross was officially created on 17 February 1863 in Geneva. From the start the Red Cross devoted itself to the protection of victims and prisoners of war with the intention of being international, neutral and humanitarian with no connection to politics. Its universally known emblem is a red Greek cross on a white background, being based on the Swiss flag (a white Greek cross on a red background).

The *Deutsches Rotes Kreuz* (the German Red Cross) was instituted in 1864, and was officially recognised in Geneva on 27 July 1929. Like other Red Cross organisations, the DRK was responsible for providing humanitarian aid and medical assistance to the German population. After January 1933, the German Red Cross did not escape the *Gleichschaltung* (nazification process). The DRK was presided over from 1933 to 1945 by Karl-Eduard Duke von Sachsen-Coburg und Gotha (1884–1954), a male-line grandson of the British Queen Victoria and Prince Albert. The Duke was a controversial figure in the United Kingdom due to his status as Sovereign Duke of Saxe-Coburg and Gotha, part of the German Empire, during the First World War. He was deprived of his British peerage, of his title of Prince and Royal Highness and of his British honours in 1919.

After the war he joined the German Nazi Party in 1935, was appointed SA Obergruppenführer (General), became 'Hitler's Favourite Royal' and was deeply embroiled in Nazi policies. Karl-Eduard, whose three sons served in Germany's armed forces, must have been aware of the Nazi euthanasia programme that murdered about 100,000 disabled people in Germany, and probably knew a great deal about the existence, plan and execution of the *Endlösung der Judenfrage* ('Final Solution of the Jewish Question'. As can easily be imagined, the Duke's conversion

◀ This *Schwester* (nurse) of the *Deutsches Rotes Kreuz* (German Red Cross) wears service dress of a light grey fedora hat, a double-breasted light grey jacket with a dark grey collar displaying Red Cross collar patches, a matching skirt and grey stocking. She wears an armband with a red cross and the words '*Deutsches Rotes Kreuz*'.

▶ This DRK *Schwester* wears the traditional ward dress of white starched cap, a grey blouse with vertical pleats with a white removable collar for washing, a matching grey shirt, a waist length white working apron, white stockings and black laced shoes. Her distinctive insignia includes the DRK armband on the left arm, a black triangular badge with the name of her home district on the right upper sleeve and a Red Cross brooch at the throat.

and commitment to Hitler's National Socialist regime caused considerable embarrassment to the British Royal Family.

The *Deutsches Rotes Kreuz* was brought into line with other Nazi uniformed bodies. Incorporated into the Nazi welfare organisation NSV, its structure was altered to fit the National Socialist model and it become de facto a Nazi entity. In December 1939, Hitler conferred a new legal status on the Red Cross by recognising it as a

national organisation with some independence from Geneva. With this new status, the German Red Cross expanded its size and remit in Germany, expanding its organisation into two distinct branches: medicine, nursing and first aid (Red Cross); and charitable and social work caring for children, the old and the homeless (Social Welfare).

Although DRK members, both male and female, were on a non-salaried basis, a full-time cadre of Nazi-selected, uniformed and salaried leaders supervised them. The DRK incorporated the omnipresent eagle and swastika with the International Red Cross symbol in the design of their own distinctive insignia. In January 1938 the German Red Cross introduced a complex rank structure, qualification badges, decorations, insignia and military-style guidelines. The DRK male ranks were:

Anwärter	Private
Helfer	Private 1st Class
Vorhelfer	Corporal
Vorhelfer mit Gruppenführerprüfung	Sergeant
Oberhelfer	Staff Sergeant
Oberhelfer mit Zugführerprüfung	Master Sergeant
Haupthelfer	Warrant Officer
Wachtführer	Second Lieutenant
Oberwachtführer	First Lieutenant
Hauptführer	Captain
Feldführer	Major
Oberfeldführer	Lieutenant Colonel
Oberstführer	Colonel
Generalführer	Brigadier General
Generalhauptführer	Major General

The DRK female ranks were as follows:

Anwärterin	Private
Helferin	Private 1st Class
Vorhelferin	Corporal
Oberhelferin	Staff Sergeant
Haupthelferin	Warrant Officer
Wachtführerin	Second Lieutenant
Oberwachtführerin	First Lieutenant
Hauptführerin	Captain
Feldführerin	Major

The DRK uniforms were also re-designed. The colour traditionally used for Red Cross service dress, other than the white nursing clothing, had always been slate-grey and this was retained until 1937 when a range of new uniforms was introduced for medical attendants, nurses and medical officers. Members

⬆ The DRK *Mantel* (overcoat) was of the standard pattern found throughout the German Army and auxiliary forces. It was worn over the service tunic by soldiers, NCOs and all other ranks alike with only detail differences to account for rank and insignia. In style the *Mantel* was a very long double-breasted garment reaching to the wearer's calf. Mostly field grey in colour, it had two rows of six grey metal buttons (gilded for generals), deep turn back cuffs and two side slash pockets. The woollen *Mantel* existed in an even thicker version for extra warmth. It had to be buttoned up to the neck and the collar could be worn turned up cold weather. The light grey RDK greatcoat was distinguished by pale dove-grey lapel facings and collar patches bearing a small red enamel cross.

◆ A Red Cross officer. Like other organisations of the Third Reich, DRK officers of the rank of *Wachtführer* (Second Lieutenant) and above had a dagger, introduced in February 1938 for evening and parade dress wear. The hilt was made of a pot metal base, having muted nickel-plated surfaces. The cross guard featured an oval medallion, which portrayed a Red Cross eagle. The bird was a closed-winged design, clutching a Red Cross symbol in the talons with a vaulted swastika superimposed on the bird's chest. The grip was a celluloid type being a yellow colour, usually toned to varying orange shades. The scabbard was steel (or silver) with matching nickel plating over pebbled panels. The DRK dagger had an overall length of 13.25 inches. Although the production of the DRK dagger ceased in 1940, officers wore it until the end of the war. Subordinates had a dagger with a toothed blade without point.

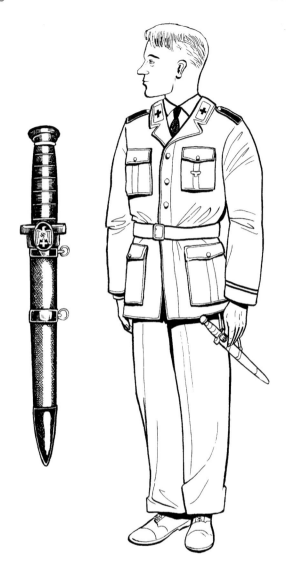

wore a dark grey uniform with a grey cap band and collar patches. Ranks for male personnel was shown by means of a system of shoulder straps, and bars of silver lace were worn on the tunic sleeve to display the length of service held by the wearer. Nurses and Sisters' ranks were indicated by a system of pips worn on a white blouse or slate-grey tunic. A tropical dress was even issued for female nursing personnel engaged in North Africa with Rommel's Afrika Korps. This included a sun helmet, light brown jacket and matching skirt. DRZ personnel who served in hazardous duty positions were issued a variety of steel helmets (e.g. standard army M35 or duty 'air Prevention' civic models). The inevitable eagle and swastika were present in emblems, badges, nurses' brooches, belt buckles, daggers and decorations.

During the Second World War, the German Red Cross became involved in both the home front and the international scene. It was the primary agency through which individual donations were funnelled to the troops, and its personnel served on both the home and combat fronts. It was active in organising first aid courses for civil defence, establishing shelters and emergency aid stations to nurse, feed and

◆ Nurses of the German Red Cross served in North Africa with Rommel's Afrika Korps. The female DRK tropical uniform included a pith sun helmet made of compressed cork covered with olive green canvas cloth, a light cotton brown tropical jacket (with tan cloth belt, and either long or short sleeves), a matching pleated tan skirt, black stockings and black shoes.

◆ Opel Blitz ambulance. Ambulances used by the German Red Cross were usually of standardised models with an average capacity of four stretchers or eight sitting patients. A common model was the Opel Blitz Typ S. In emergencies military or civilian buses could be used or converted to ambulances. In accordance with the Geneva Convention, ambulances were marked with a red cross on a white disc displayed on the sides, the back and sometimes on the roof of the vehicle for air recognition.

⬥ At the end of the Second World War, with many adult German men dead, wounded or taken prisoner, the clearing up was left to the women. *Trümmerfrauen* ('Rubble Women') were employed to shift the ruins and clean up the streets. Some 50,000 women were involved in the enterprise, which gained them extra rations. Germany's women were the true force behind the country's reconstruction in the first months of peace after May 1945. As described in Günter Grass's book *My Century*, 'they had endured too much to give up now'.

house victims of the bombing. It served as the intermediary between families and the military, notifying soldiers serving overseas of births and deaths of relatives.

The mother Red Cross organisation tried to gain access to prison camps to carry out inspections, but the Nazi-controlled German Red Cross refused to cooperate with the Geneva statutes. After Germany's defeat in 1945, the DRK, like all organisations linked to the Nazi Party, was disbanded. The German Red Cross was re-established in 1952 during the post-war reconstruction of both West Germany and the eastern DDR. As for the wartime DRK President, Karl-Eduard von Sachsen-Coburg und Gotha, he was sentenced by a denazification court, heavily fined and almost bankrupted in 1946. The former Duke spent the last years of his life in seclusion, and died a penniless war criminal in 1954.

It is interesting to note that even after the most terrible Allied attacks, the German organisations discussed in this chapter managed to respond to the aftermath very effectively. In Dresden, for example, after the terrible raids of February 1945, electricity was restored by the TeNo to most parts of the town within a few days, trams were running within four days, and factories started functioning again within a few weeks. In spite of continued bombing, German air defence, with the organisation and improvisation of industry under Minister Albert Speer, kept morale high, and production even increased until the end of 1944. Only in the very last months of the Second World War was the system brought to the point of collapse.

APPENDIX 1

MARCHING SONG OF THE GERMAN ANTI-AIRCRAFT ARTILLERY

1

We, the men of the 2cm, 3.7cm and 88cm
We protect the Fatherland against enemy coming from the sky, night and day.
Be it in Poland, France or Russia
Our fighting spirit is renowned
They know that Flak means gun fire

Refrain
Flak forwards! Shout armour and infantry
This cry, gunners, never shall we forget it!
An assault gun speeds towards the enemy
Everyone shouts 'Ready to fire!'
What was an enemy tank is now a smoking wreck
Hit by our Flak.
Yes! that's precision work
Bull's eye for our Flak!

2

Anton and Berta, Caesar and Dora
Will never part.
They're bound together 'cause they form a Flak battery,
And yet in France, Poland and Russia
They were not always together.
If a tank was in sight, one of them headed to the enemy

(Refrain)

3

Our Flak also fights bunkers, machine guns and tanks.
Such combats rejoice our soldiers.
When the enemy surrender in the end,
When the war is victorious,
A shout of combat rises from the graves.
It is the call of the 88
Our deads sing in chorus

(Refrain)

Music score of 'Flak nach vorn!' (Flak Forwards!) The lyrics and music were written by Unteroffizier Nils Cederborg, and the song was dedicated to Generalmajor Walther von Axthelm.

APPENDIX 2

RANKS OF THE LUFTWAFFE FLAK

General Officers

Reichsmarshall   no equivalent (literally Marshal of the Empire or
                                          Supreme Commander of the Luftwaffe), a title
                                          especially created for Hermann Göring
Generaloberst   Air Chief Marshal, commander of a Flakkorps
General der Flakartillerie   General in command of a Flakkorps
General der Luftnahrichtentruppe   General commanding signal units or a Luftgau
Generalleutnant   Lieutenant General or Air Marshal commander
                                          of a Flakkorps
Generalmajor   Major General or Air Vice-Marshal
                                          commanding a Flak division

Officers

Oberst   Colonel commanding a Flak regiment
Oberstleutnant   Lieutenant Colonel, commanding a Flak
                                          regiment
Major   Major commanding a Flak battalion
Hauptmann   Captain commanding a Flak battalion
Oberleutnant   Lieutenant commanding a Flak company
Leutnant   Second Lieutenant commanding a Flak
                                          company

Non-Commissioned Officers

Hauptfeldwebel, Hauptwachtmeister,
Stabsfeldwebel, Oberfeldwebel,
Oberwachtmeister, Feldwebel and
Wachtmeister   Warrant Officers Classes 1 and 2
Unterwachtmeister   Sergeant Major
Unteroffizier   Sergeant

Enlisted Men

Hauptgefreiter and *Obergefreiter*	Corporal
Gefreiter	Lance Corporal
Funker	Signalman
Kanonier	Gunner, artilleryman
Fallschirmjäger	Paratrooper
Schütze	Infantryman (only in the Herman Göring Division and Luftwaffe infantry divisions)
Sanitätsmann	Medical orderly

Musicians

Luftwaffe Obermusikinspizient	equivalent to *Oberstleutnant* (Lieutenant Colonel)
Luftwaffe Musikinspizient	equivalent to *Major* (Major)
Stabsmusikmeister	equivalent to *Hauptmann* (Captain)
Obermusikmeister	equivalent to *Oberleutnant* (Lieutenant)
Musikmeister	equivalent to *Leutnant* (Lieutenant)

APPENDIX 3

LUFTWAFFE COLOURS OF SERVICE (WAFFENFARBEN)

Flak	bright red
Air Signals	light brown
Transport and Supply	as per branch to which attached
Pioneer and Engineer	black
Air Crew and Ground Personnel	gold-yellow
Medical Personnel	dark blue
Airfield Security	light green

BIBLIOGRAPHY

Angolia J.R. and Littlejohn D., *Labour Organizations of the Reich* (R. James Bender Publishing, 1999)

Autori vari, *Histoire Universelle Larousse Tome II de 1500 à Aujourd'hui* (Librairie Larousse, 1974)

Bartov, O., *L'Armée d'Hitler, la Wehrmacht, les Nazis et la Guerre* (Hachette Littératures, 1999)

Bishop C. and Warner A., *German Weapons of WWII* (Grange Books, 2001)

Boog H., *Die deutsche Luftwaffenführung; Führungsprobleme, Spitzenliederung, Generalstabsausbildung* (Stuttgart, 1982)

Carman, W.Y., *A Dictionary of Military Uniform* (Anchor Press Ltd, 1977)

Cecil R., *Hitler's War Machine* (Salamander Books Ltd, 1976)

Chamberlain P. and Gander T. *Anti-Aircraft Guns* (McDonald & Jane's, 1975)

Chazette A., Paich B., Destouches A. and Boulard E., *Tobrouks Typologie Atlantikwall-Südwall* (Editions Histoire & Fortifications, 2004)

Deighton L., *Bomber* (Triad/Granada Publishing, 1978)

Delagarde J., *German Soldiers of World War Two* (Histoire & Collections, 2005)

Duprat F., *Les Campagnes de la Waffen SS* (Editions les Sept Couleurs, 1973)

Ehrlich C., *Uniformen und Soldaten: Ein Bildericht vom Ehrenkleid unserer Wehrmacht* (Verlag Erich Klinkhammer, 1942)

Faber H., *Luftwaffe: An Analysis by Former Generals* (Sidwick & Jackson, 1979)

Fitzsimons B., *Tanks and Weapons of World War II* (BPC Publishing Ltd, 1973)

Fleischer W., *Feldbefestigungen des deutschen Heeres 1939–1945* (Podzun-Pallas Verlag, 1998)

Foedrowitz, M., *The Flak Towers in Berlin, Hamburg, and Vienna 1940–1950* (Schiffer Publications, 1997)

Ford, B., *Duitslands Geheime Wapens, Hitlers laatste hoop* (Standaard Uitgeverij, 1990)

Fuhrmeister, J., *Der Westwall* (Weltbild GmbH, 2009)

Funcken L. and F., *L'Uniforme et les Armes des Soldats de la Guerre 1939–1945* (Editions Casterman, 1972)

Gméline P., *La Flak: 1935–1945, La D.C.A. Allemande* (Editions Heimdal, 1986)

Gordon-Douglas, S.R., *German Combat Uniforms 1939–1945* (Almark Publications, 1970)

Griehl, M., *Das Grosse Buch der Flak, Deutsche Luftverteidigung 1912–1945* (Podzun-Pallas Verlag, 2003)

Gunston B. and Wood T., *Hitler's Luftwaffe* (Salamander Books Ltd, 1977)

Harding D., *Weapons: An International Encyclopaedia from 5000 BC to 2000 AD* (Diagram Visual Information Ltd, 1980)

His Majesty's Stationary Office, *DCA, Histoire Officielle des Défenses Anti-aériennes de la Grande-Bretagne de 1939 à 1942* (London, 1943)

Hettler E., *Uniformen der Deutschen Wehrmacht Heer, Kriegsmarine und Luftwaffe* (Verlag Otto Dietrich, 1938)

Hogg I.V., *German Artillery of World War Two* (Greenhill Books, 2002)

_____, *German Secret Weapons of the Second World War* (Greenhill Books, 1999)

_____, *The Guns 1939–1945* (Ballantine Publications, 1970)

Höhne H., *Der Orden unter dem Totenkopf* (Verlag der Spiegel, 1966)

Keegan J., *A History of Warfare* (Hutchinson Publications, 1993)

_____, *The Art of War, War and Military Thought* (Smithsonian Books, 2005)

Koch, H-A., *Flak* (Podzun-Pallas-Verlag, 1965)

Kroesem F.L. and Albarda J., *Nederlands Geschut sinds 1677* (Uitgeverij van Kolkema & Warendorf, 1979)

Kuhlenkamp, A., *Flak-Kommandogeräte* (VDI Verlag, 1943)

Lepage J-D., *German Military Vehicles of World War II* (McFarland & Company Inc., 2007)

_____, *Aircraft of the Lufwaffe, 1935–1945* (McFarland & Company Inc., 2009)

Linhardt, A., *Die Technische Nothilfe in der Weimarer Republik* (Demand Gmbh, 2006)

Mabire J., *Les Paras du Reich, le Fer de Lance de la Blitzkrieg* (Grancher, 1996)

MacDonald C., *Luchtlandingstropen, Parachutisten in de strijd* (Standaard Uitgeverij, 1995)

McInnes C. and Sheffield G.D., *Warfare in the Twentieth Century: Theory and Practice* (Unwin Hyman Ltd, 1988)

Maynard C., *Luchtgevechten* (Zuidnederlandse Uigeverij N.V., 1990)

Moerkerk J.J., *Radar, een populair-wetenschappelijke Beschouwing* (Uitgeverij Wijt 1946)

Mollo A., *German Uniforms of World War II* (MacDonald & Jane's, 1976)

Montgomery B.L., *A Concise History of Warfare* (Wordsworth Editions Ltd, 2000)

Müller, W., *Horchgeräte-Komandogeräte und Scheinwerfer der schweren Flak* (Waffen Arsenal Podzun-Pallas-Verlag GMbH, 1991)

Nicolaisen H-D., *Der Einsatz der Luftwaffe und Marinehelfe im 2. Weltkrieg* (Bernard & Graefe Verlag, 1981)

Parker G., *Warfare* (Press Syndicate of Cambridge University, 1995)

Pickert, W., *Unsere Flakatillerie* (Mittler Verlag, 1940)

Price A., *Luftwaffe Handbook* (Ian Allan Publishing, 1977)

_____, *Luftwaffe* (Ballantine Books, 1970)

Rolf, R., *Atlantikwall Typenheft, Atlantic Wall Typology, Typologie du Mur de l'Atlantique* (Prak Publishing, 2008)

Ropp T., *War in the Modern World* (Duke University Press, 1959)

Sakkers, H., *Generalfeldmarschall Rommel* (Uitgeverij Zeelucht, 1993)

Schamberger R. and Hornung W., *Brandschutzgeschichte* (Kohlhammer, 2004)

von Senger und Etterlin F.M., *Die deutschen Panzer 1926–1945* (J.F. Lehmanns Verlag, 1968)

United States War Department, *Handbook on German Military Forces* (Washington, 1945)

_____, *Handbook on German Army Identification* (Washington, 1943)

Wright Q., *A Study of War* (Phoenix Books, 1965)

INDEX